CARTOON-ILLUSTRATED
TECHNOLOGY REVOLUTION

by

Kaiman Lee, PH.D.
President
VisionQuest Today

ISBN: 0-915250-84-5
www.technology-revolution.com

Published by:
CARTOON ILLUSTRATED BOOKS
A Subsidiary of
Environmental Design & Research Center

CARTOON-ILLUSTRATED TECHNOLOGY REVOLUTION
is a *Cartoon Illustrated Book*.
Another *Cartoon Illustrated Book* is
**CARTOON-ILLUSTRATED METAPHORS: Idioms, Proverbs,
Cliches and Slang**.
See it at www.MyMetaphors.com

TABLE OF CONTENTS

Cartoon Illustrated Books

Cartoon Illustrated Books are <u>revolutionizing reading and learning</u>. They make reading and learning <u>fun</u> again, so much fun that you tend to read them anywhere, in <u>bed</u>, at <u>lunch</u>, on <u>vacation</u>, or on an <u>outing</u>.

Subject matters are presented in <u>digestible bites</u> of one concept or idea per page. Every page in a *Cartoon Illustrated Book* is <u>conceptualized and written by an executive for executives</u>, and of course <u>for anyone</u> who wants to learn a <u>difficult subject in an easy and fun way</u>.

<u>Cartoon</u> illustrations are used throughout to facilitate the <u>initial understanding and later refreshing</u> of the subject matter. The <u>critical concepts</u> have been <u>highlighted</u> for you. You can <u>browse back and forth</u> with ease.

Cartoon Illustrated Books strip away the veneer of writing and give you the <u>naked substance</u>. "<u>Less is more</u>" is demonstrated so <u>effectively and entertainingly</u> that you will use *Cartoon Illustrated Books* again and again.

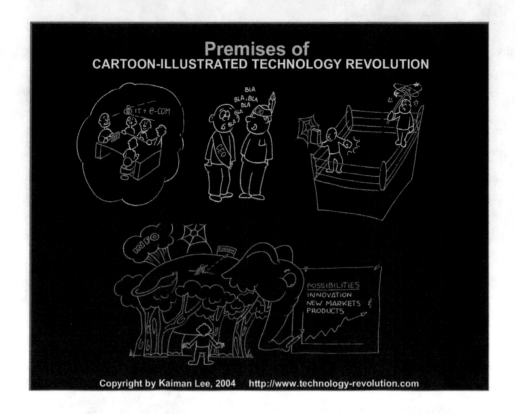

Premises of
CARTOON-ILLUSTRATED TECHNOLOGY REVOLUTION

Technology changes everything. Do you want the information technology (IT) vision to be your vision? To talk fluently with your computer staff? Ask the right questions to realize your vision? Leverage IT as your business competitive edge? And, recognize the opportunities and perils?

Big-game hunters say the hardest animal to see is an elephant! We are all surrounded by elephants we are not noticing. Among the biggest ones are:
- innovation explosion,
- universal and instantaneous communication,
- business globalization,
- customer's expectations for speed in service delivery, and
- widening gulf between the haves and have nots.

Investing in technology in answer to business requirements is a survival response, not a growth strategy. You must not only know what technology can do for you, but also could do for you so you can expand into new markets and products, and capture new customers. You must not limit your thinking to how your current processes can be automated. You must innovate your business by forward and possibilities thinking.

You must formulate your own IT vision.

Acknowledgements

Copyright by Kaiman Lee, 2004   http://www.technology-revolution.com

"Oscart" is one of the most talented cartoonists in the Silicon Valley. He would want the readers of this book to associate him with the insignia "Oscart" of his art work. I love his mural covering the whole pedestrian tunnel of a Palo Alto (California USA) train station. The other ones I enjoy are murals in restaurants. Of course, the best are in this book!

Professor Bob is my best friend. He does not want his real name in print. But he knows how much my life's purpose and accomplishments are influenced by his unselfish counsel. Without his encouragement and guidance in the development of this book, I might still have doubts about its value to you.

Mr. W. Bradley Holtz edited the first draft and provided invaluable ideas for the overall concept of the book. Mr. Holtz is the President and Principal Consultant of WBH Associates specializing on strategic consulting to the computer-aided design industry. He is the Editor of the industry standard, *The CAD Rating Guide*.

And, of course, I am grateful to Cathy, my wife. Without her encouragement and guidance in the development of this book, it would not have been published.

About Kaiman Lee, Ph.D.

Copyright by Kaiman Lee, 2004   http://www.technology-revolution.com

- President, VisionQuest Today, a technology consulting firm.

- Past Director of Information Systems of a facilities engineering organization.

- Past Chief Engineer and Director of the Engineering Group of a public works organization.

- Past Chairperson of Information Superhighway Applications Committee, Construction Industry Institute, Austin, Texas.

- Instrumental in developing the world's first turnkey computer graphics system for architects.

- Pioneer of computer aided design in the architectural, engineering and construction industry.

- Lectured around the world with innumerable conference papers, tutorials and seminars.

- Published over 20 books since the early 1970s.

PARADIGM CHANGE

Mother of All Vectors

PRE INDUSTRIAL AGE   INDUSTRIAL AGE

INFORMATION AGE   INNOVATION AGE

Copyright by Kaiman Lee, 2004   http://www.technology-revolution.com

Every economic era is based upon a key abundance and a key scarcity. They are called the Mother of All Vectors.

In the Pre-industrial Age, land was abundant and horsepower scarce.

In the Industrial Age, horsepower (now known as watts) became abundant and land scarce.

For most people of the world, now is the Information Age. Computer transistors (i.e. MIPS [million instructions per second] and bytes, or just computer capacity) join with watts as abundant resources. What is scarce is communications power we call bandwidth through wire and air. Computing power is used to compensate bandwidth limitation.

For some people, they are living in the Innovation Era. Bandwidth will be abundant and embedded appliances will make use of it to become ubiquitous. What will be scarce is time, the human's biologic time, and battery life.

Innovation will be everywhere because information will be packaged so well that people can create new knowledge easily.

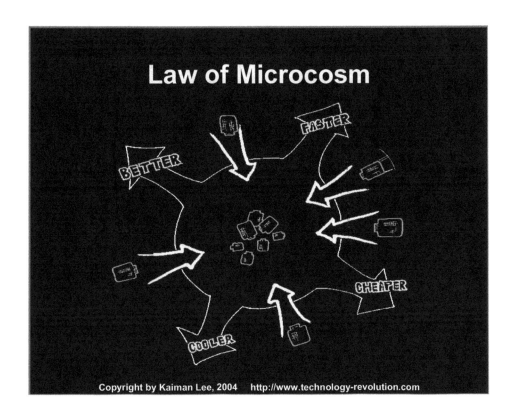

Law of Microcosm

FASTER

BETTER

CHEAPER

COOLER

Carver Mead, California Institute of Technology, said in 1960:

"Put 'n' <u>transistors</u> on a single sliver of silicon, and you will get 'n' square <u>performance</u> <u>and value</u>." That is the law of microcosm.

In other words, as <u>transistors</u> are miniaturized and jammed more <u>closely together</u>, they run <u>faster, cooler, cheaper, and better</u>.

Computer speed will increase about <u>100 fold</u> in the next decade, <u>doubling every 18 months for another 20 years</u> (unbelievable!), predicted by the legendary Gordon Moore. Until now, computer technology has been governed by the law of microcosm.

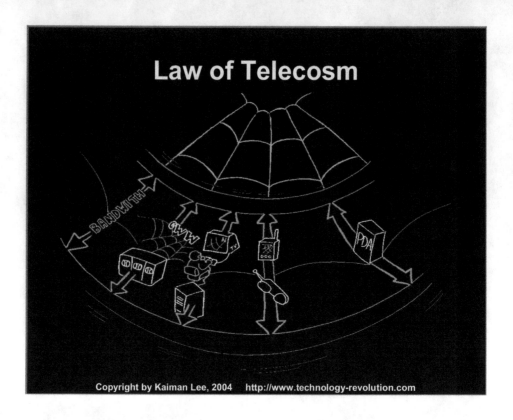

Law of Telecosm

Copyright by Kaiman Lee, 2004   http://www.technology-revolution.com

Bob Metcalfe, Inventor of Ethernet (1973) and founder of 3Com said in 1979:

"Connect 'n' machines (computers, cellular phones, pagers, etc..) to the network, and you get 'n' square potential value, performance, or cost effectiveness." That is the law of telecosm.

In other words, the performance, value or cost effectiveness of the network rises by the square of the number of digital devices connected to it.

Bandwidth will increase about 1000 fold in the next decade, doubling at least every year, predicted by George Gilder, Editor, Gilder Technology Report, December 1997.

With telecosm, the peripherals (e.g., cell phone) and the Internet are the basis for the way we do almost everything from home entertainment and banking to voice.

Microcosm, where computers are used to store, switch, and route information will give way to telecosm that enables virtually limitless, low-cost, and incredibly-fast bandwidth communication. Tomorrow, computer technology will be governed by the law of telecosm.

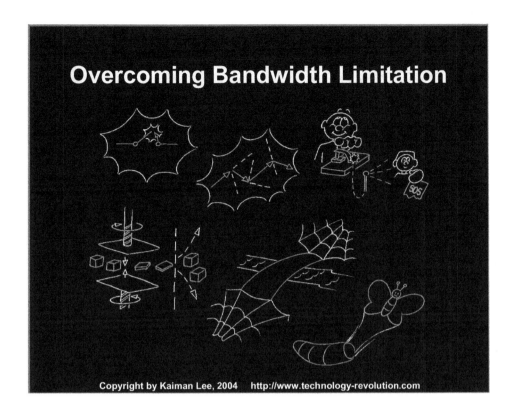

Our current paradigm is to use cheap computers and microchips to compensate for limited bandwidth by switching, routing, multiplexing, compressing/decompression, coding/decoding, buffering, caching, prioritizing, error correcting, bridging, converting and simply storing information.

We use switches as a substitute for bandwidth. The current switches use a dedicated point-to-point line between two places. The future of communication is in packet switching where information is broken down into packets, and the computer directs the packets over the Internet via the shortest routes.

Almost all of today's telephone and computer networks, and microprocessing and software for today's information technology are based upon bandwidth scarcity.

Imagine for a moment: what if the paradigm suddenly changed; bandwidth is limitless?

Power of Online Trend

The online (or real-time) trend is moving with the <u>power</u> of the <u>tsunami</u> and the <u>nuclear wave</u>.

The Internet is like an unstoppable wave that will sweep over the horizon with tremendous force, forever changing the landscape of everything in its path. The changes it is bringing about are so fundamental that you may discover that it has affected your core business or even your entire industry, as it recedes. "Can this happen to my company?" is a question every business person should ask.

View <u>Internet, Intranet and Extranet</u> as part of your <u>core business</u> strategies and you will <u>prosper</u>.

If you allow yourself to be <u>carried along by the wave</u>, you may gain some benefits, but not as many as are possible through clear vision and commitment.

If you resist the Net, you will experience an erosion of your business as the forces of the online waves continue to swell.

When the tsunami strikes, will I be on high ground, or am I at the shoreline, about to be overwhelmed?

TRANSMISSION TECHNOLOGY

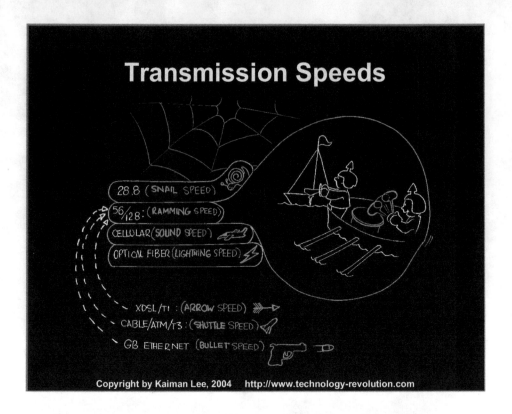

Transmission Speeds

28.8 (SNAIL SPEED)
56/128: (RAMMING SPEED)
CELLULAR (SOUND SPEED)
OPTICAL FIBER (LIGHTNING SPEED)

XDSL/T1 : (ARROW SPEED)
CABLE/ATM/T3 : (SHUTTLE SPEED)
GB ETHERNET (BULLET SPEED)

Copyright by Kaiman Lee, 2004   http://www.technology-revolution.com

MCI tripled its capacity in 1996 -- from 45 Mbps at the beginning of the year to 155 Mbps by year end. It closed out 1997 with a new dual OC-12 system capable of handling up to 1.2 Gbps. And in 1998 MCI doubled it to OC-48 (2.4 Gbps). Qwest Communications moved from its OC-48 foundation in 1999 to an OC-192 (10 GBPS) IP-over-optical nationwide backbone in 2000.

In early 1998, a new company Nexabit used a new layer-three switching scheme that could handle 16 OC-192s (that is 10 gigabits per second apiece) at the same time and run at a wire speed of 320 gigabits per second.

The future communication speed will make you feel as if you are driving a horse and buggy on the Autobahn. Bell Labs demonstrated in early 2000 a speed of 3.28 Tbps over one fiber-optic strand, the equivalent of three times the world's daily Internet traffic in one second. Fiber optic cables with 864 strands or 432 strands are being laid.

It is estimated that the Internet traffic grows 100 fold every 1000 days (three years). The bandwidth will be there to meet the challenge.

Internet users in U.S. will be trying to replace their 56 KBPS modem (ramming speed re: Ben Hur movie) en masse by 2004.

A modem speed of 28.8 KBPS (kilobits per second) is somewhat like draining Lake Tahoe through a Dixie straw. But it is the most popular modem up to the end of 1998. The majority of the world does not even have that speed.

Other metaphors for the slow speed used in the industry are "using a drinking straw to unload an oil tanker," "squeeze a fire hydrant of data through a soda straw pipeline," and "drinking from a fire hose."

In the U.S.A. the 28.8 KBPS speed has been obsolete by the year 2000 along with its predecessors 14.4 KBPS and 9,600 baud rate.

More and more American users are upgrading their telephone modem connections to high-speed digital subscriber lines (DSL) or cable modems, which are at least ten times faster.

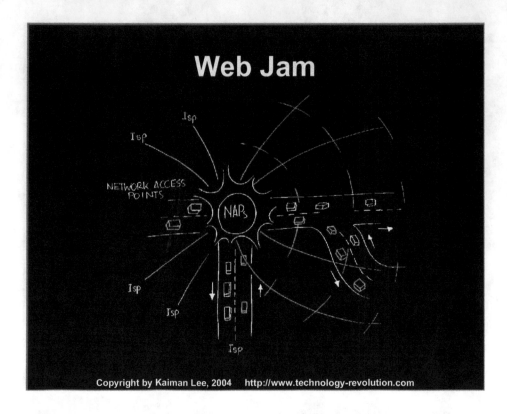

Web Jam

ISPs (Internet service providers) connect to NSPs (network service providers) by lines leased from local telephone companies.

The NSPs run their own local and national networks. In most cases they use lines leased or bought from one of these companies: AT&T, LDDS, WorldCom/MCI, and Sprint. These companies own the copper, fiber-optic, and satellite networks across which the telephone networks and Internet backbones run.

The NSPs' networks connect to one another at a variety of locations. Major ones include network access points (NAPs) near New York, Chicago, and San Francisco, plus metropolitan area exchanges on the East and West Coasts called MAE East and MAE West.

Web jams of course occur at these NAPs where data packets pack through bottlenecks.

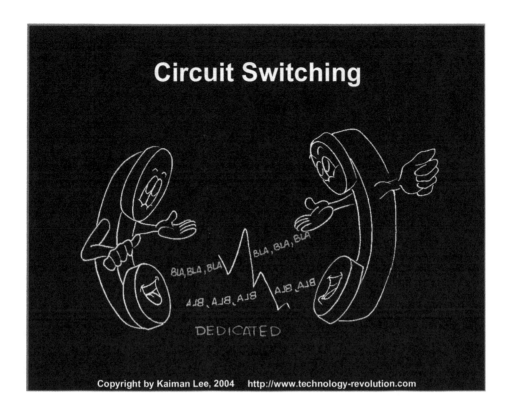

Circuit Switching

Voice transmission is moving away from the traditional circuit-switched networks to packet-switched networks.

Circuit-switched networks are designed primarily for voice communications. Calls are sent to local phone company switches. Long-distance calls are sent to long-distance networks and returned to local phone switches at the other end.

The network establishes a connection between multiple switching points and creates a straight or direct circuit for the duration of the call. Even if no conversation is taking place, the circuit is in use. If the line goes down, the call is cut off.

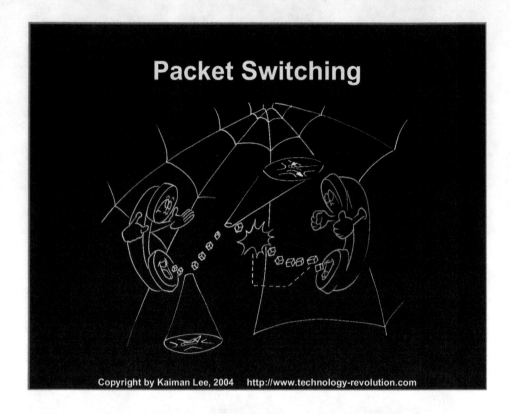

Packet Switching

Copyright by Kaiman Lee, 2004   http://www.technology-revolution.com

A file is broken into smaller chunks called IP (Internet protocol) packets. Each packet is labeled with destination address.

Packets sent via routers after routers (computers). Router tables keep track of the traffic and transmission.

Packets may go in different directions because some lines are down, and links are too busy.

On the Internet, the Transport Control Protocol (TCP) divides voice calls, video clips or other data into packets. Address information is placed on the front of each information packet.

Packet-switched networks use capacity only when there is something to be sent. This way, all available capacity can be filled with packets.

In an information superhighway analogy, telephone circuit switching allows a car going from Dallas to Atlanta to use an entire lane of Interstate 20 for the duration of the trip. Digital packet switching allows as many cars as can move safely to use the same lane at the same time. Adding data compression techniques, it is as if all the cars are transformed into minivans or buses, full of people.

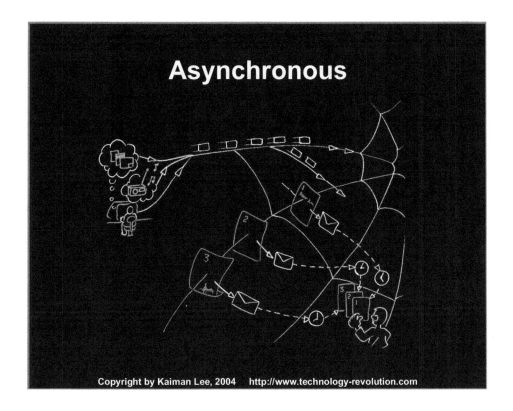

Asynchronous

"Asynchronous" means the transmission from a sender does not have to be synchronized with the receiver in order to arrive properly.

It is as if you write a long letter, then put each page in a separate envelope and drop them in the mail. Some envelopes might arrive later than others. Some might take a slightly different path to their destination. But if you number the pages, the recipient can put them in order and read the letter.

Whatever you have to send -- voice, data or video -- is broken up into small packets. These packets are sent over the Internet mostly via the method of asynchronous transmission. It is the basis of Asynchronous Transfer Mode (ATM), a means of big bandwidth transmission.

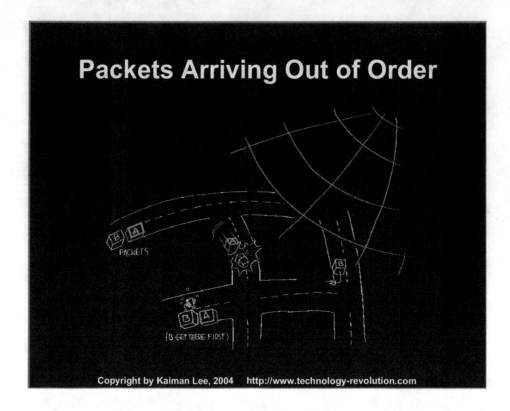

Packets Arriving Out of Order

PACKETS

(B GET THERE FIRST)

On the Internet, anyway goes, i.e., data packets will try to find the shortest route in order to get to their destinations.

The packet in front may encounter a traffic jam, so it takes another route. The packet behind suddenly finds the shortest route cleared and takes it. It arrives ahead of the front runner.

This is okay for data packets because they will be put back in order when they all arrive at the destination.

But, with voice and video streaming, there is almost no time delay. Your speech may get garbled up a bit because some of the data packets arrive a little out of order.

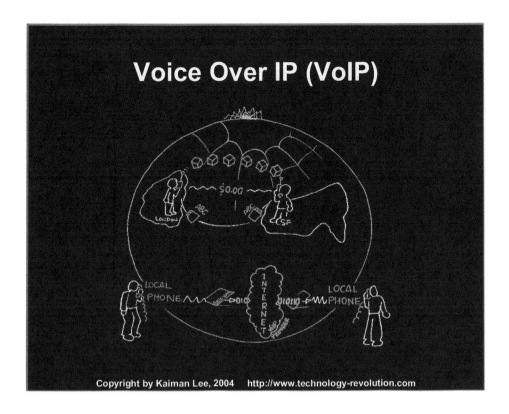

Voice Over IP (VoIP)

Sending voice as data over the Internet is called Internet telephony, voice over packets, or more commonly called voice over IP (VoIP).

The first VoIP call took place in 1995 between two PCs. Two parties arranged to be online at the same time and each had to take turns speaking, like CB radio. Next came PCs to phones. You pay nothing to make domestic U.S. long distance calls from your PC which is connected to a Web site that offers it, and some Web sites offer free international calls.

The ultimate is phone-to-phone. Wholesale IP carriers sell call minutes directly to phone companies. You place your call through your local phone company's circuit-switched network. Your local phone company decides it is cheaper to route your call through its wholesale IP carrier. The IP gateway breaks up the voice signals into compressed, syllable-sized packets. The call's destination IP gateway assembles the voice packets, puts them in the correct order, and converts them to signals so the local phone company can receive. Your call reaches your target recipient who does not know the call was routed over the Internet.

Eventually, the whole phone network could be based on IP.

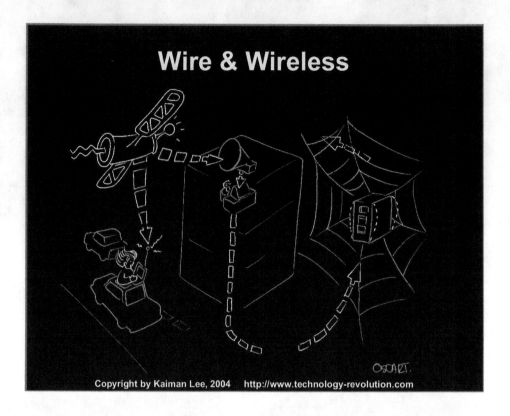

Wire & Wireless

Copyright by Kaiman Lee, 2004   http://www.technology-revolution.com

Prof. Nicholas Negroponte, Director, Media Laboratory, MIT, talked about a key vector of change in 1996: "What currently goes by air -- chiefly broadcast radio and TV -- would soon switch to wires (fiber optics and coax), while what currently goes by wires -- chiefly voice telephony -- would massively move to air."

The number of cellular phone users is multiplying like flies, started in Asian and Europe, and now in the U.S.A. With the drastic increase of mobile users by the day, there will be more and more wireless support for their data and voice transmission needs.

For example, a mobile data service lets Internet and E-mail users get connected without telephone modems. The system works by broadcasting signals back and forth from transceivers mounted on utility poles to small radio modems connected to subscribers' computers.

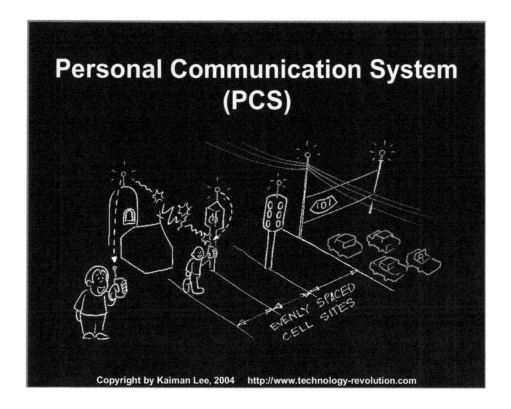

Personal Communication System (PCS)

Personal Communications Systems (PCS) started when auctions were held in 1994 for radio-frequency spectrum rights.

PCS carriers place <u>evenly spaced sets of antennas</u> and routing computers, called <u>cell sites</u>. Each cell site picks up a caller's signal when s/he enters its particular area, and then <u>seamlessly passes the call to the next station</u> when s/he leaves.

In an area where no cell site exists, called a "dead spot," a customer's call gets disconnected, a "redial opportunity."

Cell sites emit <u>radio-frequency (RF) waves</u> that operate at a wavelength on the electromagnetic spectrum between television and microwave ovens.

Although PCS antennas need to be spaced closer together than cellular ones, they do not have to be quite as high off the ground. <u>Rooftops</u> and other existing structures are used. <u>Antennas</u> can be disguised as <u>church bell towers, water-tower catwalks, lamp posts, traffic lights and highway signs, even trees</u>.

<u>Cellular-phone</u> carriers are also aggressively "<u>co-locating</u>," joining with their competitors to cluster antennas and make them seem less ubiquitous to the public.

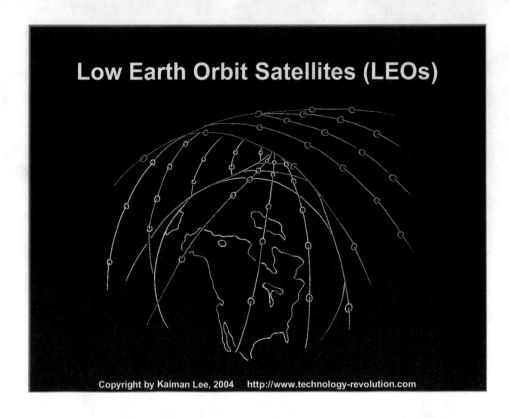

Low Earth Orbit Satellites (LEOs)

Copyright by Kaiman Lee, 2004   http://www.technology-revolution.com

Low Earth Orbit (LEO) satellites rotate with the earth at altitude about 500 to 1,400 miles from Earth. The low altitude virtually eliminates any delay in the signals going up and down. It also takes less power which means smaller satellite antennas. It takes a minimum of 12 satellites to cover the globe.

LEO's constellation of satellites work together using computerized "switchboard-in-the-sky" techniques originally developed for the Strategic Defense Initiative (SDI) -- or "Star Wars" -- missiles defense system. A LEO satellite phone call will be bounced from satellite to satellite until it reaches the other party.

Narrowband LEO applications include mobile voice, fixed rural telephony, and paging/messaging. Broadband LEO applications include virtual private networks, fixed voice, consumer multimedia, and Internet services.

LEO allows a developing nation to leapfrog copper and cable, and bring the advantages of the information age to the entire world, particularly to those being left out as a matter of cost or geography (e.g., Afghanistan).

LEO will be a boon for international travelers and people who live in areas with unreliable telecommunications.

Hurdles for LEOs

Copyright by Kaiman Lee, 2004   http://www.technology-revolution.com

LEOs "see" only a portion of the earth's surface at a given time, so the satellites must hand off signals like cellular-phone base stations do. In space, that is a complicated maneuver.

LEOs have problems serving urban canyons. If large cities you may experience signal shadowing caused by high-rise buildings. This can be signal distortion or loss. Even within a building, if you are not within a line of sight of the satellite, you may not get the signal.

Satellite communication is susceptible to weather deterioration.

If you work in a building with metallic glass, odds are the signals will not penetrate.

Even though satellite telephony services appear to be a non-starter in corporate networks, broadband satellite services could well be the next boon in wide-area data services, especially to remote locations without landlines.

Satellite technology are being deployed at the same time that fiber optics are getting laid down, so the longer it takes to get to commercial reality, the smaller the opportunity, which is the current situation in 2003.

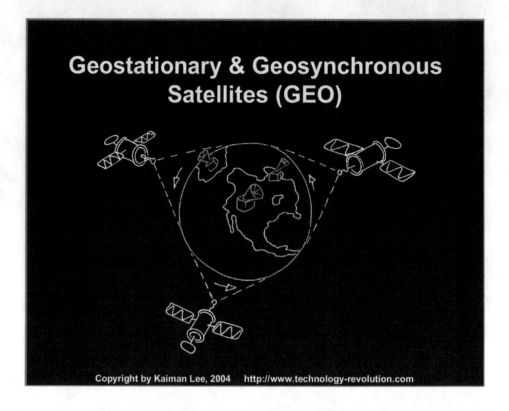

Geostationary & Geosynchronous Satellites (GEO)

Satellites that beam down television signals today are in geosynchronous or geostationary orbit 22,300 miles above fixed points on the equator. They do not rotate with the earth.

GEOs are also called High Altitude, Long Operation (HALO) platforms. It takes a minimum of three satellites to cover the globe. They require large and expensive earthbound stations.

Typical applications include corporate WANs, carrier backbones, video broadcast, and Internet services.

Signals have a half a second round-trip delay.

Net-over-satellite access like Hughes Electronics' DirecPC service can receive Web pages and e-mail on their pizza-size satellite dishes. It has speeds such as 400 KBPS downstream.   A phone line, modem and an ISP account are needed for outbound traffic, which is routed through an ISP to DirecPC's Earth station and out to the Net. Incoming e-mail and Web pages are beamed from the Earth station to a satellite and back home.

Beam It to Me

Copyright by Kaiman Lee, 2004   http://www.technology-revolution.com

You can take your personal digital assistant (PDA) out of your pocket and place it on the table. You now can beam your data and money to other people around the conference table.

Your meeting from now on could consist of this additional "beam it to me" data transfer.

The technology, code-named Bluetooth is in the form of wireless transmitters and receivers. You do not need wireless modems and cables.

Bluetooth is a specification for short-range radio links at 2.45 GHz, up to 1 MBPS, and up to 30 feet. It replaces proprietary cables with a single universal wireless link.

The transmission can be between and among digital devices such as notebooks, cellular phones, fax machines, keyboards, camera, printers and PDAs.

You will be able to set up an ad hoc peer-to-peer network almost instantly between any Bluetooth-equipped device.   And because Bluetooth conforms to the IEEE 802.11 standard for wireless communication with LANs, you will be able to connect any of these devices to LANs.

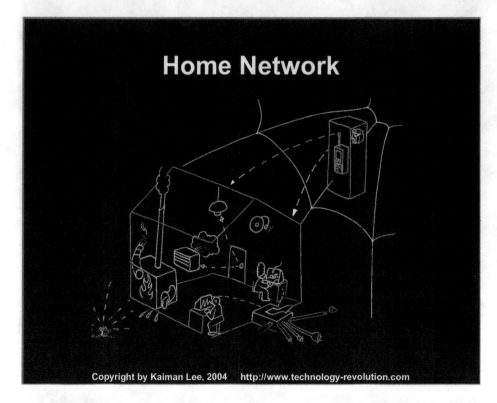

Home Network

A home network will let you share one <u>Internet connection among a few computers</u>. You can <u>share printers, cameras, and scanners</u>, etc.

You can also <u>automate your home</u>. You <u>can link heating, ventilating and air conditioning systems with the lighting, and security systems</u>. You can remotely reset fire and burglar alarms, and adjust garden sprinklers. You can have the system turn up the heat and lights as you move toward a room, dimming and cooling behind you.

Using a <u>hand-held or a PC at work</u> you can <u>check a security camera, adjust window blinds, watch live video feeds of the kids and their babysitter, and monitor what is being watched on television</u>.

You can network your home using <u>phone lines, airwaves, cable wires, electrical wires</u>, or <u>Ethernet cables</u>.

You can get a <u>high speed</u> Asymmetrical Digital Subscriber Line (<u>ADSL</u>) on your existing phone-line network.

A <u>wireless</u> network can <u>reach battery-operated independent devices</u>.

<u>Cable modems</u> <u>share lines with your neighbors</u>, thus a security issue.

<u>Electrical power lines</u> is a <u>not-yet-proven technology</u>.

<u>Ethernet cables</u> are <u>difficult to use and not readily installed</u> in homes.

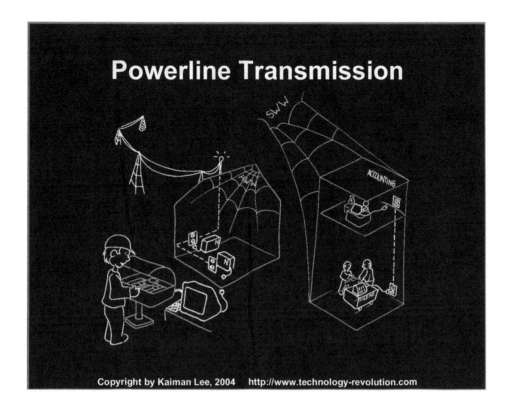

Powerline Transmission

Copyright by Kaiman Lee, 2004   http://www.technology-revolution.com

With electrical power lines, the external adapters plug into any 110-volt AC power outlet, and computers and printers connect to the adapter via parallel port cables.

Consumer Electronics Bus (CEBus) is an industry standard being developed and used in early 1998. You can use CEBus in your home network to identify, monitor, and control any CEBus-enabled plugged-in device.

Filene's and Lord and Taylor in Boston have used this technology for cash registers on wheels. Registers are plugged into the power line. All the transactions are done in real time via the power line.

There are disadvantages of electrical-power network. They were not designed to carry data. They are slower compared to other means. Sharing a common transformer with neighbors could pose a privacy issue although you can use encryption. It also requires surge protection and line conditioners to protect against power interference.

The goal of this technology is "no new wires to support home networks."

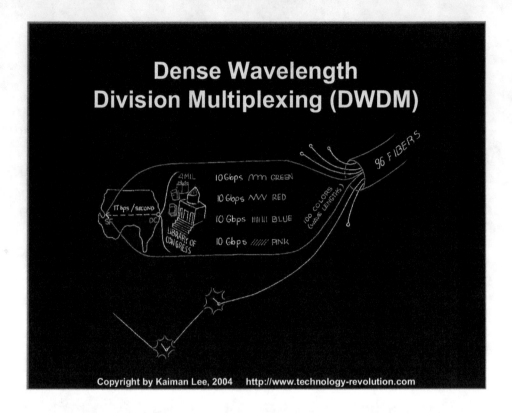

Dense Wavelength Division Multiplexing (DWDM)

In March 1998, Bell Labs, the R&D arm of Lucent Technologies demonstrated the first long-distance Tbps (terabit-per-second, trillion bits per second, 1,000 Gbps, or 1,000,000 Mbps) transmission over a single optical fiber.

That is fast enough to transport four-million books of the Library of Congress coast-to-coast in seconds on a single fiber. Or about 12 million phone calls. In May 1999, Nortel unveiled its capability of carrying 1.6 Tbps (laser pulses) -- enough to support 28 million simultaneous Internet connections.

Wavelength division multiplexing (WDM) uses a multiplexer to split the colors (or wavelengths) of light like a prism. Each fiber can then carry simultaneous multiple channels, or streams of data through different wavelengths.

Dense wavelength division multiplexing (DWDM) squeezes say 100 closely spaced wavelengths (colors or channels) each at 10 Gbps, totaling 1 Tbps on a single fiber. A typical fiber optic cable holds 96 fibers.

Bell Labs predicts 1,000 colors in a few years. However, the routers which route packets of data, and optical switches which switch between wavelengths, need to be fast enough to handle that volume of data packets.

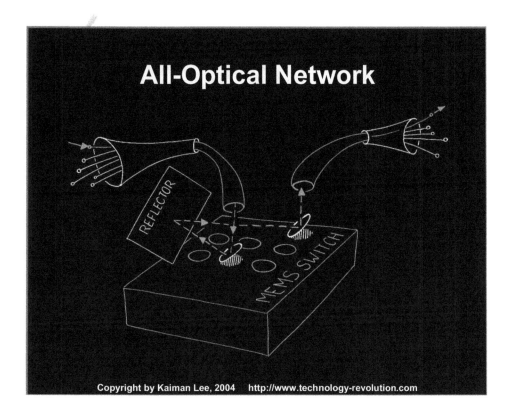

All-Optical Network

All-optical Internet requires IP (Internet Protocol) switches from one fiber to another to be all optical, i.e., without converting photons (or light waves) into electrons, and then back to photons.

In Lucent's photonic switch, micromirrors are used to redirect incoming light from one fiber to an outgoing fiber, manipulating hundreds of beams at the same time. The micro-electro-mechanical system (MEMS) relies on electronics to control the tilt of the mirrors -- and hence the route of the outgoing light.

The light wave travels through a lens at the end of each fiber. The light bounces from a tilting mirror to the reflector which then deflects the light to another tilting mirror. Finally the light goes into the lens of the target fiber and exits from the switch.

Each micromirror is several hundred micrometers in diameter. 256 of these micromirrors could fit on a few-square-centimeter silicon chip.

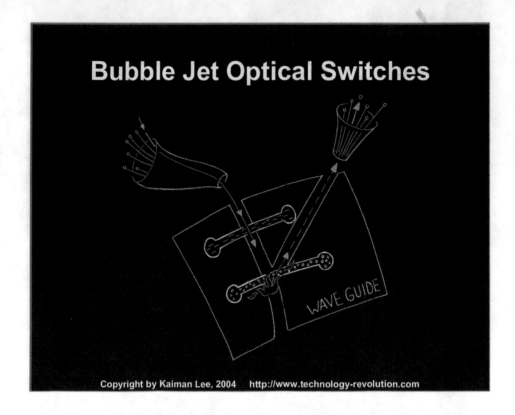

Bubble Jet Optical Switches

Agilent Technologies has developed an optical switch based on its bubble-jet printer technology, i.e., a vapor bubble to switch light signals from one optical fiber to another.

A lightwave from an incoming fiber enters a glass-channel waveguide in the switch. It passes through a fluid-filled trench that has the same optical properties as the glass.

To redirect the lightwave, a bubble-jet heater warms the trench to 65 degree Celsius, vaporizes the fluid, creates a bubble in the trench, and gives the trench a different refractive index than the glass. The lightwave bounces off the trench to a different waveguide. The lightwave then exits the waveguide to a different optical fiber.

The bubble-jet heaters can set up a switch path in less than 10 milliseconds. That number beats the 50-millisecond limit carriers set on acceptable network failures. If the networks can be restored within 50 milliseconds the failure will go undetected by customer applications running across it. This means the switch could be used in a protection-switching scheme in which traffic is routed around a broken fiber along an alternate path.

The switch can handle at least 32 input and 32 output fibers on a chip the size of a dime.

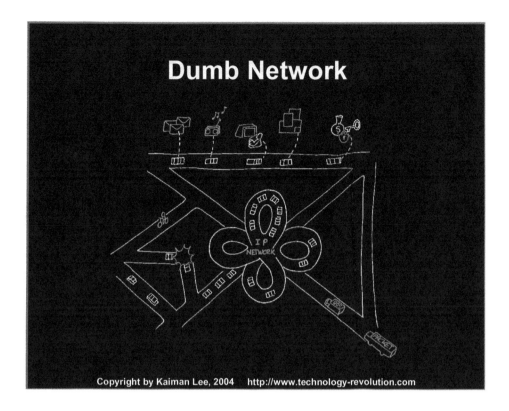

Dumb Network

In the age of <u>bandwidth scarcity</u>, we have <u>intelligent network</u>. Every <u>new feature</u> on the network must be <u>tested</u> with every other feature for "feature interactions." In the era <u>of bandwidth abundance</u>, all we need is a <u>dumb</u> network which does not need to have many features. <u>Intelligence</u> and <u>Innovation</u> occur on the <u>periphery</u> of the network.

A <u>dumb network</u> is like a <u>system of roads</u>. Its traffic can be anything from pedestrians to cars to 18-wheel trucks. The owner of each vehicle determines its contents. Each vehicle, like each packet in an IP (Internet Protocol) network, is under its own control. And like the Internet, the system of roads is a <u>self-organizing system</u>. There is <u>not a controlling authority</u> that sets up the route of every vehicle before it enters the network. And like the Internet, sometimes there is <u>congestion</u>, and sometimes there are <u>crashes</u>. But on the whole, the resulting simplicity makes the inconvenience <u>acceptable</u>.

In a dumb network, the data tells the network <u>where</u> it needs to go, and what kind of <u>services</u> it needs. The dumb network treats different data types appropriately, such as one-way voice messages, two-way voice or video, E-mail, and documents.

In a world of <u>dumb terminals and telephones</u>, <u>networks</u> had to be <u>smart</u>; but in a world <u>of smart information appliances</u>, <u>networks</u> can and should be <u>dumb</u>.

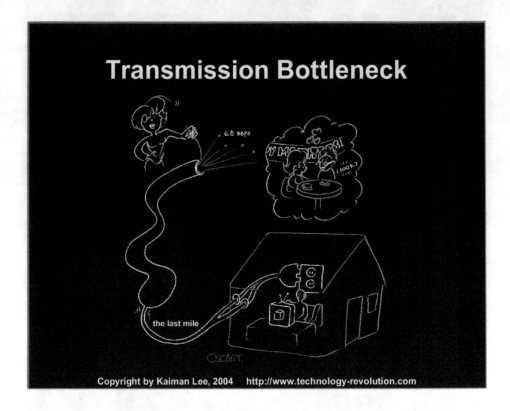

Transmission Bottleneck

the last mile

OSCART.

Copyright by Kaiman Lee, 2004   http://www.technology-revolution.com

We can have all the bandwidth in the global systems, but the <u>last mile</u> to people's homes and offices is the <u>bottleneck</u>.

Fiber optics could carry 25,000 times more information than conventional copper wires.

<u>Fiber optics</u> had the potential in 1997 of carrying <u>6.8 Giga (billion) bits per second</u> of data, or pulses of light, through a single glass strand the thickness of a hair. That is enough capacity to provide <u>simultaneous telephone service for over 100,000 calls</u>, the traffic on <u>Mother's Day</u>.

Someone said "It's the fiber, stupid." <u>One fiber</u> thread could have contained <u>three times the total traffic on the entire global telecommunication network in 1994</u>. Although the data market is growing at five times the voice market, fiber can handle it without any difficulty.

<u>Cable modems</u> and <u>DSL (digital subscriber line)</u> solutions for homes, and Gigabit Ethernet solution for enterprises are needed to alleviate the last-mile bottleneck.

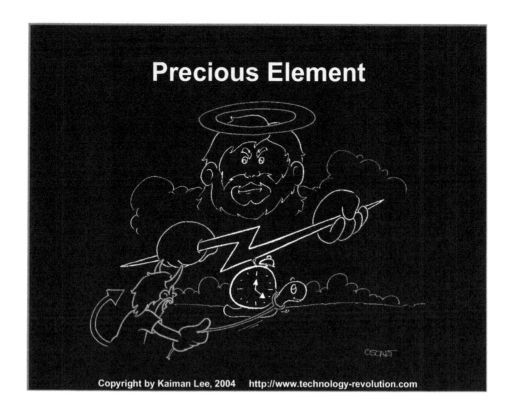

Precious Element

David Hancock, chief executive of Hitachi Corporation's portable computer division said: "Speed is God and Time is the Devil." "I focus on execute, execute, execute."

Internet has severely compressed the business cycle leading to high-speed product development that results from exchanging ideas and research over the Net. Progress is measured in Web weeks. A lost week or month can prove to be a business disaster. "You stop for lunch and you are lunch." The resultant of the accelerated speed is turmoil, opportunities and risks.

Now, we live on Internet time. We must adapt our lives, at warp speed, in a new territory.

Some engineers are working 16-hour days for months on end to get a new Java product out the door. They have more control over their time because nobody asks them why they were not in by 8 a.m. They now understand what it is like to be an options trader on Wall Street: tumult.

Internet time has blurred the boundaries between home and work life.

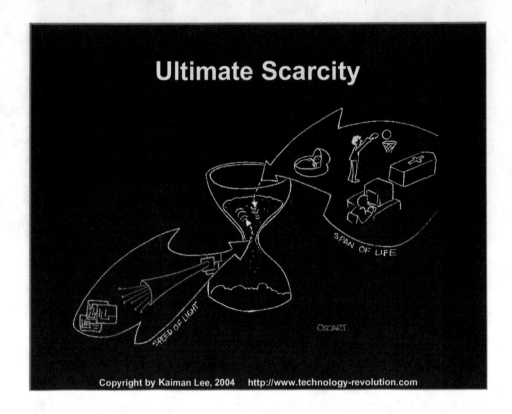

Ultimate Scarcity

SPAN OF LIFE

SPEED OF LIGHT

OSCART.

Alternative medicine is on the increase. About one-third of all doctor visits are to non-M.D.s according to the New England Journal of Medicine, 1998. More and more people are looking for holistic health.

It is quite possible to live to 100. We all know the key to long life is to stay healthy physically and mentally. One way of achieving it is to have more leisure time.

You can make use of technology to simplify your life and gain leisure time. The power of the computer and the limitless and lightning speed of the bandwidth can let you do that.

If you can get things done in half the time while others take twice the time to accomplish, you may have much more time to "live a life."

INTERNET TECHNOLOGY

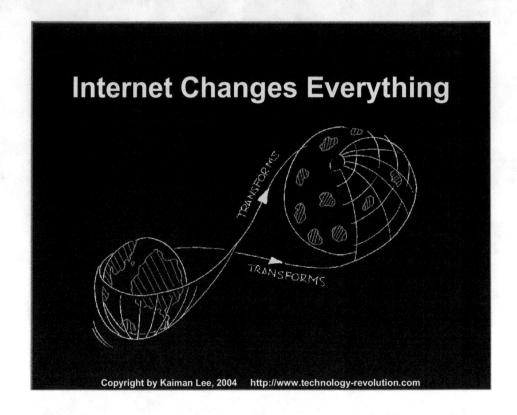

Internet is a loose collection of world networks. It can be a two-edge sword. It can drastically modify monopolies, hierarchies, pyramids and power grids of the established industrial societies. But it can also empower individuals who take full advantage of it to be enormously successful and free.

While television is primarily about our leisure time, the Internet is already transforming work, school, and play.

Virtually every business, political, and social activity will be affected and dramatically transformed by the Internet. Child rearing, consumer behavior, education, religion, and even our culture are also being changed dramatically by the Internet.

A business trip overseas used to mean distance from family and loved ones, but the Internet phone, E-mail, chat and digital pictures are changing all that.

Internet is a highly subversive phenomenon for international telecommunications, for a nation's security, and for international commerce.

As the Internet changes everything, the Internet is changed by everything.

Internet is More Important Than

We have all probably heard that the Internet is <u>more important than the printing press, automobile, TV, telephone, communication satellite, and personal computer</u>.

Some people say that the most important technological developments in the <u>last 20 years</u> are <u>PC, cable TV, and VCR</u>. Now, <u>Internet can be considered the most important technological development ever</u>.

Internet is sometimes referred to as the <u>Information Superhighway</u>. It is not quite a right metaphor because it is not measured in distance such as miles or kilometers, and it has <u>no speed limit</u>.

Internet is the "network of networks." The very basic definition of Internet is that it is a public network, a <u>global connection of TCP/IP (Transmission Control Protocol / Internet Protocol) networks</u>.

Internet itself was set up in 1969. Graphical browsers, software programs that help users mouse-click their way around the Web, were first developed in 1993. The popularity of Netscape Communications' Navigator browser caused an explosion of Web activities in 1994.

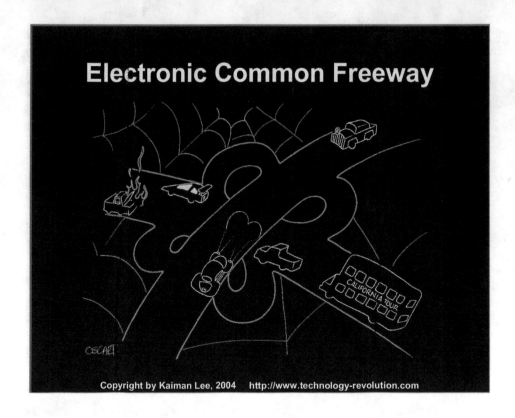

Electronic Common Freeway

Copyright by Kaiman Lee, 2004   http://www.technology-revolution.com

The Information (or electronic) Superhighway is like an interstate highway (or freeway) in the physical world. Therefore, the Internet should be and will be <u>accessible to everybody</u>.

It will carry <u>good and bad cars</u>, <u>rich and poor people</u>, and potentially <u>half of the world's commercial transactions</u>.

It is your willingness to get on the freeway and <u>drive carefully </u>that will get you somewhere.

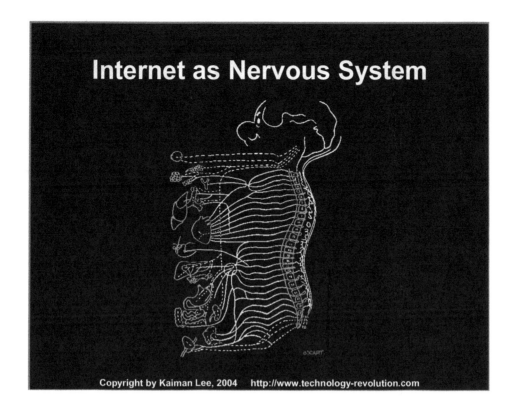

Internet as Nervous System

If <u>money is the lifeblood of business</u>, <u>Internet is its nervous system</u>.

Using the Internet, you have universal <u>connectivity to all the "organs"</u> that function for business and life. IBM's Intranet is its a digital nervous system and its knowledge-sharing medium.

To extend the metaphor further, what about adding effective <u>nervous and responsive systems</u> (information appliances) to houses, office buildings, robots and vehicles of all sorts?

Your surrounding physical environments will then <u>feel their own pain</u>, and make corrections so that you do not feel those pain.

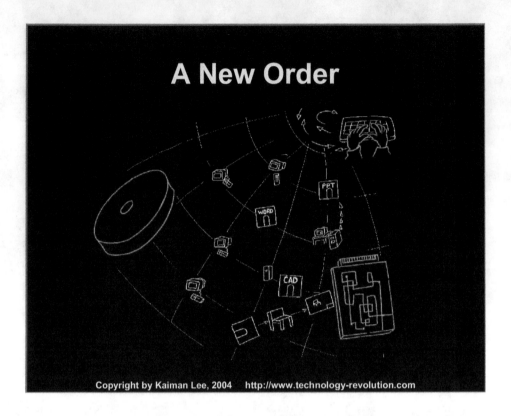

A New Order

The basis of the new order is that the programs in your machine will no longer mainly determine the functions you can perform. The computer is becoming a peripheral to the Internet.

The Web has turned the Internet into a giant virtual disk drive. Java will turn the Internet into a giant processor.

The personal computer, operating system, and applications as we know them today will dissipate into the background. They will be taken for granted the way we treat telephones and fax machines. They are just there in whatever form they might be, to be used for collaboration and communication.

A three-dimensional Web could become the "Window" or the universal interface to the world and the entry point to do anything that involves information and communication.

Bill Gates' vision (Nov. 1990) of having "information at your fingertips" is already a reality. It is not through Windows everywhere, but through Internet everywhere.

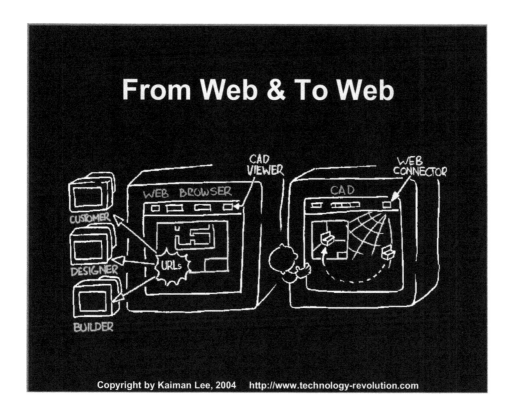

The idea of a <u>separate browser and file manager</u> will go away and be replaced by one interface. The <u>artificial dividing line between what is the Net and what is on the desktop will fade into oblivion</u>.

A Web browser has become the least common denominator front-end. It is now the universal interface. The Internet <u>browser </u>will be your <u>interface to the world all day</u>. Therefore, <u>all applications will have an Internet connection</u>.

To stretch your imagination a bit more, what about a <u>bar code address field in a browser</u>? When a bar code is scanned, it will go directly to the product's Web site or page.

Consumers will shift from print, radio, and TV media to the Internet as their primary source for product information.

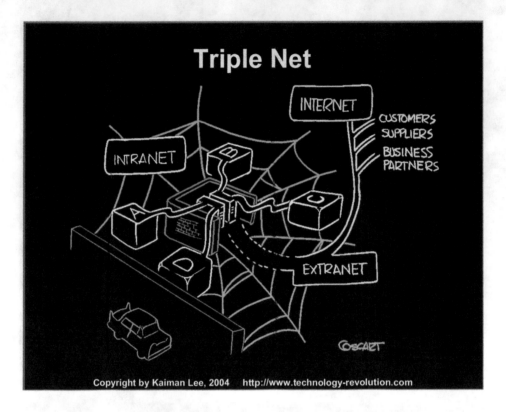

Triple Net

INTERNET

CUSTOMERS
SUPPLIERS
BUSINESS
PARTNERS

INTRANET

EXTRANET

The "Triple Net" consists of the Intranet within a company, the Internet outside of the company, and the Extranet where outsiders use encapsulated and encrypted messages through an Internet tunnel to communicate with the company.

An Intranet leverages Internet-standard technologies such as TCP/IP, HTML, HTTP and Java to develop, present and transport data within the enterprise, i.e., behind an organization's firewall.

Enterprise networks are no longer defined by the mere physical boundaries of the corporation. They encompass remote sites and offices which may be spread across the country or around the world.

They include mobile users and telecommuters of the company. They also include partners, suppliers, service providers and major customers.

The boundaries of today's enterprise networks are defined logically (vs. physically) as a security policy, a set of rules that spell out access rights to information and to information resources.

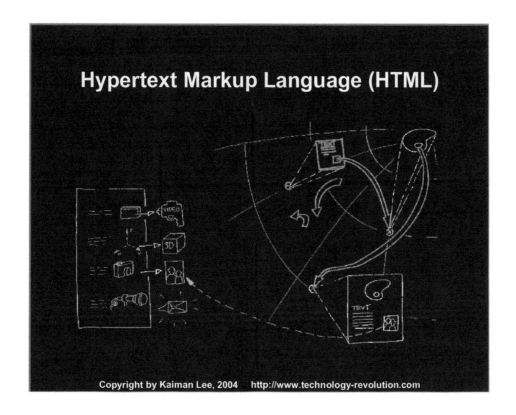

Hypertext Markup Language (HTML)

The very basic beauty of the Internet is its hyper-linking facility called hypertext markup language (HTML). Double click a highlighted URL (Uniform Resource Locator) address and you are in another site or another page. It integrates the whole world's information.

With hyper-linking, there is no need to know file names and where files are. These virtual documents are a combination of information objects that can come from any source and from anywhere in the enterprise or the Web.

HTML is a presentation format. It is not meant to be used for interactive applications. Its turn-around time is quite high.

An Internet browser allows for an interface that third parties could use to create specialized programs to increase the browser's basic functionality, such as to view larger, or more detailed images or other types of documents, such as the TIFF (tagged-image file format) images. It is called a "plug-in."

Java has mostly replaced plug-ins. It will also extend HTML to incorporate interactive and dynamic functionalities.

eXtensible Markup Language (XML)

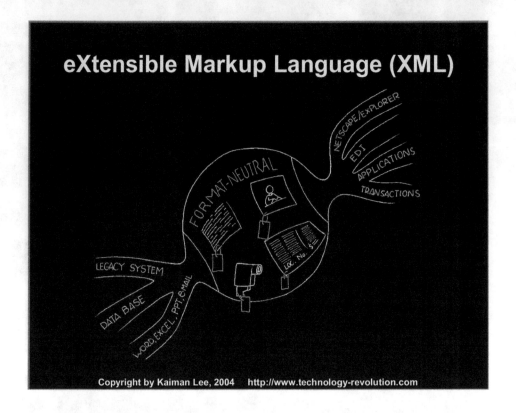

Extensible Markup Language (XML) can be considered a <u>document management tool</u> that may eventually <u>replace a big part of HTML</u> for coding the most <u>advanced Web pages</u>.

XML is a <u>meta language</u> that can be used to write <u>format-neutral</u> documents containing <u>structured data</u>. You could use XML to process <u>forms</u> or <u>database searches</u> via the Web. You could <u>convert MS Word, Excel, PowerPoint</u>, SQL Server, Windows NT directory and various E-mail programs to the XML format. Then <u>publish</u> the XML files to any desktops. XML gives developers the ability to <u>create content once and distribute it anywhere</u>.

XML lets users <u>define content</u> through <u>special tags</u> (<u>attributes</u>) to text, images, programs, etc. This is done so that any processor, from browsers to special search agents or servers, can understand what the <u>content</u> is.

XML <u>standardizes syntax</u>, a way to define tags, but it <u>does not</u> establish <u>what these tags mean</u> (<u>semantics</u>). Does the content DATE mean date of publication, date due, or date modified?

XML is emerging as a <u>middleware standard</u>. You will see a new breed of three-tiered applications in which XML servers <u>pull formatted data out of back-end or legacy databases</u>, save it as XML, and convert the data <u>into any format</u> to deliver to the client.

Java (an invention by Sun Microsystems, Inc.) applets, <u>unlike browser plug-ins</u>, which have to be downloaded and installed, are <u>delivered through the Web</u> as you use them or <u>on demand</u>.

In most cases, they <u>run inside a Java-enabled Web browser</u>.

Initially, Java applets could not do much except <u>handle graphical presentation and user interaction</u>. They would communicate only with the server they were down-loaded from.

The capabilities of applets are becoming more and more powerful, to the extent that <u>all e-commerce</u> will use some form of Java applets.

Java applets are objects that will make <u>network computing</u> (thin client: a stripped-down personal computer for mainly Internet access) commonplace.

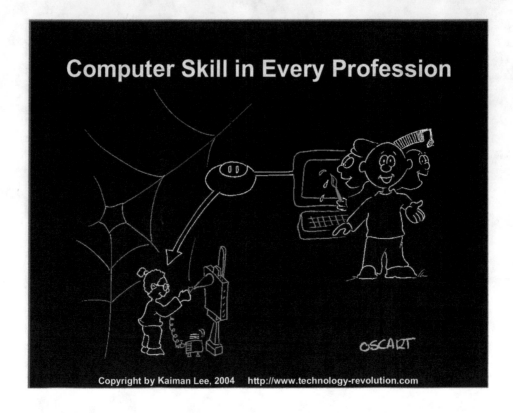

Computer Skill in Every Profession

Let us say that you are an expert in spray painting and you want to <u>sell your skill over the Net</u>. You have a couple of options.

First, you can <u>hire someone with Java programming</u> skill to learn about your field and write the Java applets. That <u>hand-off</u> will cost you time and aggravation, in going back and forth between you and the programmer.

The other option is to <u>write the applets yourself</u>, and avoid all the hassle and costs.

If you believe that almost everything that can be done on the Web will go on the Web, then you will realize that those who have something to sell over the Net should have the skill in writing Java applets.

For the new young generations, an education in computers to the extent of getting a <u>B.S. in computer science</u> may give an individual a competitive advantage in the business world. His or her chance of succeeding in a professional career (e.g., architect, medical doctor, accountant, real estate broker) will be much higher than those without it.

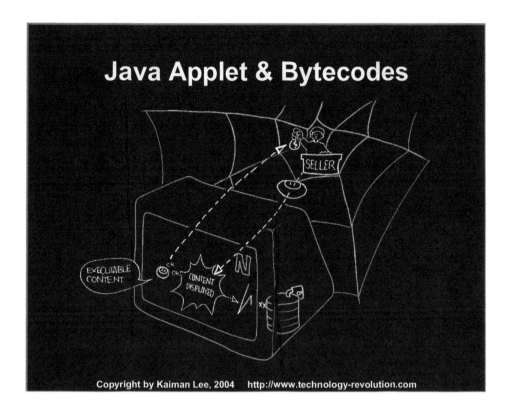

Java Applet & Bytecodes

The Java code that a programmer writes is not compiled (computer applications such as MS Word, and Excel are compiled) to the binary instruction codes that are recognized and carried out by a processor's arithmetic and logic units.

When a Java applet is written, Java statements are translated into a Java class file which contains a stream of byte codes. The byte codes are processed at run time by an intermediate program called a Java Virtual Machine (JVM).

A JVM could be built in the form of a chip for any "real" computer including embedded information appliances, or in most situations written in the form of a program for any operating system.

Java byte-code files become executable on a computer when that computer has its own version of the JVM.

A stream of byte codes can be read from a class file and transformed into instructions for the host machine in the same way a spreadsheet file can be loaded and recalculated by a user on either a PC or a Macintosh.

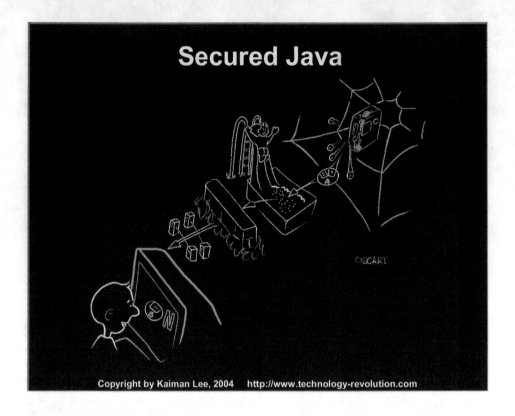

Secured Java

Java applets can be run in a virtual machine layer, a safe computer layer, or within the confines of your browser, so that they can not introduce viruses to your desktop or system.

Applets can also be executed on a security server or a "sandbox" that <u>sits outside the firewall</u>, and isolated from the operating system. The <u>"sandbox" environment is for "play" and does not worry about getting hurt</u>. It allows only the user interface portion or visual components to reach your browser.

If an applet contains some sort of vandal attack codes, any <u>damage will be done to the security server or sandbox</u>, acting as a <u>sacrificial lamb</u>, rather than to any resource inside the firewall.

The information about the breach of security is then communicated to the gateway or firewall which then establishes permanent blocking measures to deny vandals further access to the network.

Java's "write once, run anywhere" promise is based on certain premises, the JVM (Java Virtual Machine) and Java APIs (applications programming interfaces). Claims made for Java's efficiency, security or capability are subject to the limitations of each machine's JVM and Java APIs.

The API classes for Java's generic GUI (the Abstract Windowing Toolkit, or AWT) are a portable interface layer that must be supported by "native peer" code.

When a Java program needs to put a button on the screen, a programmer can write platform-independent statements to create and display that button, but somewhere API classes use a hidden connection to the local operating system to make that happen.

On Windows, the buttons look like Windows buttons. On a Macintosh, they look like Mac buttons. The appearance and behavior of a Java graphical application on different platforms is consistent with that of native applications.

Therefore, the Java promise should read "write once, run anywhere that has a JVM and a full set of Java API classes."

XML does for <u>data</u> what <u>Java</u> does for <u>applications</u>.

XML describes data, and Java describes the behavior behind the data.

XML gives Java something to do. Java lets XML do something useful. XML and Java have <u>reciprocal duties in enabling the Web of the future</u>. <u>Java</u> will become the <u>brains</u> (programs) of the Internet. <u>XML</u> documents will be how they <u>speak</u> (format) to each other.

When it comes to building distributed systems around the Internet, the standard <u>languages of choice will be XML and Java</u>.

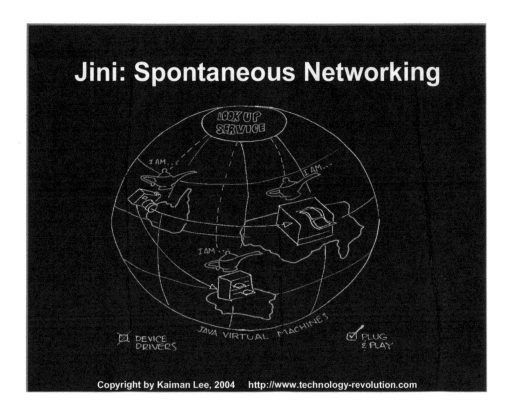

Sun Microsystems' Jini (pronounced "genie," and not an acronym) would allow any digital device, e.g., printer, projector, camera, smart card, palm top, and cell phone to plug-and-play in a network, free of device drivers and network log-in hassles.

Without the intervention of the operating system, a printer would identify itself with its characteristics. After that, any device, e.g., a camera, already on the network could use the printer.

Jini allows for ad hoc, impromptu or spontaneous networks of different services to be created. Jini makes "autodiscovery" of assets on the network possible.

Jini assumes everything is networked and everything on the network is a service. Services are found through a look-up service, a dynamically built directory that keeps track of all the devices available on the network. New services are added to the look-up service by a process called discovery. It is Java's ability to run on different types of computers that lets Jini-enabled devices send their own software code to the look-up service and receive instructions from others.

With Jini and Java, most operating systems as we know them today could be rendered obsolete. They let the Internet be the computer, the ultimate distributed system.

WEBCAM
TECHNOLOGY

"You've got a video call" ... on your desktop!

Desktop videoconferencing (DVC) is a technique of streaming live video and audio between geographically separated PCs or network computers (NCs) using a monitor-mounted camera, a network connection and software to exchange images.

DVC usually means a "talking head" application, where people are mostly sitting at their desks and not giving elaborate presentations.

Employees scattered around many floors, buildings, or even countries, for example, are perfect candidates for a DVC system. This has applicability to direct sales, customer service, technical support, help desk support, electronic shopping, medical applications, and distance learning.

DVC is usually equipped with document-sharing or whiteboard applications. The whiteboard is a built-in, shared drawing program that lets multiple users collaborate on projects by modifying images and text in real-time.

Large bandwidth is required for you to experience smooth, high-quality video and listen to synchronized audio that does not sound like it comes from the bottom of a well.

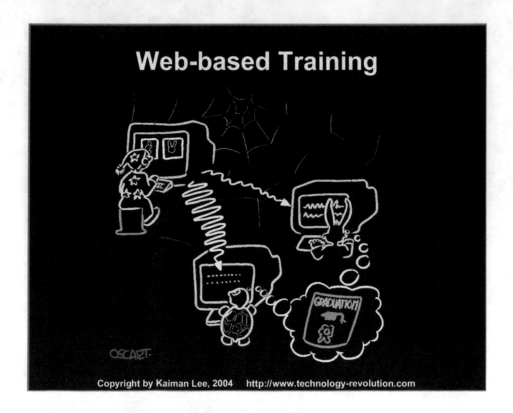

Web-based Training

Copyright by Kaiman Lee, 2004   http://www.technology-revolution.com

Studies show that people learn better when they are participating in the learning experience. Web-based training allows people to <u>learn interactively on their own time and location</u>.

You can think of it as <u>learning on call, just-in-time course work, or a pay-per-use training</u> program. Other terms used are <u>Internet-based training, online training, just-in-time continuous learning, and remote training</u>.

With course work installed at a Web site, all you need do is fire up a Web browser, access the URL (Uniform Resource Locator) and start reading, watching demos and answering questions.

Project team members can go through training at their own pace. <u>Slow and fast learners</u> can all achieve the same measure of competency. The <u>course work</u> is <u>tailor made</u> for each student. A <u>live instructor</u> on the other end can appear when s/he is needed.

Web-based training is likely to be <u>less expensive than CD-ROM-based or computer-based training (CBT)</u>, and far more flexible. The real savings come in eliminating the costs of tracking and handling the CD-ROMs.

Web-based training equalizes the opportunity and responsibility for employee learning. Training can also be <u>decentralized</u>.

Employee Recruiting

Many industries are using the Internet and Webcams as an interview medium to recruit recent college graduates and experienced employees.

Employee recruiting can be done on a company's own Web site or by using common job listing sites.

A career fulfillment site uses searching technologies to allow people to search the advertisements from several newspapers using categories such as geographic location, position level, etc. and key words.

Another way is to let users fill out a form that profiles their experience, abilities, and what they are looking for in a new position.

These electronic resumes can then be searched and matched up with available positions.

Summer Camp

With ubiquitous and inexpensive multimedia running over the Internet, anxious parents can see what their <u>children at a summer camp</u> look like, or in a day-care center through a Webcam.

Your child in college can make a <u>video call home and beg for money</u>. A <u>hospital</u> can use an Intranet-based Webcam to <u>monitor patients</u>, and <u>mom can check on her baby</u>.

A computer chip manufacturer can keep an eye on activities in a clean-room environment. <u>Convenience stores</u> can use Webcams for <u>security</u> purposes.

Webcams could <u>force telecommuters to get dressed for work</u>. Webcams in Intranets can be used for <u>remote monitoring of employees</u>.

You can monitor your beach house during winter months. You can check out the scene inside a nightclub before you stand in line, or help you steer clear of traffic using highway Webcams that can beam gridlock conditions to your moving car.

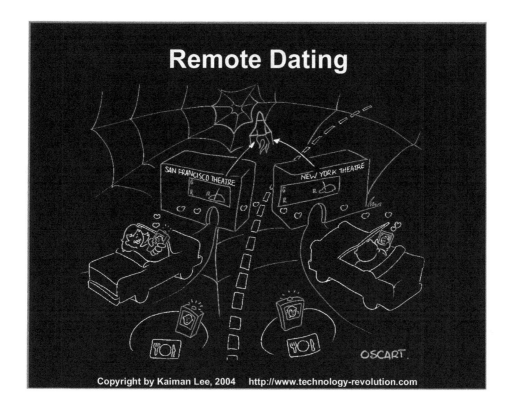

Remote Dating

In Bill Gate's book "The Road Ahead," he visualized a <u>long-distance romance</u>.

Lovers could <u>watch a movie</u> playing in their respective cities at about the same time.

Driving to the theater, they would talk to each other on their car cellular phones.

After the movie, they could re-establish the Webcam connection on their PDA (Personal Digital Assistant) or other handheld devices and talk about the movie, or anything else.

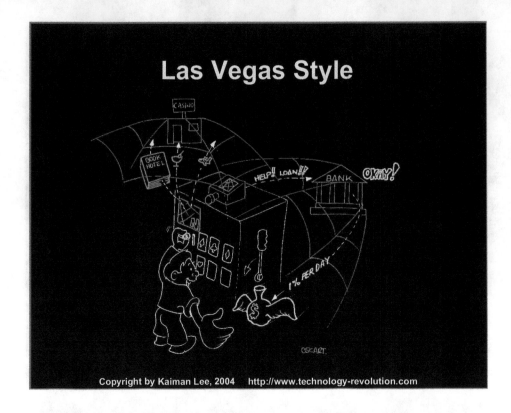

In Las Vegas, it is conceivable that, <u>without leaving your electronic slot machine</u>, you can place a <u>video call</u> to the concierge via an Intranet and <u>order a drink</u>, extend your stay in the hotel one more night, order <u>tickets to a show</u>, or make a <u>dinner reservation</u>.

For those who gamble a lot, they could be feeding dollars into the machine with one hand while, with the other, calling up the closest bank that offers <u>quick loans</u> using the Internet!

The idea here is that Internet access will be ubiquitous just like the telephones.

Internet Live Shows

In 1998, about 2 million people observed the <u>first-ever live birth on the Web</u>.

Two people claiming to be virgins said they would have <u>their first sexual intercourse on the Web</u>. After weeks of courtship shown on the Web, it was then proven a <u>hoax</u>.

You could've <u>observe the life</u> of Jennifer Kaye Ringley <u>24</u> <u>hours</u> a day via a <u>Webcam</u>. People were <u>fascinated, enraged, entranced or obsessed</u> by being able to see another person's whole life.

<u>College students</u> received <u>free room and board</u>, tuition and a stipend by living in a house where <u>cameras were all around, including the bathrooms</u>. Web surfers paid to view the site.

Tiny and affordable <u>video cameras</u> are embedded into <u>smoke detectors, exit signs, cellular phones, stuffed animals, shoes and showerheads</u>.

These inexpensive hidden video cameras are part of a "<u>third wave</u>" of technological advances that are changing how we live. The first two waves are <u>inexpensive computer processors and inexpensive computer networks</u>.

Site Cam

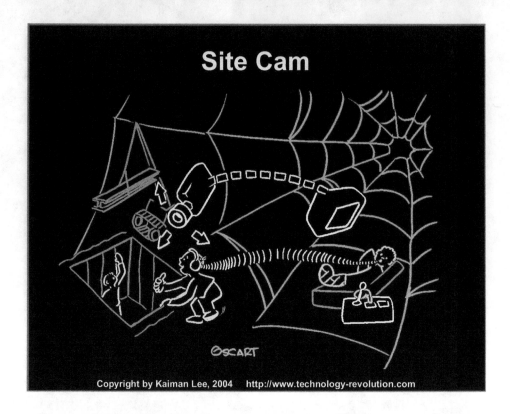

Webcam (also known as CyberCam or NetCam) technology uses an embedded video camera linked to the Internet/Intranet. It provides remote vision beamed from offices and construction sites.

A site cam can take pictures continuously or every few seconds/minutes. A telerobotic Webcam can allow you to remotely control the view, zoom in or out, and select interested parts of the scene.

Construction site applications include safety inspections and monitoring critical construction stages such as excavation and concrete pouring. A foreman could supervise the construction remotely if s/he can not get to the site.

A Webcam can also be placed to record unforeseen conditions for claims purposes. It can be used to measure precise earth and retaining wall movement.

You can create a movie which records the daily construction progress on the site. It can be used as an archive of the construction project.

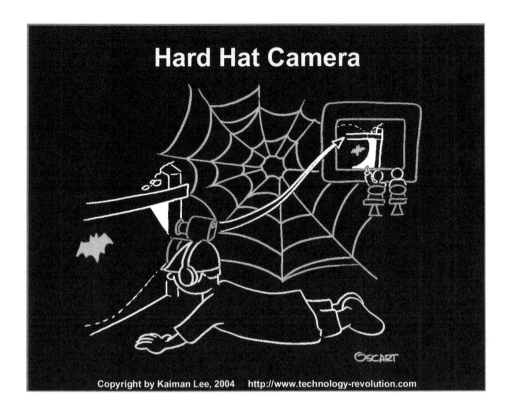

Hard Hat Camera

Copyright by Kaiman Lee, 2004   http://www.technology-revolution.com

A hard hat camera refers to a small video camera mounted on a worker's <u>hard hat</u>.

These cameras are usually designed to help increase safety and mobility. If the cameras are embedded with GPS devices, their use can enhance field personnel's knowledge of their location in the field .

Such use would support improved communications between the inspector in the field and the engineers in the main office. The enhanced communication capabilities make <u>real-time decisions</u> possible.

They are capable of operating in an <u>explosive atmosphere</u>. When mounted on <u>mobile robots</u>, they can serve as a warning system that detects levels of radiation, carbon monoxide, and other <u>hazards</u>.

Remote Field Testing

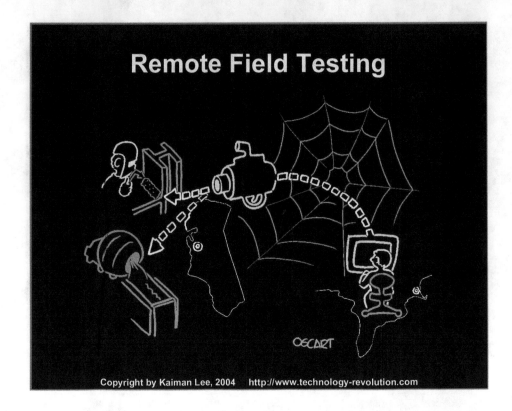

An expert can remotely observe the field testing of <u>concrete</u> and <u>steel welding</u> for quality control. You can have <u>instant expert's advice</u> on unforeseen site conditions.

A remote expert can also see if a site condition is compatible with the design intent.

These concepts can be projected to manufacturing environments where Webcams will allow remote experts to observe the critical stages in an assembly line.

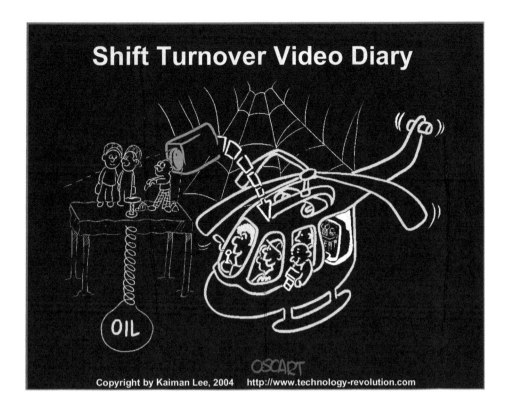

Shift Turnover Video Diary

Copyright by Kaiman Lee, 2004   http://www.technology-revolution.com

A shift turnover video diary is an efficient way for different shifts to communicate progress and problems at a construction site. Personnel on one shift record their progress, <u>visually and verbally, with a Webcam</u>.

The video can be saved for later broadcast or viewing. It can also be concurrently viewed by the replacement crew while they are <u>en route</u> to the site.

It is quicker and easier to produce and review a video diary than it is to create and read traditional <u>written shift turnover diaries</u>.

Construction staff members are able to <u>express</u> themselves <u>more easily and fully</u> using speech and gestures.

Punch List

Copyright by Kaiman Lee, 2004   http://www.technology-revolution.com

The <u>owner</u> can do a <u>virtual walk through</u> remotely with other parties such as the architect, real estate broker and contractor, present at the site, while the punch list is being generated.

Same concepts can be applied to all kinds of inspections, e.g., <u>environmental compliance</u>, and <u>hazardous waste disposal</u>, etc.

The Federal Aviation Administration (FAA) is considering installing <u>video recorders in airplanes</u> so they do not have to search for the black box in 5,000-foot deep sea, in case of an airplane crash.

COLLABORATION TECHNOLOGY

Hiding Information

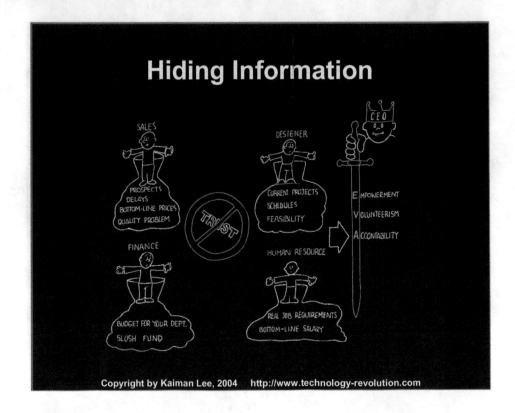

Salespeople hide information on prospects from the boss and other salespeople. They hide delays, bottom-line prices and potential quality problems from customers. Customers hide their real plans and priorities from sales people.

Product designers hide what they are working on, and how long it will take. Human resources hide from applicants about real job requirements.

Finance people hide how much money will actually be available. Production departments hide how much they really need. We hide our data and software tricks from each other.

People hide information because they do not trust people. Everybody has an agenda that is most likely not the same as any other's. People fear that if they reveal their real intentions to the wrong people, their quotas might be jacked up, and their schedules shortened.

A successful business inherently has a culture where knowledge sharing is embedded. Only the top executive has a chance against the culture of information hiding. Without that leadership, all you can do to uncover information is to do your homework, listen at the watercooler, make friends, cut deals, and swap secrets.

Copyright by Kaiman Lee, 2004   http://www.technology-revolution.com

Do you know what is <u>talked about</u> in the <u>board room</u>? Do you know <u>right away</u> the decisions that could affect your project or career?

You do not, if you depend on news from the <u>paper medium</u>.

You do if you frequently look at the <u>Intranet</u>, and if it is the "<u>single source</u>" for information distribution. <u>Intranets</u> are making it much easier for employees to find information from a "single source."

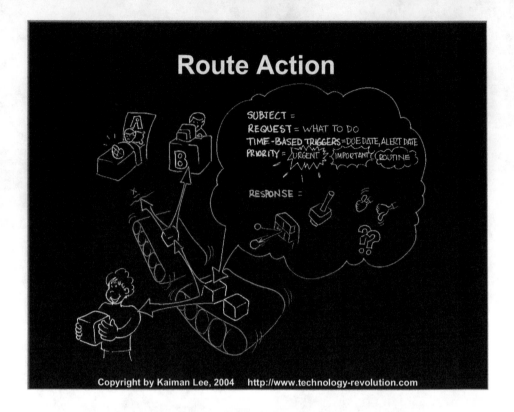

Route Action

SUBJECT =
REQUEST = WHAT TO DO
TIME-BASED TRIGGERS = DUE DATE, ALERT DATE
PRIORITY = URGENT, IMPORTANT, ROUTINE

RESPONSE =

You can think of electronic routing being very similar to manual routing. You have a "routing slip." It may contain the following routing actions:

- subject: what project and task,
- reference: background,
- request: note what to do,
- time-based triggers: due date, alert date,
- priority: urgent/important, important, routine, and
- response: approve, vote, reject, more information.

Routing can be done through <u>serial or parallel distribution</u>. You may route to <u>alternate users</u>, and optional reviewers. You may also use <u>conditional routing</u>, i.e., if this happens, then ...

You should route the work to specific <u>roles or functions</u>, <u>rather than to a specific person</u>. If the person who would normally do the work is not available to act on it, the system can find someone else with similar qualifications to perform it.

When an individual leaves a company, the routing does not need to be changed. The table that maps a person to one or more roles and functions will be updated with the replacement person.

Single Source

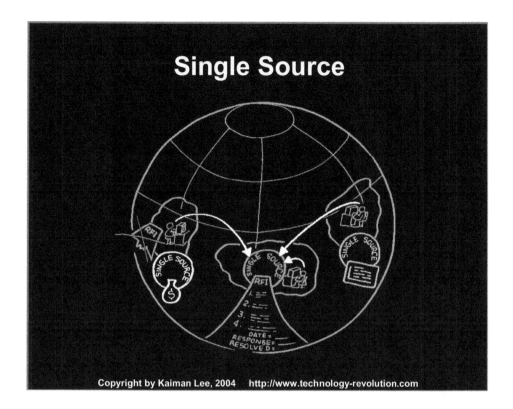

You can put an <u>end</u> to the <u>"why didn't someone tell me" syndrome</u> by implementing the concept of "single source."

It is a <u>single place</u> where a particular piece of information is located, and from which people can handle all of their work. Single source documents everything with <u>integrity</u> so people do not <u>second guess each other</u>.

As an example, single source provides a common view of the "state of the work." A request for information (RFI) on an Extranet does not leave the online database. It <u>exists in one place only</u>. As a result, its transaction history is generated automatically.

Single source does <u>not mean all information is to be located in one place</u>. Enterprise data to be shared by all groups may be centrally maintained while parochial data can be locally maintained.

As long as the same information is <u>not duplicated at several places</u>, it fits the single source concept.

Check In & Check Out

In a traditional workflow process, the original document does not usually move from place to place. A copy of it is sent to the next person in line to do something to it. When the work is done, the copy is checked back in to replace the original and given a new version number.

With single source in an Intranet and Extranet environment, the workspace is always available to anyone, anywhere and anytime. Instead of even thinking about a copy of a document moving anywhere, it does not move at all. The "material," e.g., documents, do not check in and out of the workplace -- the individual or team does.

While you are editing it, other people can see it if you let them. Or the others will see the previous version until you hit "save" or check out of the document.

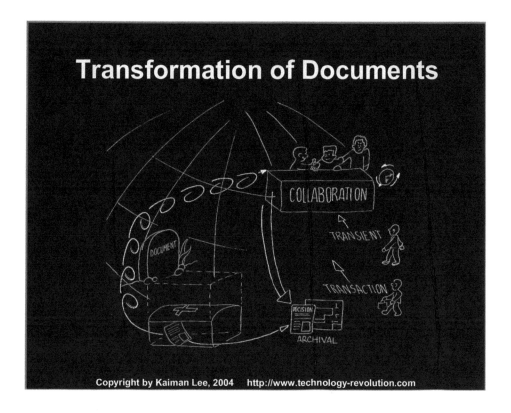

Transformation of Documents

Traditionally, when you are <u>writing</u>, say a business proposal, you do some <u>research</u>, put together a <u>draft</u>, <u>think</u> about it, <u>check</u> with people, and <u>modify</u> the draft again and again. When you are satisfied with what you have done, you distribute it. With this <u>document</u> you take <u>accountability</u>, good or bad.

With the <u>Intranet</u>, you create a <u>Web page</u> with your quick <u>draft</u> on it. You send an <u>E-mail</u> with the universal resource locator (<u>URL</u>) to people you want to involve with. You preface it with something like, <u>"Here is my first cut, what do you think?"</u>

Your <u>team members respond</u>, posting their own thoughts. Some discussions and real-time chat are captured and saved. <u>In the end, a document for which you take accountability for comes to being</u>.

<u>Documents have value when they are done</u>.

<u>Intranet project sites have value while the project is underway</u>. Business <u>documents</u> will primarily be records of <u>decisions</u> made, or "<u>archives</u>" of business. <u>The real work of business will be in collaboration</u> revolving <u>around Web sites</u> rather than documents.

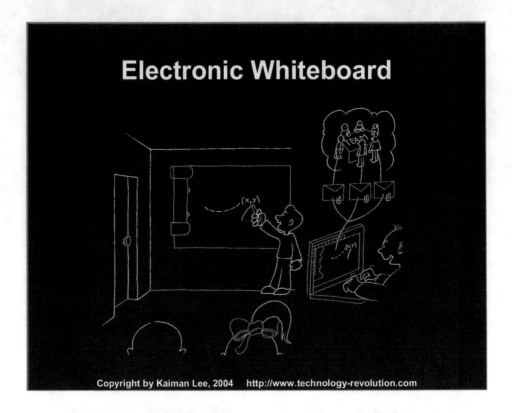

Electronic Whiteboard

Turn an inexpensive whiteboard, a wall or window glass into a data-sharing collaboration tool. An electronic capture bar (portable sensor bar) can record everything you have written and erased.

The bar is about 24 inches long and can be folded in half and stored in a bag. It weighs about 2.5 pounds. You can easily set up a whiteboard in an office on the road. Two suction cups attach the bar vertically to the leftmost portion of a flat surface.

Ordinary markers are held in special ultrasound-emitting jackets. As the marker moves, two sensors on the capture bar track its motion by computing the ultrasound's travel time. The jackets emit an infrared signal that indicates the marker's color.

This is a line-of-sight system, so you can not lean against the board between the marker and data capture port. The tip of the marker must be "seen" by the capture bar in order to work. The strokes of the marker and dry eraser are transferred to the PC via a serial cable.

You can attach comments via a notes section to any of the screens. You can export data as an image or an HTML file. This is an excellent way to prevent data loss. You can now have ad hoc discussion recorded and shared.

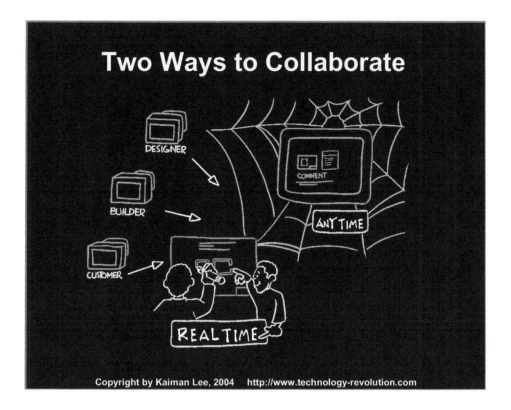

Project members including clients, architects and contractors can work on a <u>single-source database</u> in two different ways: anytime and real-time.

<u>Anytime collaboration</u> is when one person checks into a document at anytime and does something to it, then checks out. Another person repeats the process at another time. While the CAD (computer-aided design) drawings stay in one place, people can <u>review them and make comments anytime</u> they want.

<u>Real-time collaboration</u> is when people work on a document at the same time. Now it is possible to <u>review, comment and make decision</u> on CAD information in <u>real-time</u> over the Web or on an Intranet.

It will be possible to <u>identify, then correct, errors at an earlier stage</u> in the construction process. Modifications to construction plans or designs will be based on current project activities, rather than on outdated information.

Real-time collaboration requires <u>big bandwidth</u>, a limiting factor, but explosive bandwidth expansion is just around the corner.

Real-time collaboration has also been called <u>simultaneous collaboration, team-design, and co-creation</u>.

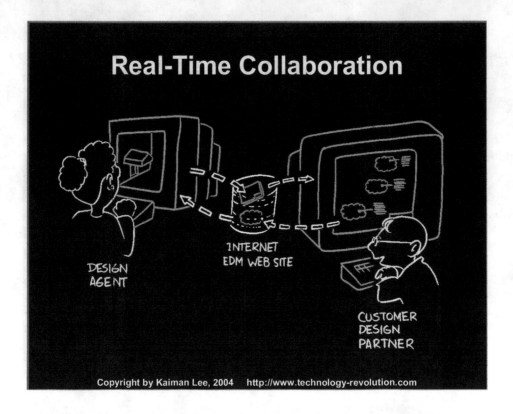

Real-Time Collaboration

DESIGN
AGENT

INTERNET
EDM WEB SITE

CUSTOMER
DESIGN
PARTNER

Copyright by Kaiman Lee, 2004   http://www.technology-revolution.com

Real-time collaboration is when several people work on a document at the same time. Designers, suppliers, and contractors who are scattered geographically comment and make decision on product development over the Web.

Any team member can have control of the mouse while all others see the product evolving and changing. They start together and finish together, with full understanding based on the information available at the time. And in the end, they all sign off on the result.

In real-time collaboration, someone is making a sketch, while other team members are building a computer aided design (CAD) model, and doing stress analysis, manufacturing productivity analysis, and cost analysis. Since these people are all on the Web together, they can talk about potential problems, pros and cons of a design.

In addition to allowing product developers to catch errors quickly, real-time collaboration also makes it easier to pull experts onto a given project. Real-time design collaboration can make use of say five percent of an expert's day and not wasting the rest with meetings and travel. Experts meet the team members virtually while remaining in their own work spaces, surrounded by all the tools they normally work with.

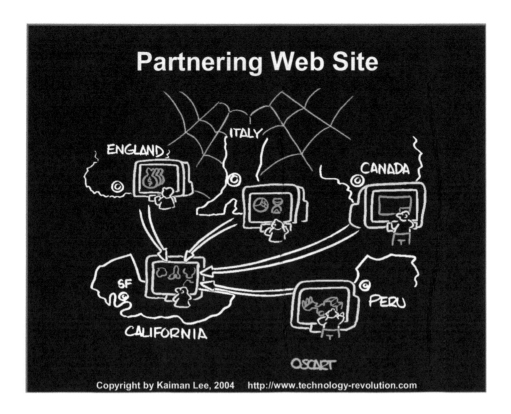

A partnering Web site helps partnering members communicate effectively despite geographical limitations.

The owner in San Francisco can have a project's <u>financial company in England</u>, the <u>project management company in Italy</u>, the <u>construction firm in Peru</u> and the <u>A-E (architectural-engineering) firm in Canada</u>.

Securities such as the simple form of <u>passwords</u> can prevent unauthorized people from seeing specific parts of the partnering site. General parts of the site can be left public on the Web to act as a marketing tool for all companies involved.

The Web site can also provide <u>links</u> to similar construction projects or to other construction projects in which project partners are involved.

The Web site can also function as a <u>virtual marketplace</u> where <u>project managers post their projects and contractors post their availability and work interests</u>. It will <u>match projects and people</u> on an <u>as-needed basis</u>. It enables projects to be managed in what can be called producer-style management, or just-in-time manufacturing, through finding the best people for specific tasks.

Construction Project Web Site

A project Web site can act as a collaboration portal, making all current project information available at every wired desktop and wireless device.

It is an efficient method of letting project members view new developments online 24 hours a day. It provides information on the plans and progress of a specific construction project to those actually involved in the project.

The projects Web site provides a single, current, credible source for project information to all interested parties. The Web site can replace (or supplement) print project bulletins. The Web site can also provide links to experts in areas related to technical aspects of the project.

With a project Web site there will be less physical face-to-face meetings needed. That keeps people working at their desks rather than on travel. A project Web site is a great marketing tool. You can broadcast to the world the work your company is doing on a project.

While the project manager is far away on vacation, s/he remains connected to the project Web site all the time. S/he would be alerted when "gold" is struck back home.

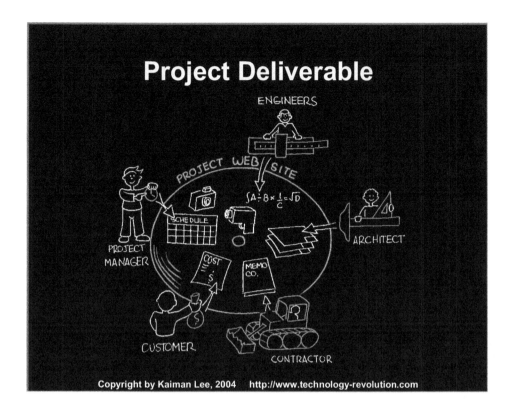

Project Deliverable

The project Web site will become the client's project deliverable. All communications, e-mail, collaboration messaging, and such is recorded. You can trace the progress and route of every document.

The project Web site does not have to be physically located at one place. It could be made up of several Web sites. At the end of the project, you can pull all the information from the various Web sites and combine them into one Web site stored on a CD. You may leave some of the information where they are for project life cycle management.

Since CDs can be configured so that they cannot be altered, why not have a date-stamped CD-ROM of the project Web site serve as the project deliverable? These are valid archival records according to the GAO's (General Accounting Office) "images-as-records decision."

If the value and concern are high enough, you could even place the CD in a date-controlled storage vault for safekeeping.

Intranet is Nakedness

Copyright by Kaiman Lee, 2004   http://www.technology-revolution.com

Those positioned at the <u>top of the stovepipe</u> usually <u>look down </u>the pipe to see what is happening in their fiefdoms. They <u>do not look across</u> and see that all the stovepipes must work in harmony to make the mission work.

The <u>old technology</u> plays well into the stovepipe management philosophy.   As long as the individuals inside the stovepipe are able to perform their individual jobs better, faster, cheaper, the head of the stovepipe is happy.

But competitiveness with the outside world is not going well because of <u>lack of interaction</u>. The processes that required activity from multiple stovepipes become stuck.   When one gets stuck, more than likely it is at the boundary between two stovepipes.

We must change the way we do business so that people are not <u>afraid of others knowing what they are doing</u>. It is like walking around <u>without clothes</u>. It might take a week or two in the <u>nude beach</u> for people to be comfortable with their clothes off.

The issue for success is <u>not technology</u>. The <u>critical path is cultural</u>! <u>Intranet</u> will <u>transform the workplace</u>, the way employees <u>work</u> and even <u>socialize</u>.

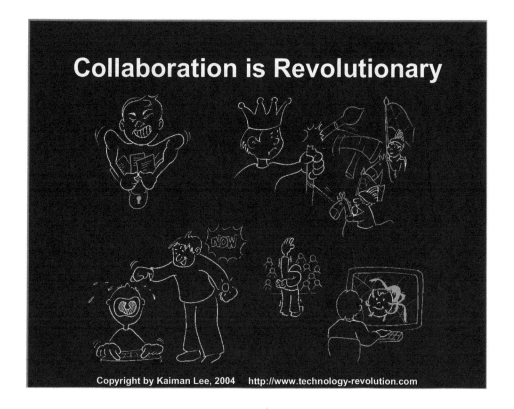

Collaboration is Revolutionary

Copyright by Kaiman Lee, 2004   http://www.technology-revolution.com

There are few key reasons why collaboration is revolutionary:
- <u>Sharing data</u>: workers are reluctant to share information; a new policy may be required.

- <u>Distributed decision-making</u>: opposite to what executives are used to.

- <u>Immediacy</u>: psychic float of time is gone.

- <u>Participation of large audiences</u>: potential bottleneck.

- <u>Software monitors</u> the flow of work across workers' desktops: <u>nowhere to hide</u>.

- <u>Liability</u>: sensitive information leaks, lawsuits over offensive content, the janitor's learning the big boss' salary, and a Pandora's box of potential problems regarding <u>information control, access and security</u>.

<u>Only the leader can create the collaboration environment</u>. The next generation of leaders are not going to earn their big offices by the number of people they manage. They will earn their respect by <u>being out in the fray</u>, by being able to <u>laugh at mistakes</u> and especially at their own mistakes, by being a participant just like everybody else. That builds collaboration.

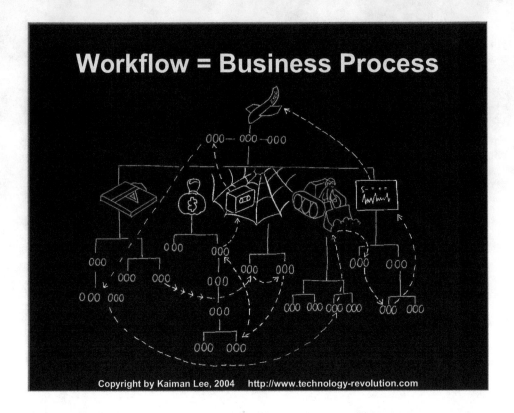

Workflow = Business Process

Copyright by Kaiman Lee, 2004   http://www.technology-revolution.com

Your business can be defined by the knowledge and skills of your people, and by your business processes.

Workflow or coordination applications track actions, and are people-driven rather than data driven. Therefore, workflow can become an online extension of the organization's business process.

There is a strong connection between workflow and business process redesign (BPR).

Workflow can be thought of as taking down the door of a toilet stall. People do not like to be seen or exposed, thus the resistance to change.

Even the more successful managers cannot articulate their business processes. Competent people can draw a blank when it comes time to describe existing processes and the rationale behind their existence.

They may be the real reason for the cultural resistance to workflow and why up to 70% of reengineering efforts fail -- few managers understand what the problem is, much less the solution.

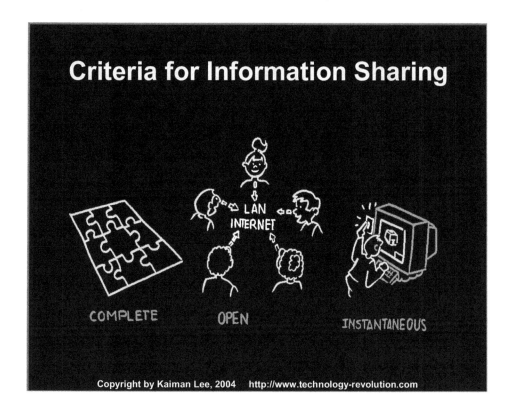

Criteria for Information Sharing

COMPLETE   OPEN   INSTANTANEOUS

A complete, open and instantaneous collaborative sharing environment should be the goal of every business. Complete because a specific piece of information is in a single source and not duplicated. That single-source information uses Internet standards, and is open to all those having specific rights, e.g., read only, or edit. The single source information is Instantaneously updated when changed.

Telephone callers are now used to becoming self-served telephone operators, with a menu for them to choose from.

Now, computers, software, and networks are turning people into researchers, publishers, order clerks, and bank tellers. That can only be customer friendly if the information necessary is complete and open to everybody with the proper access rights.

In a service-oriented world, you service customers by creating an environment of information, assurance, and comfort for them. This means being in touch with customers all the time, addressing their individual needs and responding without delay.

Service is "time value" to the customer. When you deliver products or service promptly with the philosophy of "complete, open and instantaneous," you are telling your customers that you value their time. You will then gain their trust.

Productivity Focus

Copyright by Kaiman Lee, 2004   http://www.technology-revolution.com

You must move from individual productivity to enterprise productivity.

How much productivity improvement can you expect? You can achieve multiples if you do it right using collaboration technology.

Imagine project team members that look at the same document, start at the same time and finish at the same time. Does this revolutionary and synergistic process not give you multiple productivities?

Collaboration technology enables the shift from hierarchical, bureaucratic organizations to networked organizations where information and decision making move horizontally within flat organizations.

The productivity shift we can achieve should be of a magnitude matched only by the industrial revolution.

The world will be so competitive that you would only get the output you want from your workers if your focus is "enterprise productivity."

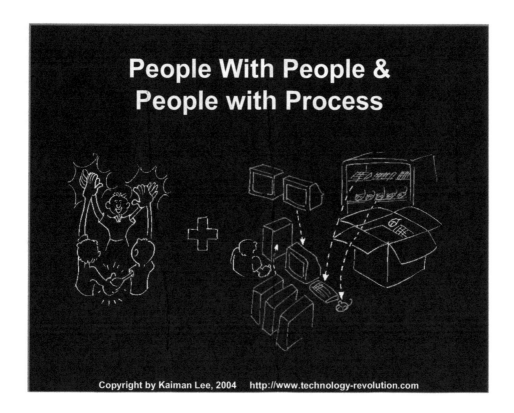

**People With People &
People with Process**

The benefits of collaboration come when you engage people with people and people with processes.

Traditional applications are information-oriented. They are maintained by departments named information technology, management information systems and information processing.

In other words, in all of these traditional applications people do not interact with other people. They interact with machines and data.

But, data addresses the past, while people work towards the future.

The purpose of interaction is basically to convert tacit knowledge to explicit knowledge. Tacit knowledge is what people know, and explicit knowledge is what is documented.

Once you have aggregated the explicit knowledge, you can share it through formal and informal processes of your business.

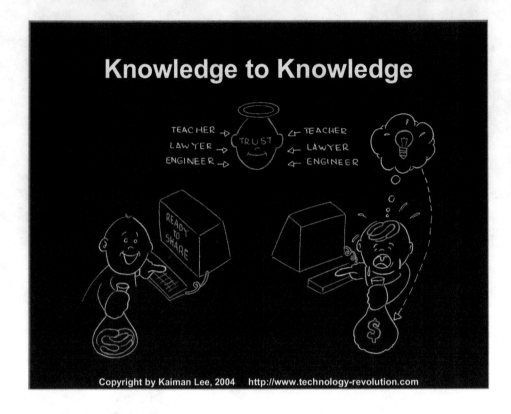

Knowledge to Knowledge

With too much content on the Internet, users want quality content which could only come from people with direct knowledge of the subject. Most chat rooms, bulletin boards, and online auction sites are somewhat based on users exchanging knowledge. Knowledge, shared between users, is knowledge-to-knowledge (K2K), and it is becoming the Internet's currency.

There will be Web sites for exchanging knowledge between teachers, between engineers, and between lawyers, etc. The content will be about ideas, experience, and thought sharing.

Sharing knowledge requires you to reflect and think about what you know before you share it with others. It is in this process of reflection that knowledge is developed. It is hard work and "What's in it for me?"

On the Net, jaded users will want some form of reward for contributing their knowledge to a site. Users with branded content will become their own broadcasters, and start earning money from sharing their knowledge.

In the corporate world, people are not often credited for the knowledge they contribute, which is why they do not share knowledge. Paying for knowledge is too hard to measure. Trust is therefore a prerequisite for K2K within an enterprise.

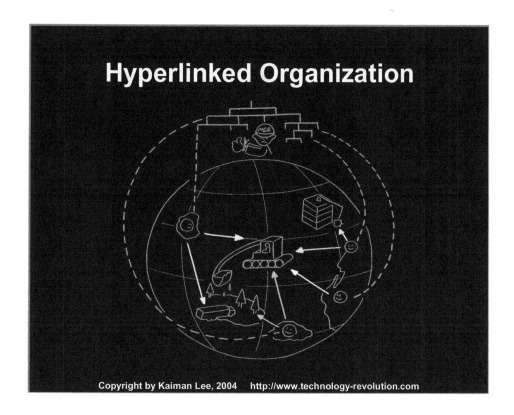

Hyperlinked Organization

A hyperlinked organization or "soft-wired" organization uses the Internet to allow employees to form ad hoc project teams, break apart, and regroup. It lets employees work on many projects of their choice simultaneously without much managerial direction.

These teams can complete complex projects that used to be done by large hierarchical corporations. Members coming from all over the world because they have the necessary skills and shared interests, not because they are in the chain of command. They volunteer to participate in specific projects and commit to project schedules and amount of time for their tasks.

Traditional hierarchical organizations are prime grounds for asymmetries of information, i.e., senior executives have a grasp and control of the "big picture," while subordinates have a more detailed, but departmentally constricted, knowledge base. These asymmetries of information result in asymmetries of power, manifested in the political games revolving around monopolizing various sources of knowledge.

When information is richer and more free flowing in a hyperlinked organization, everyone's actions become more transparent. Disgruntled subordinates and poor performers are harder to hide. Reputation substitutes a lot of formal review and control.

KNOWLEDGE MANAGEMENT

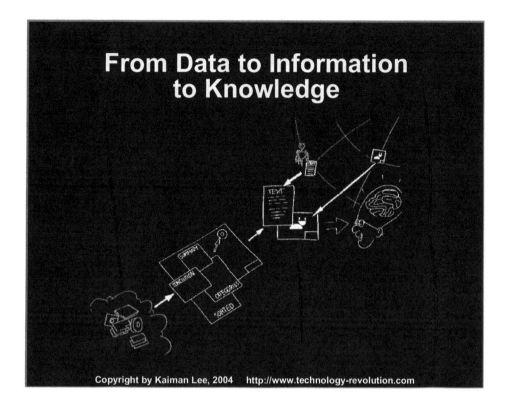

From Data to Information to Knowledge

Data are facts or figures from which conclusions can be inferred. Data implies syntax, how the numbers and text are structured.

Information has context and semantics. It represents data that are relevant and useful. It is processed and filtered data. It recognizes meaning and purpose. Information is informing or being informed.

The state of knowing or understanding information is knowledge. It separates information from meaningful to not meaningful, and from usable to not usable. "If I can extract from the sea of information that which helps me do my job, that is knowledge."

What comes after knowledge is smartness, cleverness, or intelligence. It involves learning, improving, and innovating.

The difference between the amount of information available and our ability to process it, analyze it and do something with it is the knowledge gap. Our success hinges on our ability to narrow that gap.

Wisdom may be defined as useful knowledge with a long shelf life, e.g., timeless statements. Knowledge is information in use and wisdom is the combination of knowledge and values. Being wise is the ability to apply wisdom in practice.

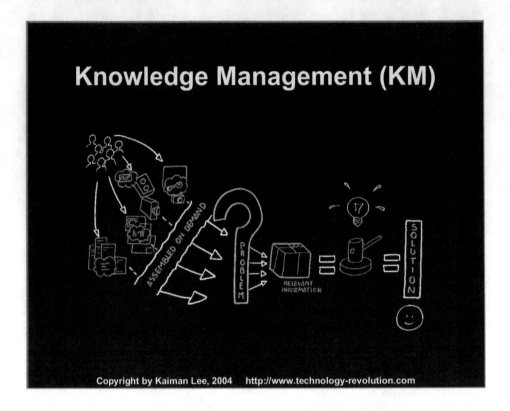

Knowledge Management (KM)

Knowledge is the information resident in people's minds that is used for making decisions in different contexts. Knowledge management (KM), in turn, refers to the <u>practices and technologies</u> that facilitate the efficient <u>creation and exchange of knowledge</u> on an organization-wide level to enhance the <u>quality of decision making</u>.

In other words, KM can be defined as the ability of an organization to leverage <u>collective wisdom to increase responsiveness and innovation</u>.

Perhaps the biggest difference between information management (i.e. the capture and retrieval of information) and KM is the ability of KM to <u>match the information to a particular set of circumstances</u> to actively promote the development of new ideas, products and actions, i.e., innovation.

KM is the ability to <u>dynamically link structured and unstructured information</u> with the changing <u>rules</u> by which people apply it. KM requires that documents are <u>assembled on demand</u> according to business rules.

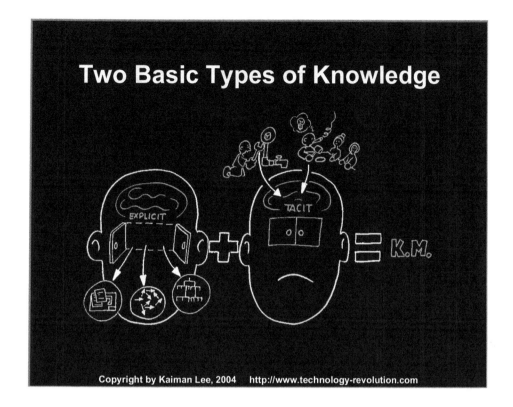

Two Basic Types of Knowledge

Copyright by Kaiman Lee, 2004   http://www.technology-revolution.com

Too much emphasis has been placed on managing information, i.e., explicit knowledge. Knowledge management must provide a means to capture and leverage the tacit knowledge that is embodied in the actions and experience of the people in an organization.

Business systems must be knowledge-based, not just information-based, if they are to cope with the incompleteness and ambiguity of real business processes and workflow.

Unexpected or tacit data often provides the key knowledge that will give you a competitive advantage.

It used to be the more you knew and the less you told, the more valuable you were and the less likely it was you could get laid off. Knowledge management is about making cultural changes.

Are there end-to-end knowledge management solutions? No. There is no single product that will solve your knowledge-sharing issues. Are there knowledge-management enablers? Yes.

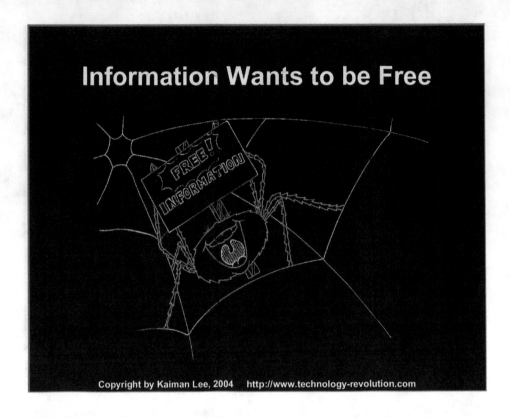

Information Wants to be Free

FREE ! INFORMATION

Copyright by Kaiman Lee, 2004   http://www.technology-revolution.com

You can find almost any information you want on the Internet because almost all information is free. They are there for those who have the patience to look for them. The smart ones will find the effective search tools first before trying to find information.

Information wants to be free, but your time is not.

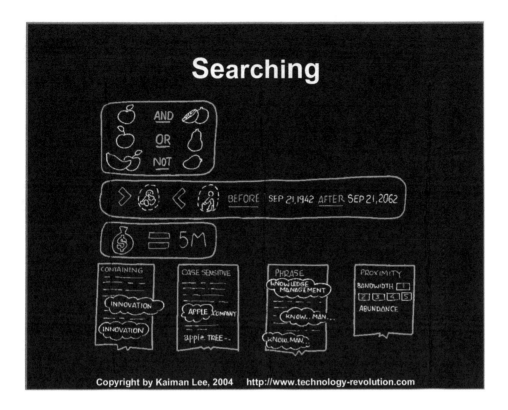

Searching

Traditional search methods are based on Boolean functions: And, Or, Not , Bigger/Smaller Than, Before/After, Equal, Containing, Case Sensitive, Phrase, Proximity.

You can search from all texts in a drawing, or all text in a word document.

You can search part of a word (truncation).

You can specify that two words are in a given proximity, i.e., they are a specified number of words apart in a sentence or paragraph.

You can search forward with new criteria and go backwards, trying out all combinations to find what you want.

You can save the search criteria or scripts for future reuse.

Advanced search lets you find out more about any word that appears anywhere on your desktop. Point your mouse over the word, press the Alt key, and click your mouse. In very short order, the computer returns dictionary, thesaurus, and encyclopedia definitions, biographies, weather forecasts, stock quotes, press releases, and book searches, etc.

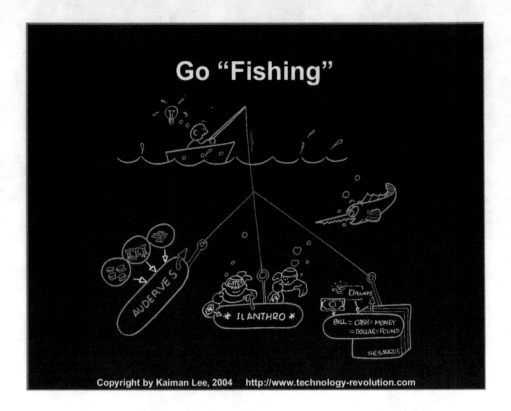

You can "go fishing" and see what you will get, e.g., search for a word that sounds like "auderves" but which you can not spell. It is called fuzzy search.

You can use a wildcard, i.e., an asterisk -- in the middle, or at the beginning or end of a word. In this case, you are specifying a partial word with any prefix or suffix. They are called embedded and trailing wildcards. "*ilanthro*" would give you "philanthropy" in return.

You can use the thesaurus and find words that are of similar meaning, or synonyms.

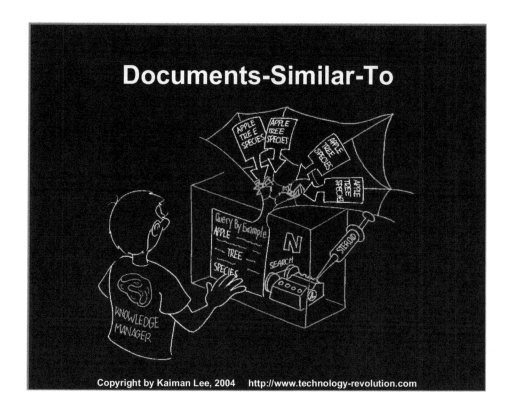

Documents-Similar-To

You do not want to interact with a search engine much beyond keying in a few words and letting it go out to get results.

You want to be able to find a general set of documents you need without checking each document one at a time.

You want to <u>use the result of one search to find more</u> documents similar to it.

This capability is also called <u>Query-by-Example (QBE)</u>. You might call them search engines on steroid!

New Search Technologies

Copyright by Kalman Lee, 2004   http://www.technology-revolution.com

A document is redefined as "any package of data structured for use as information." This means a document can be almost anything: holograms, CD-ROMs, video segments. As soon as the author calls it a document, it is.

It is currently much easier to search for text on the Web than for graphics, audio, or video. But when a user wants the best information, it should not matter what form it is in, whether it is a text document or a video document.

With video and multimedia indexing technologies, you can begin to search video recordings. You could search for the phrase "high crimes and misdemeanors" on a special site and quickly locate and play streaming video clips of the impeachment proceedings where that phrase appears.

You can search for specific faces. Researchers are also working on technologies for identifying sounds, such as gunfire.

You can use optical character recognition (OCR) features to extract text that appears on screen, such as a news correspondent's name. C-SPAN has used closed-captioning information as well as raw audio data to match the video to the text.

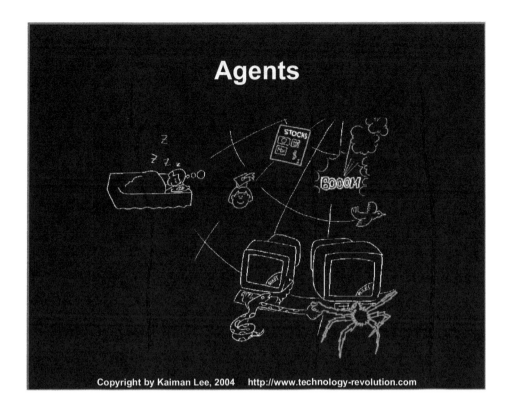

Agents

Information clutter is already overwhelming. <u>Agent technology</u>, or <u>deep computing technology</u>, will emerge to help you <u>find and filter</u> the information that you care about.

Web-search engines are also known as <u>software agents, software robots, softbots, personal assistants, knowbots, automatons, brokers, spiders or crawlers</u>. You can send them out to crawl and prowl the nooks and crannies of the Internet and collect useful information for you. They <u>build indexes</u> and update them from all the Web pages out there.

Smart agents can <u>sense surroundings, gauge circumstances</u>, and <u>feel the environment</u>. They are trained to behave in certain manners: <u>shake hands politely, nod the head, do not walk out, do not kill the messenger, keep talking or negotiating, look for win-win, do not wake up the master unless it is an emergency or the deal of a century</u>.

Imagine your agent <u>earning a degree</u> for you, investing for you, or even making <u>war or peace</u>, all while you are asleep. Intelligent agent technology is the <u>next wave</u> for the Web.

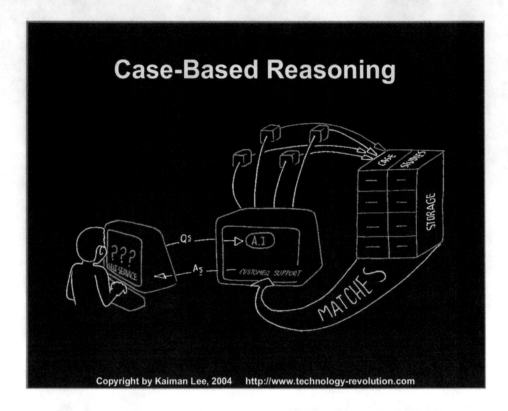

Case-Based Reasoning

Case-based reasoning, or CBR is an artificial intelligence (AI) application. CBR stores case studies, responds to a problem by finding similar cases in its memory, and adapts the solution that worked in the past to the current problem.

Automated customer-support systems uses CBR. It is growing as companies seek to reduce product support costs by encouraging customers to find their own answers on a Web site instead of calling toll-free numbers for live person support.

Help Desk uses CBR. It works by asking customers to describe their problem in plain words. It then leads customers through a series of questions until it can match a description of the problem to descriptions of similar, previously solved problems in its case base. Help Desk then offers a solution.

Typically, a CBR search is based on three kinds of values: text matching, which searches for similar words; numerical similarity; and discreet or symbolic values, which are values such as "yes," "no," "high," "medium," or "low."

Other uses of CBR include diagnosis in process-control applications, such as network monitoring; in medical applications, such as patient diagnosis; and in general knowledge-management applications, such as complex scheduling, planning, and design programs.

Your business may have mountains of raw data on <u>demographics, product sales, inventory, contacts and human resources</u>. How do you organize and <u>transform them into useful information</u>?

Business intelligence (BI) tools can <u>transform daily transactions into detailed customer profiles</u>, including such variables as <u>spending habits which might indicate product loyalty</u>. BI tools can help develop insights and improve decision-making, and that is why they are in the <u>"decision support" market</u>.

The simple concept behind BI is to get the right information into the right hands, and virtually every aspect of your business will benefit from the reduced redundant work and maintenance burdens. For example, your <u>sales department</u> can now accurately determine what is driving business. Your <u>finance department</u> can conduct analyses and identify trends. Your <u>marketing department</u> can maximize profitability by developing targeted strategies derived from information provided by BI applications.

BI tools allow for <u>query, analysis and reporting</u>. They include <u>online analytical processing</u> (OLAP), <u>data mining</u> and <u>knowledge management</u> (KM) tools. While KM is an organization-wide cultural effort involving a wide range of processes, BI is a key component that makes KM possible.

Corporate Portal

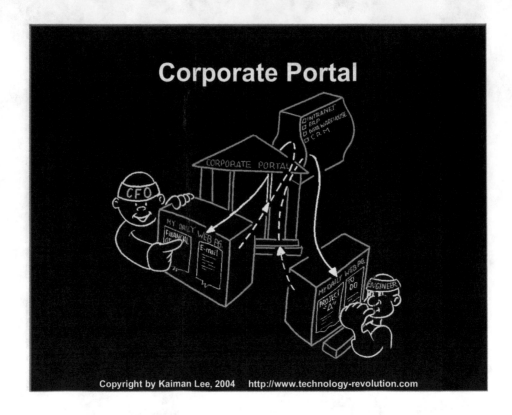

The corporate portal is where you <u>enter</u> when they arrive at work with a <u>single sign-on password</u>. You see what is <u>pertinent to you</u>, e.g., <u>project schedule</u>, announcements, what is new, tip of the day, etc.

A sophisticated profiling system alerts you to the arrival of new information that matches your profile and suggests related documents or subject matters. It can also use your profile to automatically <u>connect you to people with similar interests</u>.

A corporate portal can <u>combine information from multiple sources</u> such as Intranet, data warehouses, enterprise resource planning (ERP) system, and the Web based on your <u>role, profile and preferences</u>.

It uses <u>browser</u> interfaces to offer <u>personalization</u> similar to those used on portal sites such as <u>My Yahoo</u>.

Corporate portals are also called <u>enterprise portals, company portals, business portals</u>, etc.

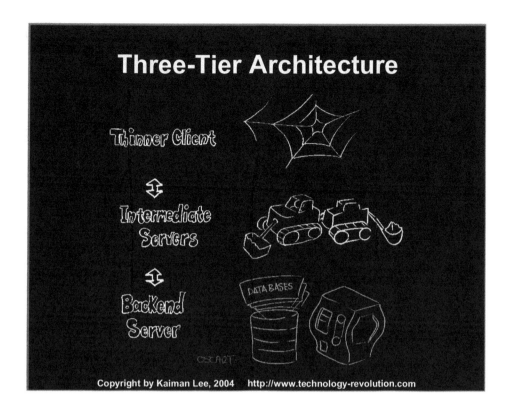

Three-Tier Architecture

Thinner Client

Intermediate Servers

Backend Server

DATA BASES

Client/server technology is two tiers. The client, i.e., PC, stores the application or computer program and the data could come from the server.

The overwhelming majority of mission critical information still resides on IBM and IBM-compatible mainframes.

The growth of the Internet has forced a transition from client/server and mainframe operations to TCP/IP-centric operations.

This requires a three-tier architecture that consists of the mainframe, middleware server, and client. Their relative functions are access to the database, execution of business logic, and presentation to the user.

In a simple sense, the concept is browser-based access to existing client/server and mainframe applications. The Web acts as a display mechanism for legacy data that is turned into HTML.

However, just wrapping a better, Web-based interface around the existing infrastructure or providing access to old, inefficient databases will not improve the situation much.

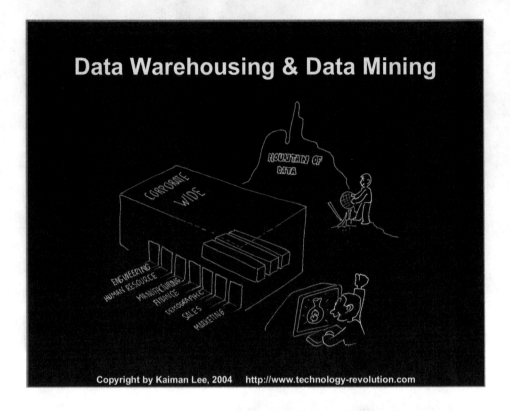

Data Warehousing & Data Mining

A data warehouse is designed for strategic business support such as customer service and retention. It is largely built from operational databases including sales and demographics. Its database grows over time. One day you may find that 70 to 90 percent of the data is not being used.

A key to data warehousing is to decide what to delete and what not to save. Maybe you can get rid of all summary data after six months, and entire columns that have never been accessed in a year. Maybe only the last two or three months of data are really useful for most business analyses.

Data warehouses are classified into two broad categories depending upon the scope of the data stored in them:
- an enterprise data warehouse represents corporate-wide data from operational systems, and it is cross functional.
- a data mart contains a subset of corporate-wide data that is of value to a specific user or a functional group of users.

Data mining uses pattern recognition to sift through large amounts of data stored in a data warehouse or data mart, such as purchasing history, and reveal meaningful correlation, patterns and trends. Data mining can rate your customers as good, bad and ugly, so you keep the good, improve the bad, and have nothing to do with the ugly.

PUSH
TECHNOLOGY

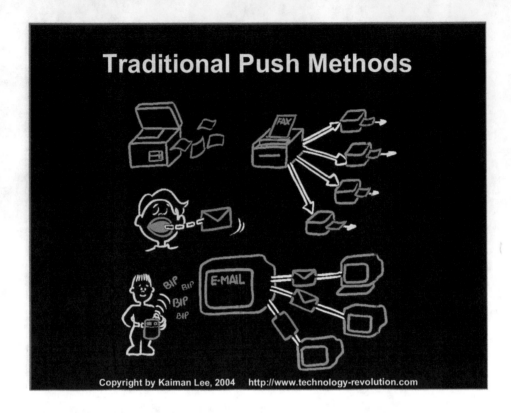

Traditional Push Methods

E-Mail is a type of push technology. Others are paper copying, fax, voice mail, beeper, pager, etc.

Web-based push technology is also called <u>broadcasting, narrowcasting, Webcasting, Web data blasts, channels, and personal broadcast</u>. They use display techniques such as <u>on-screen alert, ticker tapes and pop-up windows</u>.

You can use push technology to deliver regular updates of anti-virus software. Potential applications of push technology are <u>project status changes</u> and alerting workers to <u>emergencies</u> or problems.

Push technology can be a <u>front end to legacy databases</u> residing in client/server and mainframe computers.

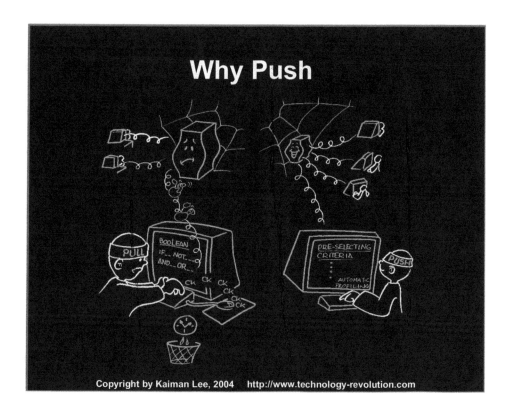

Why Push

"Finding information on today's www is like drinking from a fire hose. With push, you cut the fire hose down to a nice glass of cold water."

The concern for "pull" technology is information overload and too much "clicking" and "fooling around" with Boolean logic. There is a lot of time-wasted searching for information, and it consumes a lot of network bandwidth.

Also pulling can drag back bad data or viruses, along with usable data.

Where appropriate push technology could reduce congestion on the Internet and reduce the cost of providing information online.

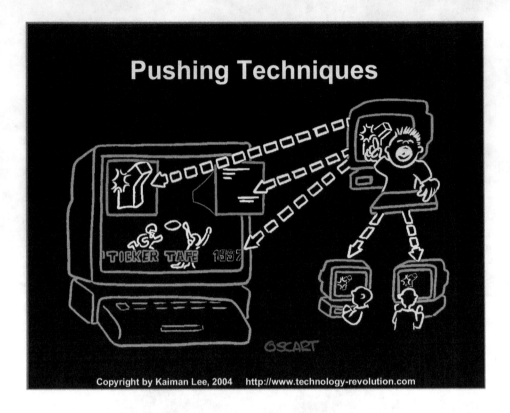

Pushing Techniques

"Push technology" is often used to distribute up-to-the-minute and specific information automatically to multiple subscribers. In an international engineering organization, for example, a seismic engineer can push the news of an earthquake happening to subscribers in real time.

In a commercial setting, a push broadcaster can ask you detailed questions about your interests and then provide a regularly updated Web page of news summaries, stock prices, weather forecasts or sports news. The personalized page can be programmed to appear as the default page when you log on to the Internet instead of your online service provider's home page.

On the negative side, why do some people say that "push" should be termed "shove"? The answer is that most push technologies are packed with advertisements because push broadcasters are funded mainly by advertising.

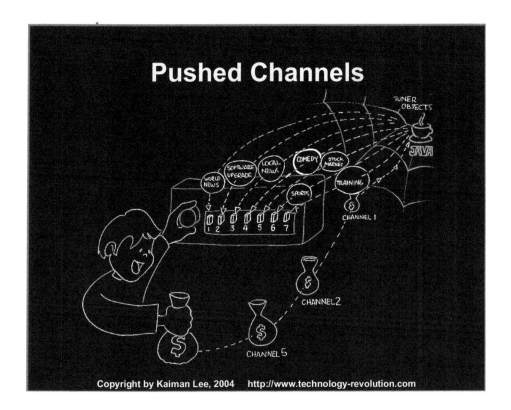

Push technology uses a <u>television or radio broadcasting model</u> in which subscribers <u>'tune in' to channels such as ski, hobbies, collector, occupation, local news, world news, software upgrades, comedy, sports, stock market and training</u>.

Subscribers can down load a free "tuner," a piece of software that helps them subscribe to their desired channels of information. Once they have subscribed, information is "pushed" to their systems during Internet connect time, usually in the background. The software notifies users that new information from a channel has been received.

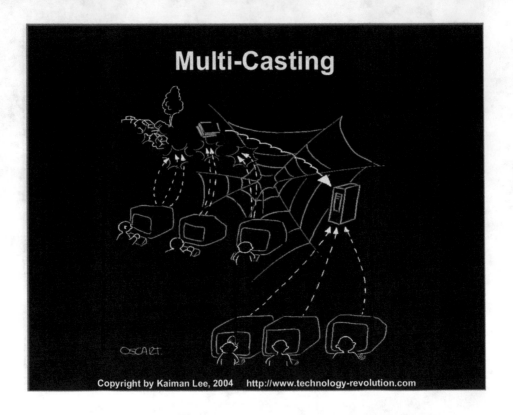

Multi-Casting

Multicasting or data broadcasting is defined as the transmission of data, audio and video from <u>one source to many users</u> over the Internet.

Current networking solutions send the <u>same data repeatedly</u> <u>from the source</u>, resulting in <u>heavy network traffic</u>.

Multicasting works by analyzing the network routes to users and sending <u>a single stream of data to local servers</u> rather than a stream of data to each user. The stream is then duplicated by local servers to reach each user, cutting the total amount of data that has to be carried by the entire network.

Think of the <u>network server as a "transmitter," intermediary servers as "repeaters" and the client as a "tuner."</u>

The local servers are also called <u>traffic servers and network caches</u>. They are <u>strategically located</u> to ensure that the data is stored as close as possible to the user, minimizing user access time.

This way, you can deliver <u>live feeds</u> of full-motion <u>executive addresses</u>, television broadcasts or corporate training efficiently.

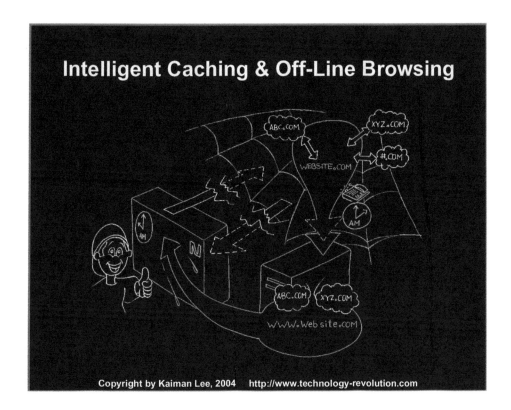

Normally, a Web browser software stores Web pages you have visited recently in cache memory, and pulls them out for return visits. The so-called intelligent caching automatically tracks the Web sites you visit regularly and during idle modem time visits those sites, <u>updates the images</u> and stores them in the cache so they are there when you want to see them.

When you are reading a Web page, the browser scans the page for <u>hot links</u> to related pages, then <u>down loads</u> those pages to cache memory so they will load faster if you decide to view them.

Packaged Web pages can be collected and exported to another computer during off hours for office browsing, such as <u>office presentation or home viewing</u>.

Off-line browsing of preloaded Web sites has not made the Web faster, you just experience it faster.

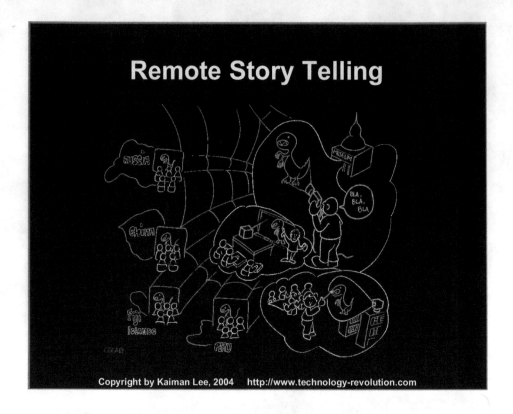

Remote Story Telling

Copyright by Kaiman Lee, 2004   http://www.technology-revolution.com

Using push technology, multimedia story telling or informational sessions held in major libraries and <u>museums</u> can be provided to other <u>libraries</u> and <u>schools</u> worldwide.

You can <u>chat with scuba divers</u> who are exploring the kelp forests of Monterey Bay in California or the coral reefs of Bermuda.

A computer monitor feeds live questions from students nationwide or worldwide to a diver at the bottom of the sea.

A diver uses an underwater camera to transmit live scenes and conversation over the Web to thousands of school children, who could even <u>control</u> which way the <u>cameras</u> point.

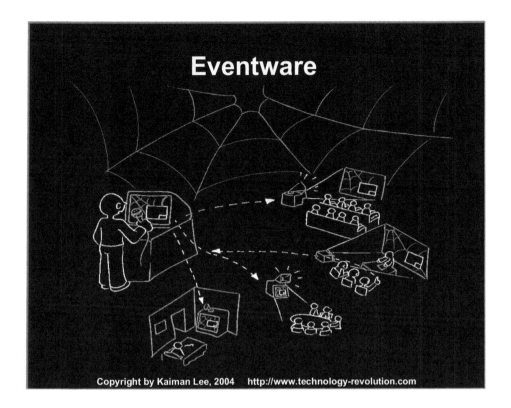

Eventware

Remote learning and training can be done in three different ways. The first is unidirectional, in which a presenter speaks to an unknown and often unresponsive audience.

The second is bi-directional, in which the audience can be seen and heard by the presenter.

The third category is in between the first two. It not only supports one-to-many communication, but it also offers the capability for some limited real-time interaction.

The generic name for the third category of products is "eventware." It uses the auditorium or classroom metaphor. The presenter can deliver his or her voice over streaming audio, while the audience can see PowerPoint slides on the screen and ask questions or make comments.

These technologies are great for presentations, demonstrations, training, and even classroom learning.

You can update your sales force on new products while the salespeople are in their hotel rooms or at client sites.

Push & Pull, We Want Both!

Copyright by Kaiman Lee, 2004   http://www.technology-revolution.com

Even though push and pull technologies are moving in opposite directions, there is <u>not a conflict</u> here. Skilled Internet users would probably want to pull information specific to their ad hoc needs from the Net, by using search engines of their choice. Less skilled users might want to specify what they are looking for in general and let the agents push the findings to them on a periodic basic.

Choosing between pull or push is like deciding between the <u>burger and the soft drink</u>. We <u>want both</u>, and we can have both.

Companies that understand how to make these two work in harmony are going to be the winners in the years to come. For instance, a company's Web site might allow a frequent user find things on a self serve basis, and push relevant information to the new visitors.

EMBEDDED TECHNOLOGY

Ubiquitous Information Appliances

Information appliances, also called Embedded Internet Devices (EID) could end the PC-Centric Era.

You will soon be able to turn on the microwave from your office using the Web. Appliances will be Web-enabled, including your television set-top box, telephones, video game consoles, VCRs, copiers, burglar alarms, even blenders and door locks. How about dictating your thoughts to your shower head?

Computers are embedded into everyday objects. These computers are not only ubiquitous but invisible, behind the scenes. A fridge reads bar codes and reorders from online grocers when the food supply runs low. An alarm clock turns off the electric blanket and a scale sends your weight to the gym! Web browsing on your blender! E-mail on your humidifier!

The network will be the computer. The network appliances (including PCs) will just be nodes on the network. They will reduce the headaches of administration, maintenance, service and support.

There are three revolutions in computing: mainframe computer, PC, and ubiquitous computing, which is just the opposite of the mainframe era. Instead of one computer shared by many people, you have one person owning many computers.

Silicon Cockroaches

"Silicon cockroaches are wireless devices that can communicate with each other and the Internet," said John Sidgmore, Vice chairman and chief operating officer of MCI WorldCom, during his keynote address at Comdex/Fall '98.

"These silicon devices will multiply, becoming the Internet's biggest growth driver," Sidgmore said. "Everyone will have an average of five IP (internet protocol) objects on their body by 2000." Although this has not happened, the implication of multiple wireless information appliances we carry is profound.

An employee's embedded name badge can communicate via a wireless network to wired network access points scattered throughout a company's building. The badge-computer could let someone on the network know where the employee is, or unlock doors the employee is allowed to access.

Other places for these tiny embedded computers might be cellular phones and personal digital assistants (PDAs).

Another example might be a small display on your eyeglasses and speaker on your ear. It has a built-in camera that, at your request can tell you about the person who is approaching you. Everything from motorcycle helmets, to ski goggles to clothing can be embedded with a computer.

119

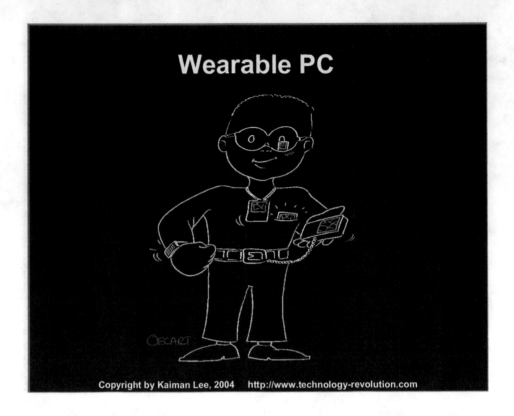

Wearable PC

Imagine a miniature <u>liquid-crystal display screen</u>, worn around the <u>wrist</u>, <u>neck</u> or on a <u>belt</u> with a <u>magnifying mirror</u> system that brings images to full size.

<u>Java chips</u> can be <u>embedded in a watch, ring, key chain, necklace and wallet</u>. A Java applet updates your "<u>ornament</u>" every time it is connected to the web. They could be <u>networked together via clothes</u>. Tiny earphones could be embedded in a headband, sending waves to a microphone pinned to the shirt -- both of which would be wirelessly linked to a tiny cell phone snapped to a sleeve or pants leg. <u>Flat batteries</u> could be incorporated in your <u>underwear</u>.

These information appliances are also called "<u>connected information devices</u>" or <u>CID</u>s. They will be found in your cars, walls, desks, kitchens and stereos, etc.

<u>Credit cards</u> will know when they have been <u>stolen</u>, and <u>self destruct</u> when used by the thief.

Airline mechanics wear computers linked to <u>display glasses</u> so they can read from a <u>repair manual</u> with both <u>hands free</u>.

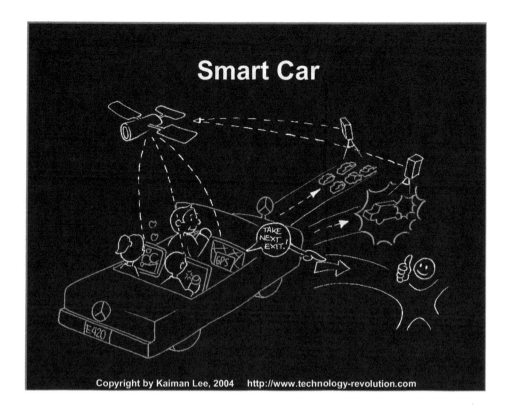

Your car can soon have a 5" computer screen on the <u>dashboard</u> between the front two seats, plus <u>computer screens embedded in the head restraints</u> for use by passengers in the back.

When your car is Internet-enabled, it can <u>show accidents or traffic jams</u> on a map displayed on the computer screen. Or when you have engine trouble on the road, <u>engineers</u> at the manufacturing plant could <u>comment on the car's condition</u>.

A trusty agent -- talking to you through a microphone embedded in the windshield visor -- figures out where you are and immediately dispatches a tow truck to the rescue.

With a <u>built-in Global Positioning System</u> (GPS), you can <u>hear directions</u> such as the freeway exit coming up, and weather conditions miles ahead.

Your auto dealer can <u>remotely lock and unlock power doors</u> if you lose your car key, and <u>start or stop the engine</u> on your behalf. S/he can also disable a vehicle and <u>engage the horn and flashing lights</u> in the event of a theft. What happens to the thief driving the stolen car?

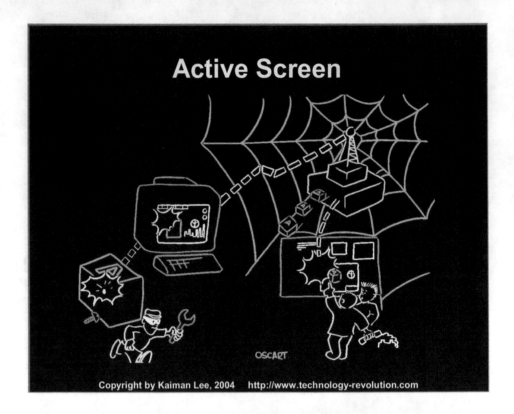

Active Screen

An "active screen" of a machine is where all the machine's <u>functions</u> are shown with their <u>current status</u>. It can be <u>linked to the original manufacturer</u> who can then <u>monitor</u> the unit's <u>performance</u>.

Whenever there is a <u>problem</u>, the manufacturer can be <u>immediately</u> and <u>automatically notified</u> without someone calling. The manufacturer already has all of the data on the screen.

<u>Solutions</u> in the forms of <u>Java applets</u>, for example, can then be sent to the active screen and the problem could automatically be fixed.

An example of an active screen can be a color <u>laser printer</u> with its <u>built-in Intranet</u> server. It provides status, configuration and reference information through a Web browser.

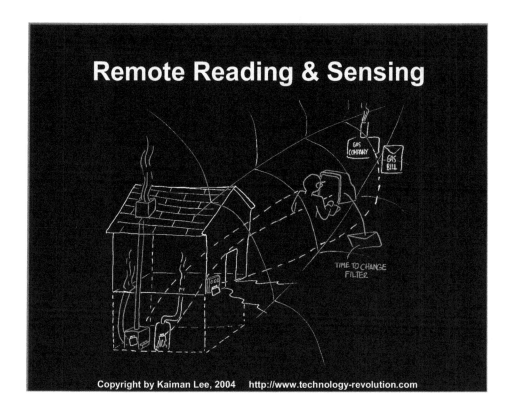

Utility companies might use embedded technology to put Web servers in meters and use push technology to send back usage instead of having to send out workers to read them each month.

Devices that can be Web-embedded are infinite, including: photocopiers, fax machines, cameras, microphones, handheld PCs, cell phones, pagers, vending machines, card readers, thermostats, pressure gauges, lighting monitors, door locks, toys, set-top boxes, game consoles, and coffeepots, etc.

Every device that consumes or dispenses something, whether it is toner, paper or soft drink, requires human beings to replenish its supply. Web-embedding those devices makes it possible to see in real time exactly what device needs re-supplying. Parking meters can radio in when they are full of coins.

When your appliances are embedded with intelligent chips, you will be reminded from time to time what you need to do in terms of maintenance and repair, or even replacement.

Embedded light bulbs will know when bulb need replacement. The manufacturer will know how many to manufacture ahead of time. An embedded airplane black box does not need to be found. It beams instant information to server elsewhere wirelessly.

Garbage Can Shopping List

When you toss your empty cans and boxes into the trash can, a shopping list is automatically generated.

A device in the trash can is embedded with a microprocessor that reads product identification codes. The information is transmitted wirelessly either to a computer or special electronic box, which compiles a list of the discarded items.

For this to work, it will require the industry to move away from bar codes to widespread use of radio frequency identification technology -- a tiny computer chip and antenna embedded in product labels -- which carries more information than bar codes.

The technology has been little used because it is too expensive to put on inexpensive products. Compare that to a less expensive embedded refrigerator where you can keep shopping lists.

An embedded refrigerator with a bar code scanner and a touch screen integrated into it will allow you to type in a shopping list, or scan products into the computer. You would then be able to send the list online to a grocery store, which will deliver the order.

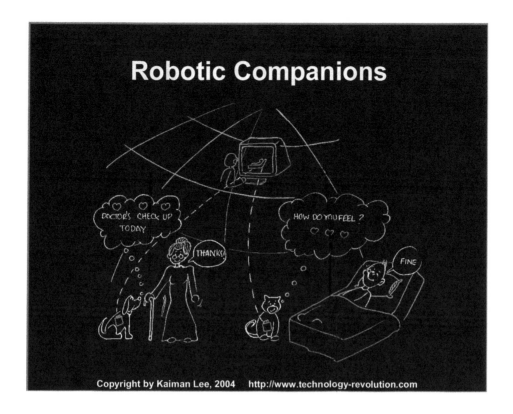

Robotic pets can speak to the elderly, especially to people who are living alone, in a natural way, and this can make them feel less lonesome.

Robotic pets can say things like, "Today is the karaoke party. Let's sing." "Today is Thursday. It is your day to get a check up." Workers at a network system center can upload messages into an elderly person's pet and then determine when it will deliver the messages. The center can also monitor elderly people's interaction with the robotic pet, allowing a health or social worker to spot potential problems.

The robotic pet is basically supposed to be a conversation partner for the elderly. If the pet starts talking and there is no response for a long time, the center might conclude that there is something amiss, and could conceivably call the person or notify a health worker.

Robotic pets can have a variety of animal shapes. With artificial intelligence added, robotic pets could become autonomous agents that can predict when they should become active and engage in conversation. They could also have different expressions and movements of head, legs, ears, and tails.

Biochip Implant

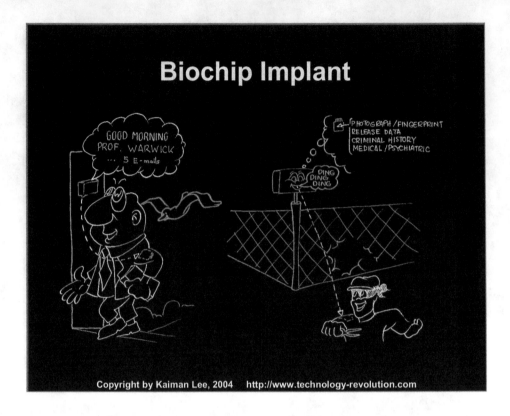

In 1998, Kevin Warwick, a professor of cybernetics at Reading University in England was the world's first to have a computer chip implanted into his arm. It contains an electromagnetic coil and a silicon chip.

When he walked through the front door of his department, the radio signal energized the coil. It produced an electric current, which the chips used to send out an identifying signal, which the computer recognized as being him. "Good morning, Professor Warwick. You have five new E-mails," said a computerized voice activated by the inserted chip. Lights went on when he entered a room.

Applications in a totalitarian society could be such that anyone who wants to buy a gun must have one of these implants. A school security alarm could sound off if a student's implant triggers a warning signal. Prisoners could be monitored.

Implants can contain large amounts of personal information, so that people could carry their passport, health records, or other official documents wherever they go. What would happen if an implant is connected to the human nervous system?

Do we want to hand over control to machinery or to have buildings telling us what we can do or can not do?

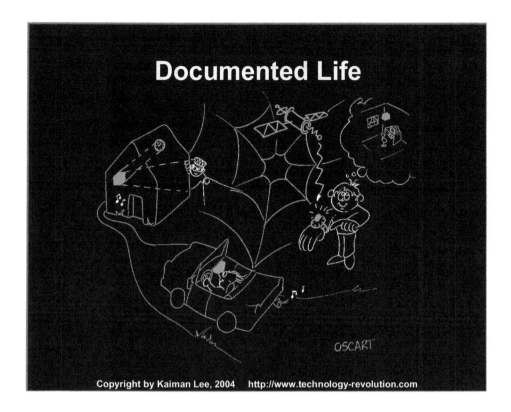

Imagine black boxes everywhere, in the car, at home, in the office and in the watch. Everything we say and do might be recorded somewhere.

Your toilet weighs you. A small electric current measures the proportion of your body fat. A sensor in the bowl measures the sugar content of urine. All this vital data is sent to the central server -- or to your doctor.

Rooms heat, cool, light up, or darken automatically as you walk through, with each movement picked up by infrared motion detectors in the ceiling.

The video phone at the entrance door records the image of anyone outside it, displays it on monitors throughout the house.

Home management software can use your PC to send data signals around the house, tracking your everyday living patterns. When you are away, you can set a routine to simulate your life-style pattern to make your home look lived-in -- in case a bad guy is watching.

Is an automatically documented life a good idea, or is privacy a big concern? The latter seems to be the issue that is blocking the technological progress of these black boxes.

INTERNET BUSINESS STRATEGIES

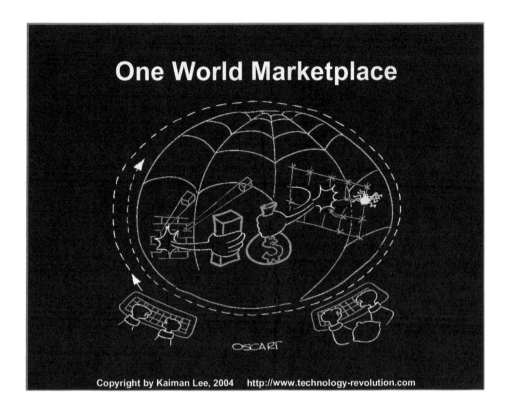

One World Marketplace

OSCART

Copyright by Kaiman Lee, 2004   http://www.technology-revolution.com

The world is becoming a single market. <u>Physical walls and fences</u> bordering the countries of the world are no longer hurdles for commerce.

Businesses are leveraging the Internet for <u>round-the-clock/ round-the-world operations</u>. As one part of the world <u>rests</u> for the night, another area is just <u>waking up</u> to shop.

Think of the Internet as an <u>endless mall</u>, with unlimited accessibility, with almost no fee for setting up shop and relatively little labor cost to maintain it. It is the beginning of the biggest market in history. However, as the world's businesses become <u>more competitive</u>, the costs of setting up virtual shops and maintaining them will become more and <u>more expensive</u>.

Not only should we think that the "<u>network is the computer</u>," now the <u>network could be the business</u>.

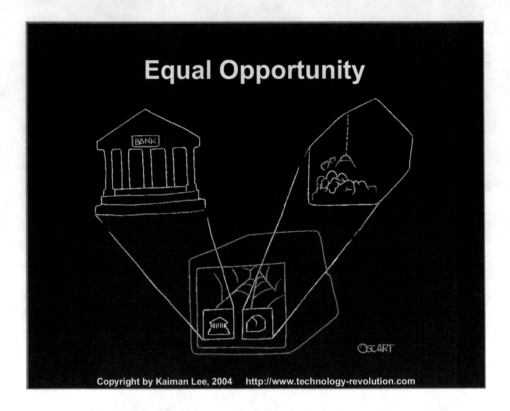

Equal Opportunity

Copyright by Kaiman Lee, 2004   http://www.technology-revolution.com

In the physical world, <u>banks</u> are perceived to be housed in massive, <u>marble-fronted buildings</u>, and <u>sex shops</u> are in low, dingy shop fronts with <u>blacked out windows</u> and <u>neon lights</u>.

Viewed through an Internet browser, <u>both</u> are reduced to <u>just a screen</u> with some pictures and text. This allows for "friction-free capitalism" that enables even the most humble business to reach a worldwide audience.

The Web enables <u>small businesses to look and act like big businesses</u>. "On the Internet, nobody knows you are a dog." You can be just <u>as good as the giants -- or better</u>, because you do not have to go through <u>28 committees</u>, and you can move quickly to reach a large group of people.

The Web revolution creates a <u>level playing field</u>. The days when a few giants call the shots could be gone forever. Changes wrought by the Internet are called <u>"deconstruction" of old business models</u>. During times of rapid change (deconstruction), <u>insurgent companies have an advantage over incumbent companies</u>, no matter how well the incumbents are run or how powerful they are.

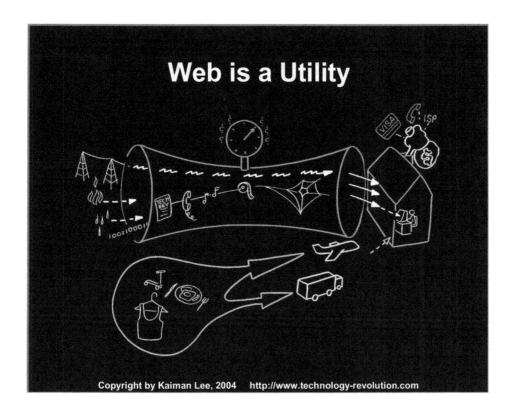

Molecules of anything -- <u>water, gas, electricity, data</u> -- flowing through a conduit or pipeline, requires a <u>metered delivery system</u>. <u>Hard or physical goods</u> such as computers, furniture, and clothing <u>can not</u> be sent over a metered delivery system. The Web is a metered delivery system. <u>Products that exist in time rather than space</u> -- <u>phone calls, data, music, movies</u> -- can be sent over the Internet efficiently.

The perception of <u>Web-as-store</u> must give way to <u>Web-as-pipeline</u>. And the services such as articles on specific topics, online games, Java applets, and streamed video content require <u>incremental payments</u> rather than large one-time payments.

<u>Micropayments</u>, or incremental charges for <u>exactly the content</u> customers want, lower the threshold for <u>fee-for-content</u> Web sites. Charging small payments means users do not have to pay a sizable chunk of cash in order to subscribe before reaping the benefit of the desired content.

Electronic micropayments can be <u>aggregated monthly</u>, and billed via a <u>credit card, ISPs or telephone companies</u>. They can be <u>funded</u> by stored-value smart cards, universal electronic wallet, loyalty or incentive programs, or <u>bank accounts</u>.

131

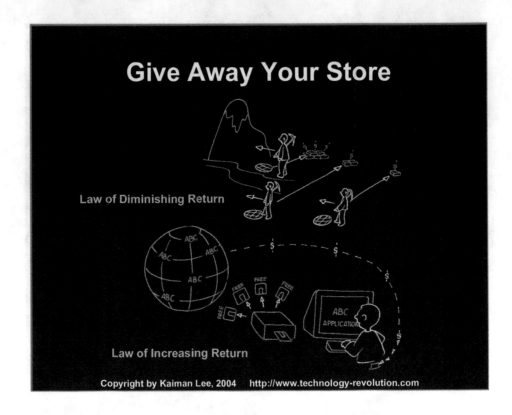

Give Away Your Store

Law of Diminishing Return

Law of Increasing Return

Copyright by Kaiman Lee, 2004   http://www.technology-revolution.com

If you discovered a large deposit of <u>silver ore</u>, you <u>would not give lots of it away</u> at first. The reason is that each <u>additional</u> ton of silver is <u>harder to extract</u> and thus more expensive. This is the <u>law of diminishing returns</u>.

The information age is changing our time-honored economic theory. A <u>software</u>, for example, has <u>expensive up-front</u> costs but, once created, can be <u>duplicated at almost no cost</u>. The law of diminishing returns becomes the <u>law of increasing returns</u>.

Most <u>profit</u> of a new innovative software product is <u>taken in during the first few months</u> on the market. Soon after, <u>competing products</u> will have <u>flooded</u> your niche so few can make money on the same concept any more.

The new software, Internet business or e-commerce <u>paradigm</u> is to <u>get big fast, subjugate profit -- even revenues</u>. Get your product out there. <u>Lure new customers like crazy</u> and try to keep up with them. The <u>malcontents</u> who expect better will be <u>replaced by newcomers</u> who do not know much.

Here is the sequence of this business model. <u>Give away first. Give away more. They like your product. They are addicted to your product. You captured their mind share. You got the market share. Start charging them</u>.

Incentive Advertisement

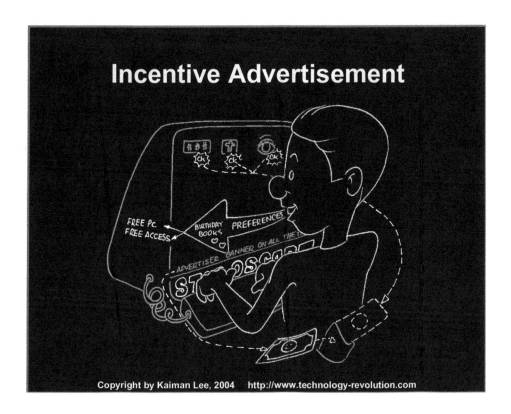

The Internet's current <u>hot business model</u> involves <u>attracting eyeballs</u> to Web sites and then <u>selling page views to advertisers</u>.

You can get a <u>free PC</u> if you <u>subscribe for Internet access</u> with an ISP for say three years. You can get <u>free Internet access</u> if you can <u>put up with the ads</u>. Personal information supplied by you will let the company target ads directly to you based on your profile and geographic region. You can also make money by <u>referring others</u> to do the same, a scheme similar to traditional <u>network marketing</u>.

The <u>Impulse-enabled ads</u> are incorporated in attention-getting devices such as <u>banners</u> that wink, blink, and talk, and animated icons. They entice you to <u>click through</u> to the information underneath, and make <u>spur-of-the-moment purchases</u>.

The move towards an <u>advertising-based economy</u> lowers <u>Internet access</u> barriers, and allows for profitable creation and distribution of content that would otherwise not be feasible.

The <u>losers</u> could be <u>traditional media companies</u>, who see wide competitions for a finite number of advertising dollars.

Free Messaging

Here comes <u>free voice mail, E-mail and faxing over the Internet</u>. You sign up for a free account. The service assigns you a telephone number that your friends can call to leave you messages. You call to retrieve messages. <u>The phone numbers are either local or toll-free</u>.

When someone leaves you a <u>voice message</u>, it is forwarded as <u>an audio attachment to an E-mail</u> in-box or kept on a Web site where you can retrieve it. Some services also let you send free outbound and inbound faxes.

The service providers' goal is to keep you coming back to their sites. They get their <u>revenue from advertisements and extra services</u> that you may buy. They are such as information-management functions like <u>a calendar and an address book</u>.

You not only can punch in codes using the telephone keypad, you could also <u>talk </u>over the phone to the computer <u>for navigation</u>.

You could be allotted say 45 minutes per day of free telephone time to send, retrieve, and receive voice mail and faxes by phone. When your 45 minutes are up, you would pay for more minutes for say 10 cents a minute. The computer accessed Web-based services could remain free and without any time limit.

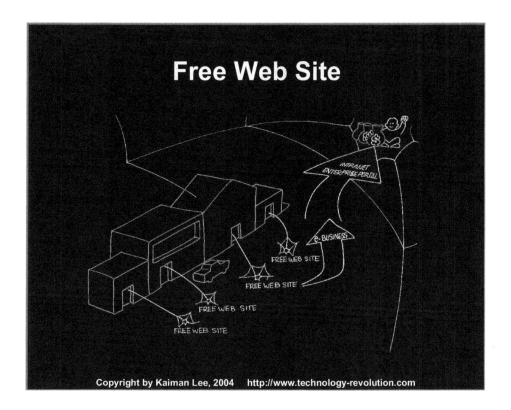

Free Web Site

An Internet company will host your company's Web site for nothing. The service is geared to departments, associations, workgroups and small and medium-size businesses. It would earn money through advertising and sponsorships.

It will also give away some free technologies and services that you would not normally get when implementing a first-generation site.

Some of the advanced functionality include tracking customer contacts; creating customer profiles and analysis; targeted marketing and loyalty programs; managing communications, inventory and logistics; etc.

The Internet company wants to turn small businesses into e-businesses, and their Web sites to Intranets. The small businesses will then buy more software, hardware and services from the Internet company.

Sooner or later, the "old economy (analog commerce) concepts" such as market share, brand equity, distribution channels, financial control, operational integrity, and excellence will come back to measure the success of the e-commerce you are running.

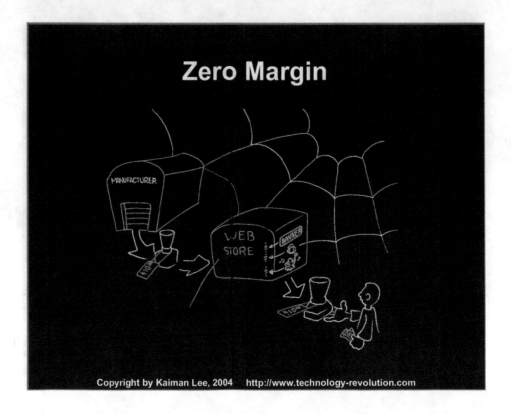

Zero Margin

"Zero margin" business model is based on little or no profit margin in selling products. Almost all the revenue comes from ad space it sells. By bringing eager consumers to its site, the company figures it will be able to entice advertisers.

Some companies sell computers and accessories at cost, plus, say $10 per transaction on their Web sites. They expect to make money on the service on top of the ad revenue.

Zero margins could create two angry sets of folks: the customers and the suppliers. The business model is built around little or no customer service, which is bound to alienate consumers. Suppliers do not want their products to be perceived as of little value.

Although the Net's advertising pie is growing rapidly, the dollar amount is still pretty small. And there is not an unlimited supply of ad dollars.

Can an online retailer really give away products and still make money? The answer could be that the Internet has changed things -- but most likely not that much. Sooner rather than later, the stock holders would want to see the company making real money.

Online Auction

Online auctions allow individual customers to <u>buy</u> goods from and <u>sell</u> goods to other customers.

It is an easy way to get your products -- whether it is your <u>branded merchandise</u> or <u>excess</u> office or computing equipment -- <u>exposed to the masses</u> without geographical boundaries.

You can <u>set a price</u> and not accept bids lower than the fixed price, or you can let bids <u>start at $1</u>. And, you can set your auction to last for <u>an hour, a day, or a week</u>.

<u>All sales are final; no buyer's remorse</u>. <u>Shipping and handling</u> charges will be added to the final cost.

Online auctions makes a <u>fundamental change</u> in pricing that will complicate the government's <u>cost-of-living models</u>. How will the Fed monitor changes in the cost of living when an overwhelming portion of the population is <u>haggling for the best prices</u> they can get at any moment?

The <u>business model has changed</u>. Online auction is enabling a buyer to get <u>the rock-bottom price for the best product from qualified suppliers</u>. It takes out some of the advantage for the <u>incumbent supplier</u> to large companies. It will change the meaning of "<u>suggested retail price</u>."

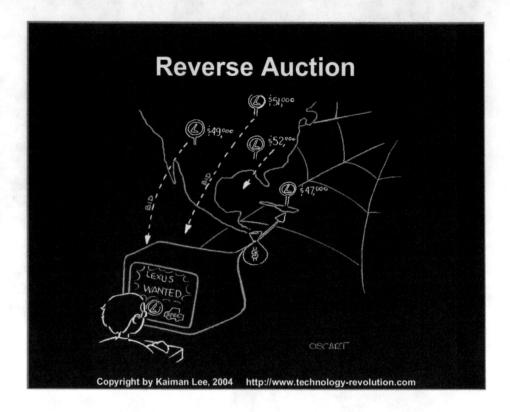

Reverse Auction

Reverse auction is a buyer-initiated online marketplace. You put in the product specifics and the price you want to pay. When your price is met, the sale goes through.

It is a business revolution, the reversal of the traditional model of seller marketing. Power has shifted to the consumer. The customer is telling the merchant what s/he will pay. It is not a traditional supply-and-demand market anymore.

At a reverse-auction company's Web site, you simply type in a description of what you want, the price you are willing to pay, and your deadline. If any of the participating merchants accepts, you get what you seek at the price you want.

On a "car-purchasing" Web site, you can order a car with your unique specifications, including the price you are willing to pay. Dealers around the world can bid on it.

Reverse auction revolutionizes pricing. Price tags are an anachronism for the brick-and-mortar world. What is my price if I am willing to wait, if I can not return it, if I take any of the colors, and if I come to pick it up right now? Reverse auction makes "one-to-one pricing" and "policy for one" possible.

Reverse auction is also called "name-your-price" auction.

Name-Your-Price Auction

Copyright by Kaiman Lee, 2004   http://www.technology-revolution.com

In the plane ticket example, you enter in your dates, destination and maximum spending amount. The site matches the price you bid against the prices various airlines have agreed to sell their distressed inventory. If the airline's price is, say, $10 less, the site buys the ticket, sells it to you at your price, and pockets the difference, on top of the normal commission. It is not really an auction; it is more like an online discount bid.

This type of sites are designed to bring buyers and sellers together in any market where there are multiple pricing options, e.g., plane tickets, hotel rooms, cars, credit cards and home mortgages, groceries, even expert consulting.

You can specify how much you will spend for items such as milk, chips, and batteries – but cannot specify the exact brand. If your prices are accepted, your credit card is charged. You can pick the items up or have them delivered by your neighborhood store.

You can "name your price" for a piece of advice, say, "What is the value for the inverted airplane stamp?" Consultants and experts dream of being able to sit on a beach and deliver advice from their laptop, and anonymously. Think about teachers and professors moonlighting. The potential is beyond imagination.

Point-of-Sale Advertising

Copyright by Kaiman Lee, 2004   http://www.technology-revolution.com

Customers may <u>stand at a checkout counter</u> for as long as <u>10 minutes</u>. That time is valuable consumer "<u>touch time</u>."

A merchant can make use of a Web-enabled <u>point-of-sale terminal to "touch" the customers</u>. The terminal can include <u>advertising, surveys and promotions</u>. While the customers are waiting, they will see and read ads and promotions at point-of-sale terminals more so than banner ads on the Web.

Web-enabled point-of-sale terminals will <u>blur the lines between brick-and-mortar and online stores</u>. They will help preserve the standing that offline retail destinations still hold with the public.

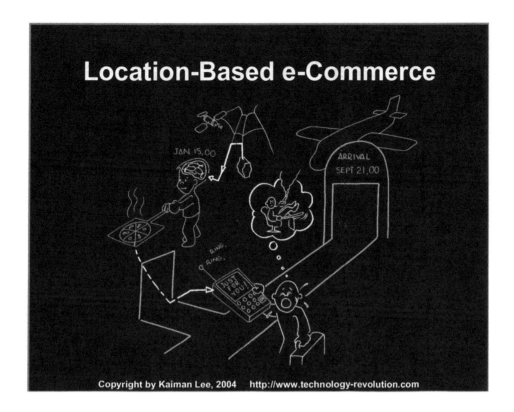

When a consumer searches for a <u>pizza restaurant</u>, a pizza shop <u>near by</u> knows it and sends the consumer a message of <u>advertisement</u> with a discount. Similarly, you can project this scenario to flower shops, shoe repair, etc.

You get off the <u>airplane</u> and turn on your <u>cell phone</u>. As you pass the <u>pizza shop</u> in the hallway, it rings. It could be the client, so you rush to answer it. "I see you haven't been here since <u>last January</u>. How about a Pizza Supreme that you had last time. We have a deal for you …" The pizza merchant knows you because you paid for your last pizza supreme by <u>credit card</u>.

Your <u>cell phone</u> <u>with or without</u> a global positioning system (<u>GPS</u>) reports your location to merchants and vending machines close to where you are. They know who you are and what you buy, and they hone the ads to your <u>Web browser, E-mail or cell phone</u>.

This could be a reality of <u>pain or convenience</u> of the new <u>wireless technology</u>.

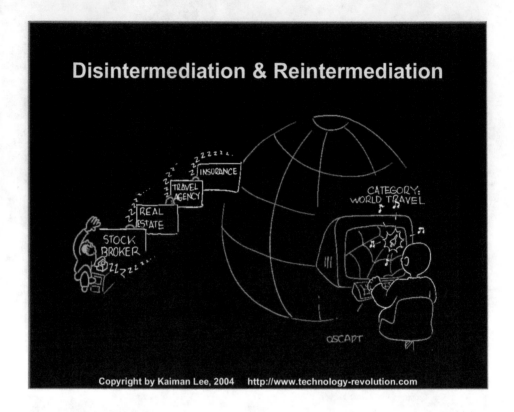

Disintermediation & Reintermediation

Opportunities lie in the <u>discontinuity of the Internet</u>. Some of the equivalent words used are <u>disintermediation, disaggregation and unbundling</u>.

Disintermediation is eliminating the <u>middle person (the hand off)</u>, and bringing the <u>producer and consumer closer</u> together. It reduces <u>three players in a transaction to two</u>. It is also called "one-to-end," e.g., a computer manufacturer sells custom-built computers to end users.

Today there are intermediaries: brokers, wholesalers, distributors, retailers, and resellers. They increase cost to the consumer. And they put the supplier at a distance from their ultimate customer.

You do not want to spend a lot of time <u>clicking the Web</u> trying to find something. You often <u>want less information, but the target information</u>. Here comes <u>reintermediation</u>. They are <u>guides, directories, and agents</u> alike.

Consumers may be willing to invest a lot of time and effort seeing everything there is to see on very few specific topics. They want both <u>convenience</u> and <u>comprehensiveness</u>. The new breed of middle person directories provides that added value.

Affiliate Marketing

A retailer signs up <u>affiliates who sell the retailer's products on their own sites</u> in return for a <u>commission</u>, usually between 8 and 15 percent of sales. That is affiliate marketing in a nutshell, or the practice of making anyone who runs a Web site an extended part of your sales team. You get the referred sales, the affiliates get a reward.

Affiliates that have <u>highly focused Web sites</u> would do well. Because they <u>know their audiences very well</u>, they can select subsets of the retailer's products and market them directly at their audiences. In this way, the retailer not only increases its distribution, it also gains some effective <u>niche marketers</u>.

This is not multilevel marketing because most of these programs <u>do not pay</u> their affiliates for <u>recruiting</u> other affiliates into their programs. However, it is only a matter of time before the affiliate program retailers <u>realize</u> that providing incentives for their affiliates to recruit still more affiliates is one of the <u>cheapest ways to expand their network</u>. When that happens, affiliate programs will start looking like <u>network marketing online</u>.

Affinity Marketing

In the traditional world of affinity, you charge to your credit cards (affinity card) what you buy. The organization (airline or your college) sponsoring the credit card would get a percentage of your charge from the bank holding the account.

In affinity marketing which is a variant of the affiliate model, the affiliate company pays a commission to a school when friends, family, relatives, and co-workers purchase CDs, magazines, food, and other items through the school's customized web store.

Say you support the goals of an organization called Heaven On Earth, which has a portal site. You go through the portal and buy all sorts of things, Levi jeans, Lexus, anything!

Heaven On Earth in turn gets 4 or 5 percent of your purchase price for providing Levi and Lexus access to its supporters.

Affinity marketing can be lucrative for brand-name products where loyalty counts. It will probably work miracles for non-profit and political organizations as a new source for funding. It is a win-win situation for consumers and fund organizations.

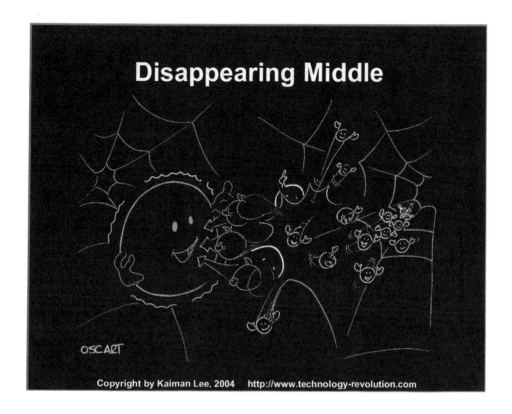

Disappearing Middle

OSCART

The <u>convenience of one-stop shopping favors superstores</u>, while independent <u>boutiques</u> are best able to <u>customize</u>. The <u>middle is being squeezed</u> as superstores and boutiques prosper.

In e-commerce, the <u>big brands will get even bigger</u>. The power of <u>gaining the attention of consumers en mass</u> will be even more powerful than it is today.

Consumers who once abandoned the Main Street butcher, baker and candlestick maker for giant stores in the suburbs are now eager to <u>trade in their insurance agencies, bank branches and securities brokers for financial supermarkets</u>: stocks and bonds in aisle 1, property and casualty policies in aisle 3, mortgages in aisle 7, all passing through the same checkout counter.

Power is diluted by time and scale. Middle-tier companies are the most sensitive to the <u>shrinking time scale phenomenon</u> because of their <u>administrative burdens and momentum</u>.

The small companies can specialize and roll out new products fast. They are free to beta test their ideas. Overhead can be low when they use electronic distribution. <u>New niche</u> businesses will flourish because <u>consumers can get exactly what they want</u> online, e.g., exact color and style they want.

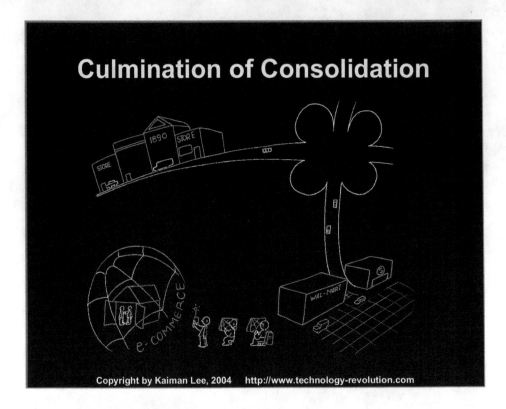

Culmination of Consolidation

A hundred years ago most retail sales came from small, neighborhood "mom and pop" stores. In the early 1900s, large department stores entered the marketplace, and many small independent shops could not compete and had to close their doors.

Department stores gave way to strip-malls and shopping centers that fit well into the suburbanization of America. Then these businesses evolved into the huge, shopping malls of today. Customer convenience was the driving force behind them.

With e-commerce, some analysts predict that retailing, as we now know it, will be mostly non-existent by the year 2015! Shopping for products from all over the world through the convenience of the Internet is the new generation of retailing.

Decades ago, books were sold by your typical "Mom and Pop" retail outlets. In the last couple of decades, large book store chains, such as Barnes and Noble, entered the scene carrying hundreds of thousands of titles in each location.

In a couple of years, Amazon.com had become the largest book "store" in the world providing millions of titles to its customers.

And it does so without a lot of the buildings, salespeople, inventory and other overhead costs associated with typical retail distribution models.

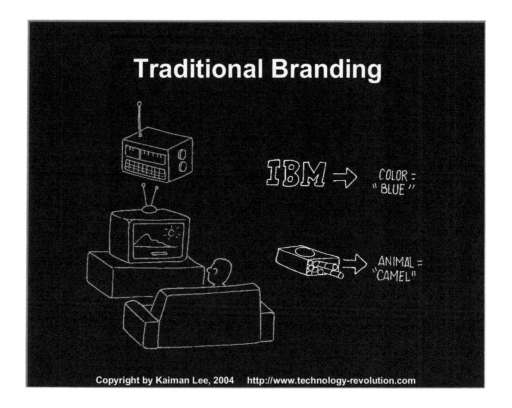

What color is IBM … Blue. What animal relates to cigarette …
Camel. You know the answers right away because you have been
imprinted. Those companies have burned their brands into your brain
by years of repetitive advertising.

Branding, for these old-line companies, means sending out endless
visual and textual messages to the consumers of the world, all in the
hope of generating a positive aura around their products. Consumers
take them in a passive manner.

The current prevalent branding of giving potential customers free stuff
may not last. Brand-building has never been free, it very seldom
works through the use of free incentives, and is, unfortunately, only
getting more expensive every day. At first, people may be excited by
the free stuff associated with required reading of advertisements, but
the enthusiasm will die down quickly. When the value of time comes
back to their head, people will ignore the free stuff en masse.

Compared to Internet advertisement, traditional advertisement has
become prohibitively expensive. Branding through traditional
advertisement will continue to shrink.

A new branding paradigm has surfaced which involves a customer's
total experience of a company.

147

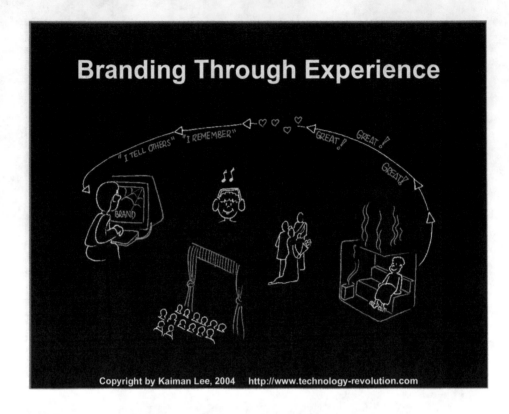

Branding Through Experience

Branding on the Web means something entirely different from traditional brand advertisement. Online branding is about an active experience -- the consumers' experience -- expressed through dialogue between consumers and retailers.

Online branding could be as simple as an easy-to-use and gentle navigation service, such as putting a CD in your shopping cart, keeping track of everything without a miss, and offering you something you are interested in. If the experience is so painless and convenient, you will become brand-loyal.

Branding is not just about image anymore. Everything you do online is part of the brand-building experience. Brand building is no longer a one-way street, but a two-way highway, with traffic zipping in both directions.

Create brand experiences – not by telling people about the brand, but letting them enter the brand. Make them feel the sensation of attending a concert, relaxing in a spa, listening to their preferred music or even getting married. Now you can be sure you get them hooked to your brand.

To further your brand, It is wise to let consumers drive the supply.

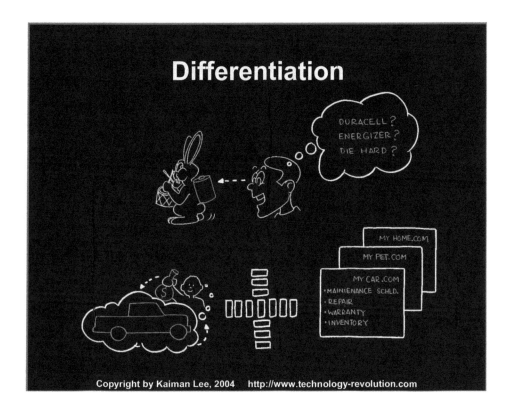

Differentiation can create barriers to exit. Is there one thing you can say that makes you the only choice for a buyer, or at the top of your customer's mind, i.e., your unique selling proposition? Energizer battery's drum-beating bunny advertisement does not differentiate qualities from the competing Duracell batteries. Consumers remember the unique commercials but not necessarily the brand.

If you use words such as robust, turnkey, best-of-breed, next-generation, leading, scalable, and end-to-end solutions to describe your product, journalists and venture capitalists will laugh at you because the new venture is not clearly differentiated.

To differentiate, you can give free Web pages for products you have sold, e.g., home page for a car that lists service history, maintenance schedule, and a place to ask questions or schedule a service appointment, or home pages for a pet, or real estate. The owner has a vested interest in continuing to visit the Web site, an exit-prevention strategy.

You can differentiate your shopping cart with others by installing in it video games for kids while the adults are shopping. You can give frequent flyer miles while others do not.

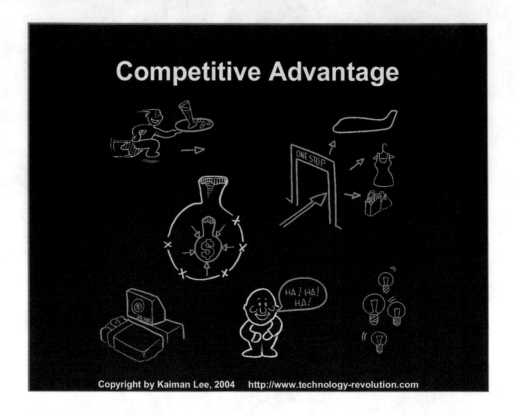

Competitive Advantage

Excellent service, fast delivery or best price can be a competitive advantage that could create barriers to exit.

Giving your customer a pain reducer vs. pain inducer can be a competitive advantage. "Wow" your customer based on any or all four fundamentals: convenience, information, entertainment and savings, and it can be a competitive advantage.

Responding to complaints and inbound help messages immediately and professionally can be a competitive advantage.

Meeting customer expectations will effectively manage dissatisfaction. Exceeding customer expectations will let you manage loyalty and attract a greater share of the market, and it is a competitive advantage. Executive talent is a competitive advantage. Speed is. One-stop shopping is.

Providing access to critical information once the phone is answered can give you a competitive advantage. With it, you can make fast and accurate decisions. Today's high-tech call centers can identify who is calling before the call is answered. All the previously gathered data about the caller can be analyzed and a prediction made about what the customer is calling about, or what he or she might want to buy. The call can then be routed automatically to a specialist.

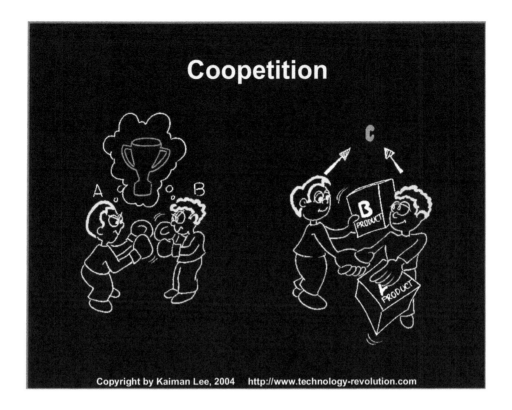

Because of the global nature of business today, e-commerce is now conducted with a mixture of organizations that many firms did not view as trading partners just a few years ago.

The new relationship has coined a new word in the business world, "coopetition." It means that <u>firms are both competing and cooperating</u> with each other for <u>win-win</u>.

A lot of the <u>new technology</u> comes from the <u>smallest companies</u>. You can work with them -- or you can try to <u>do everything yourself</u> and be <u>18 months behind</u>.

The Internet is the cradle of cooperation. If it looks like a competitor, figure out how to turn it into coopetition. If that can not be done, how about a <u>flat out purchase</u>?

According to a 1997 study by Newton, MA-based Cahners Research, <u>40% of the business transactions</u> are conducted <u>between competitors</u>.

As soon as you <u>sell somebody the whole thing</u>, e.g., software application, you <u>eliminate</u> him/her as a <u>customer</u>. Just sell what the customers need at the time. Then you can <u>sell them over and over</u> again on an as needed basis.

This strategy may be called <u>unbundling</u>.

An added advantage is that you do not have to produce a monolithic application. Get <u>one part working</u>, and <u>release</u> it over the Net as it becomes debugged. The same principle can be applied to a Web site.

It costs very little overhead for each change, improvement or transaction over the Web since they are done electronically and automatically.

Selling an application service (re: metering use of software via an application service provider) as opposed to selling the whole application is another way of selling "a piece at a time."

The key to making money is to make it any way you can.

A little here, a little there, and pretty soon it adds up. Get pennies for a recipe (snippet), not $20 for a cookbook.

You need multiple revenue streams to survive the ever-changing Internet business environment.

For example, you are more likely to make a profit if you charge for content, offer premium services, offer useful advertising, and offer Internet access, instead of just one of them.

There are basically three ways to grow your business: find new customers, get existing customers to buy more frequently, and get them to buy bigger amount.

So, Ask yourself if you are doing something to grow your base of customers, offer them more buying opportunities or expand ways they can spend more.

Upside Surprises

"An entrepreneur should always <u>heed the upside surprises</u>. Upside surprises <u>distract</u> business leaders from deadening focus on <u>problems</u> and <u>target</u> them on their <u>opportunities</u>. In the information economy, the best opportunities stem from the exponential rise in the <u>power of computers and computer networks, microcosm and telecosm</u>."
--- Peter Drucker, management guru

The power of computers and computer networks will <u>free up a lot of time</u> for the techno-business entrepreneurs.

Entrepreneurial people use their liberated time to <u>perform more valuable economic activities</u>.

Using the Web, they will be able to work far more <u>efficiently</u>, <u>collaborating</u> with the best experts anywhere and serving markets around the globe.

These entrepreneurs will build successful <u>"Cottage" industries </u>and many of them will <u>become giant</u> corporations, e.g., American Online (AOL), amazon.com, e-bay, etc.

You must <u>heed the upside surprises of what the Web will and could do for you</u>.

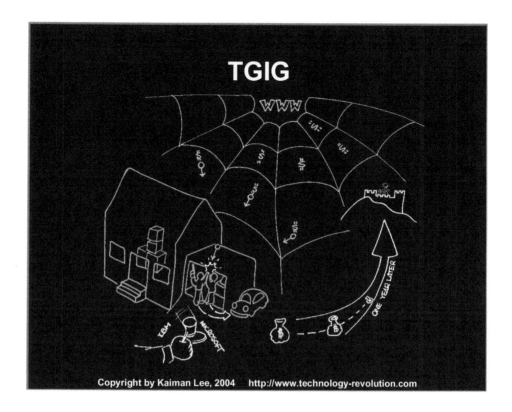

TGIG

A great deal of innovation in the online world is coming from firms that are just two guys in a garage (TGIG).

These people have innovative ideas. They are not bound by the status quo. They form companies that float their IPOs (initial public offerings) before they are even blips on the business world's radar screens.

But, before they realize their full potential, they may be purchased by Microsoft or other companies.

Here are some of the philosophies TGIG holds:
- Business models are a paradigm a dozen.
- The Internet is a minefield of opportunities.
- Step carefully, or another opportunity will go off right in your face.
- Adapt and adopt.

"$100 million dollars is way too much to pay for Microsoft."
--- IBM, 1982

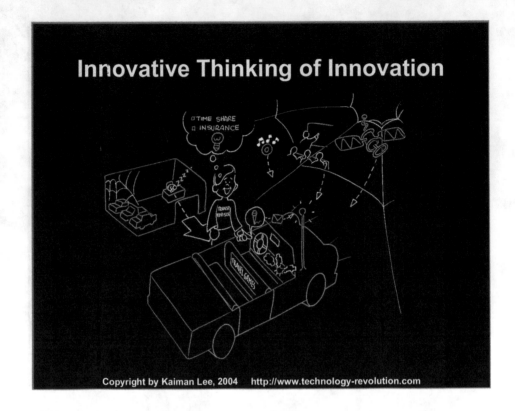

Innovative Thinking of Innovation

Copyright by Kaiman Lee, 2004   http://www.technology-revolution.com

Auto dealers could exploit the Internet to expand their role. They could reposition themselves as ongoing transportation advisers, providing new services for which the public will pay.

Imagine cars evolving into networked information appliances providing users with a place to work, learn and be entertained. Increasingly, services and content of cars will differentiate them.

In-car computers will not only play CDs, but also will take voice memos, access the Global Positioning System, display maps, dial a cell phone, read E-mail, display traffic and weather warnings, etc. Theft alarms may require ongoing monthly payments. Dealers could play a role in offering one-stop shopping for all the new services as they become available.

Dealers could help their customers develop new forms of vehicle ownership, an automotive equivalent of timeshare vacations. Customers can choose a different vehicle from week to week or month to month.

What about providing auto insurance packages?

Real estate brokers could become "relocation consultants," providing home buying, selling, loan, insurance, and moving services.

An Idea

The most valuable asset is an idea. A single idea can launch a new initiative. It then evolves to generate new markets and Initial Public Offerings (IPOs).

Most successful ideas can often be summarized in a couple of words or even a single word: insurance, auction, bills, etc.

How simply can you express your ideas? If it takes more than two minutes to explain it, the value of your proposition may not be there. The Dale Carnegie course requires students to tell a story in exactly two minutes.

What is required to become an e-business revolutionary? You need to have an utmost sense of urgency. And a dedication to continue developing the idea relentlessly until it has been brought to fruition.

Internet has generated new rules with no boundaries. Both the individual and the corporation can innovate and create e-business revolution. Are you having your troops thinking?

With the idea, what comes next is risk taking. Businesses must develop risk-taking cultures. A company that will not take risks is taking the biggest risk of all.

First Mover

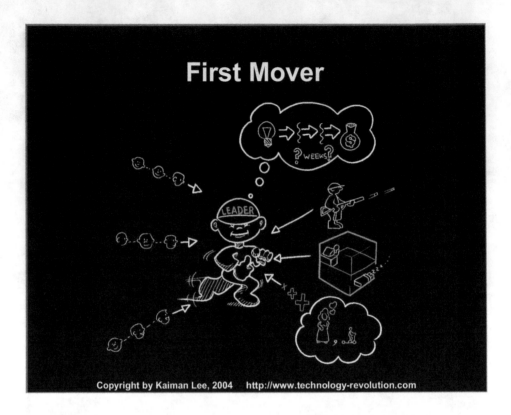

"Ready, fire, aim" is the motto of first movers. "Me too" is a bad strategy, because YahooX and AmazonY still belong to Yahoo and Amazon. First movers have focus; nobody moves faster.

First-generation (1G) start-ups raised seed money, developed a proof-of-concept version, and went back for more money. 1G staff assumed no task is beneath you -- they would do whatever it takes. 1G staff came from brand-manager positions in physical companies or MBA students on leave. Nobody had Internet experience, and everyone learned by making mistakes.

Second-generation (2G) Web companies are lightning faster -- idea, finance, prototype, demo, alpha, and voila -- business, all in twelve weeks. 2G's business plan may consist of 16 slides, with no financial projections and no budget. Financing means one-breakfast time for say $8 million, enough to last until just after IPO. 2G staff synergize not from friendships but from respect for mutually complementary skill sets. They skip the garage phase, bid on three office spaces hoping one comes through. They move in over the weekend and by Monday have it decorated.

2G companies need less strategists but leaders who are execution machines. 2G employees should have zero drag coefficient. A full hour's commute to the office is a full unit of drag. A spouse is one unit, and half unit to each kid.

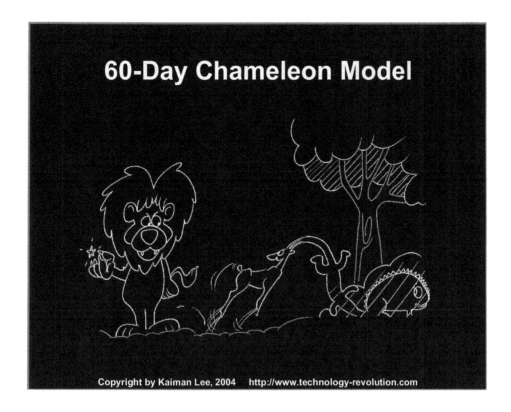

60-Day Chameleon Model

On the day Frank Sinatra died, a media firm's five-person development team assembled and posted a lifetime tribute to the legendary singer, and featured special offers on every one of his recordings -- all in six hours.

With today's rapid changes, the agility of a gazelle may not be good enough. You need to be a chameleon to succeed in the Internet economy. That means having the ability to change strategy about every two months.

Companies now receive customer feedback at warp speed. Companies that do not quickly respond with products or services run the risk of deletion from customers' bookmark lists. Customers are a click away from going to competitors.

Over the course of about 60 days, deliver different and personalized pricing offers. Offer customized buy recommendations on a daily basis. Show a top-sellers' list that is updated daily.

A software company can launch five new product versions within a few days. Enabling that breakneck pace of product rollouts is an incremental software development model under which a product is never finished. You can release something that works but not as well as you would like it to work, and then update it.

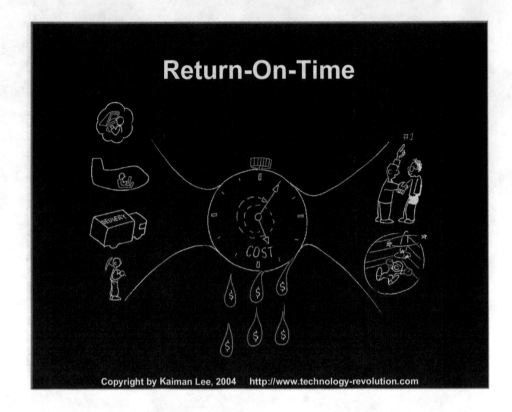

Return-On-Time

In productivity analysis, almost <u>all costs</u> ultimately <u>hinge on time</u>. The question therefore, is "how much <u>value is returned</u> from the <u>time invested</u>?"

One way to look at a business process is to consider <u>how much value is returned from a period of time invested</u>. In a literal sense, an individual's time can be measured as the number of heartbeats invested.

Time can be translated into speed also. Let us look at the phenomenon of "<u>escape velocity</u>" as an analogy. It is the speed an object must attain to escape the gravitational pull and enter the Earth's orbit. A <u>slightly lesser speed simply will not work</u>. Increasingly in the fast speed marketplace, a slightly slower speed in an endeavor may not be competitive enough.

Many success factors can be measured in those terms since <u>no less than a specific measure will attain the values of customer satisfaction, or competitiveness</u>. Most often, <u>that measure is the time, amount and speed</u>.

160

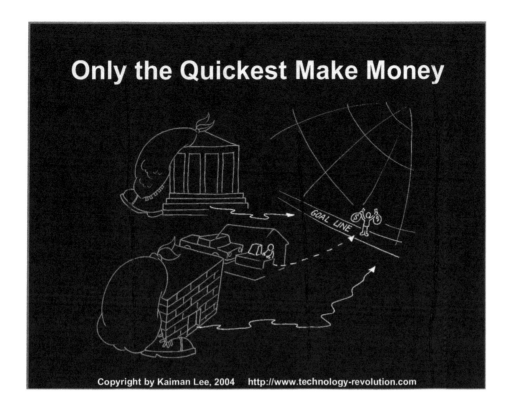

Only the Quickest Make Money

Copyright by Kaiman Lee, 2004   http://www.technology-revolution.com

Cisco Systems President and CEO John Chambers said "For the first time there is truly <u>a level playing field between small companies and big companies</u>. That doesn't mean that the small companies will necessarily win, it means <u>the fast will beat the slow</u> in this new economy." "You are going to see <u>winners and losers determined in not years, but one year</u>. It's <u>not a question of growth</u> with the Internet, it's a <u>question about how fast you are going to grow</u>."

Every month of delay today puts you further behind in this quickly evolving race. As Federal Express and amazon.com have proven, the <u>mindshare goes to those who arrive first, the first mover</u>.

To those <u>brick-and-mortar companies</u> who have so much <u>baggage</u> they are carrying in the physical world, the first step to e-commerce is the hardest but they must <u>make that first step quickly</u>, and learn that speed and agility are paramount.

Changes <u>will only accelerate</u>. Only those who are able to <u>keep up with that pace</u> will thrive.

Develop <u>scenarios for as many plausible versions of the future</u> as possible. <u>Anticipate or predict change, not react</u> to it. Fight with a <u>street tactics</u>.

Be a Real-Time Something

Copyright by Kaiman Lee, 2004   http://www.technology-revolution.com

Be a <u>real-time manager</u>. You must respond to changing circumstances and, more importantly, customer expectations in the smallest possible lapse of time. Produce <u>exceptional responsiveness</u>. Consumers want products right here, right now, served up the way they like them.

Since real time shortens our horizons, we have <u>less time to plan</u>. Therefore, we must learn how to <u>think and act in real time</u>.

Become a <u>real-time company</u>. Real time waits for no one. <u>Change</u> is moving <u>in real time</u> even if you are not. Your customers are ready for real time. You must too.

<u>Real-time technology</u> will help you ensure that your organization monitors, adapts, initiates, verifies, and reacts based on a constant exchange of information.

Be a Worrier and Paranoid

Copyright by Kaiman Lee, 2004   http://www.technology-revolution.com

"The mentality of Microsoft is to always look for what we should be worried about. ... Even though there is no financial crisis, we are very good at creating a crisis atmosphere." -- Microsoft Chairman Bill Gates (Feb. 3, 1998)

Bill Gates said in early February 1999, "In terms of size, our shadow is bigger than our body." Referring to the group's many competitors, Gates said that part of his job, as chairman is "to fear everything."

In the mid-1990s, Intel Corp.'s CEO Andy Grove made his famous observation that "only the paranoid survive" (book title).

Ted Turner, the cable legend said in 1999, "Why did I merge Turner Broadcasting with Time Warner? Because I am scared to death of the future!"

"I think Sun and Microsoft will be totally changed in the future. You can take half the people at Microsoft and half the people at Sun and write them off." -- John Gage, chief scientist at Sun (Sept. 9, 98)

Broadcast.com President and Chairman Mark Cuban invented "The Little Kid Effect" -- that a 15-year-old will think up a new media type or business model they can not imagine today.

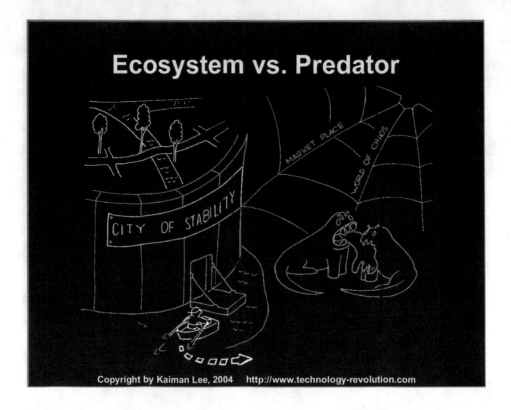

Ecosystem vs. Predator

Copyright by Kaiman Lee, 2004   http://www.technology-revolution.com

An <u>ecosystem can be a stable organization</u> composed of independent organisms. Each organism focuses on its own purposes. It sees to it that free resources find a use.

As an ecosystem becomes more stable over time, species diversity increases and the flow of nutrients and energy within it becomes <u>increasingly complex</u>.

A business that acts as an ecosystem can hardly compete in the <u>new world of business where change is a constant</u>.

A <u>predator</u> has its own purposes, which it achieves through organized and focused activities. If it does not achieve its goals, it will not have food to eat. A predator eats its competitors and <u>takes food away from them</u>. The territory of a predator company is the <u>marketplace</u>.

A company that acts as a stabilized ecosystem will not change fast enough to be competitive in this fast-paced marketplace. <u>Only the CEO has any chance</u> at all to change an ecosystem company. Even for a CEO, the road to a predator system can be a hard one.

You do not have to be a predator to have a successful business; just create something that you are the only one doing it.

Self Cannibalization

The process of <u>continuous business innovation</u> requires that you must be willing to <u>cut out</u> operations that are <u>mistakes</u>. You must be able to recognize them and take action <u>without delay</u>. Not doing so will drain resources from profitable operations and prolong the agony of the inevitable demise of the losers.

Bank One went into competition with itself by creating a "new" Internet bank called WingspanBank.com. The thinking is that it is better to cannibalize itself than to let others cannibalize you.

You must continuously and <u>deliberately attack the assumptions</u> of the existence of various operations. The business environment changes so fast that yesterday's winners may become tomorrow's deadweight.

You must <u>purge the idols</u> you might have been <u>worshipping</u> -- for example, <u>multiple-tiered distribution systems</u>. Dell Computer Corporation is a great example of this world-class <u>curve jumping</u>. It built a company that would kill the old company. In a sense, it is <u>better to be cannibals than to be carrion</u>.

The metaphor of <u>pruning a rosebush</u> can be used to illustrate the idea that a "<u>continuous process of creative destruction</u>" is a way to <u>avoid the typical business boom-and-bust cycle</u>.

E-BUSINESS

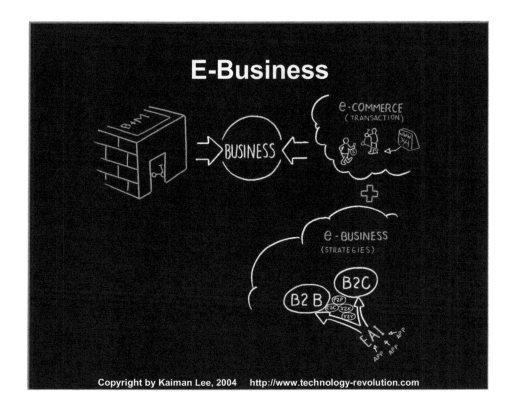

E-business and e-Commerce seem interchangeable, but e-business is all-encompassing while e-commerce is mainly for transaction. What distinguishes e-business from e-commerce is how companies develop strategies for successful e-business and how they maintain a desirable level of e-commerce through Web site development and innovative technologies.

E-business encompasses business-to-consumer (B2C: spontaneous transaction through Internet), and business-to-business (B2B: between two parties with a pre-existing relationship through Extranet).

New data sources are: Web logs, on-line marketplaces, e-procurement applications, content servers, transaction servers, and personalization servers. They generate the Web-related information needed for e-business intelligence.

E-businesses must be able to track and extract those data, then integrate them with information that exists in their traditional supply chain management, customer relationship management and sales force automation, etc. They are also loaded at high speed into data warehouses, then presented for analysis by the analytic applications that feed into the executive business-intelligence processes.

B2B Exchanges

B2B marketplaces allow customers to act as both buyers and sellers. They can deal with a particular (vertical) industry, or across (horizontal) a particular common business activity, to exchange goods, services and information. These sites go by many names -- e-hubs, e-marketplaces, e-market makers, vertical portals, business-to-business trade communities, intermediaries and even metamediaries.

B2B exchanges are neutral B2B marketplaces that let industry players trade commodities -- excess chemicals or energy capacity -- in a spot, or last-minute, market, with both buyer and seller going back and forth on prices.

One B2B business model is to charge buyers and/or sellers a percentage of the transaction value.

B2B marketplaces have a tendency to reduce products to commodities where buyers can easily compare prices across hundreds of suppliers. But when they get more technologically sophisticated, they will enable traders to search on attributes other than price.

B2B (relationship driven) is not the same as B2C (advertising, branding, one to one). B2B is about making business better.

Virtual Supermarket

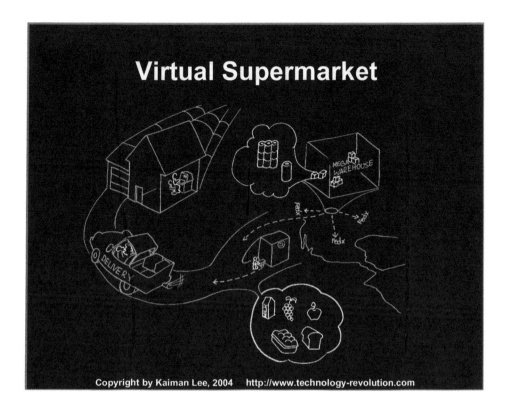

Home shopping is easy. You fill out your order on the Web. Your order then appears at your doorstep.

Non-store-based virtual supermarkets focus on non-perishable groceries. They are located at the cheapest locations but are convenient for express delivery pick up.

Virtual supermarkets are connected to the inventory system in their warehouse. Products listed online have guaranteed availability. Orders are picked from warehouse bins and boxed for immediate shipping.

They buy their products from wholesalers and manufacturers as other supermarkets do, but have no costs associated with stocking shelves or creating attractive displays. Their prices can be lower than the traditional supermarkets.

Other cyber supermarkets that are local-store-based do offer perishable goods such as milk and eggs. They arrange for delivery of goods from neighborhood supermarkets.

Shopping for a Home

House hunters using the Web will get to <u>know the new listings the moment they are listed</u>, while others will have to wait for the <u>newspaper drop off</u> or the <u>mail truck</u> to arrive.

In the near future, you can isolate an <u>area of interest on a map</u>, and find all the properties that meet your criteria. You will then have a <u>virtual house tour</u> of the homes you are interested in.

You can look at <u>360-degree photos</u> of the living rooms, kitchens and master suites. If you see one you like, you do not even need to leave the Web site to <u>set up an appointment</u> for a physical walk through. With a click of the mouse, you can enter a private <u>chat room</u> and converse with a real estate broker.

Or you can go to the real estate agent's office and experience <u>virtual reality</u>. You will wear special goggles and gloves. How does it feel to have a bath in the master suite, <u>touch the walls,</u> open doors, peek into closets, <u>sit down on the back porch</u>, and jog around the house, all virtually?

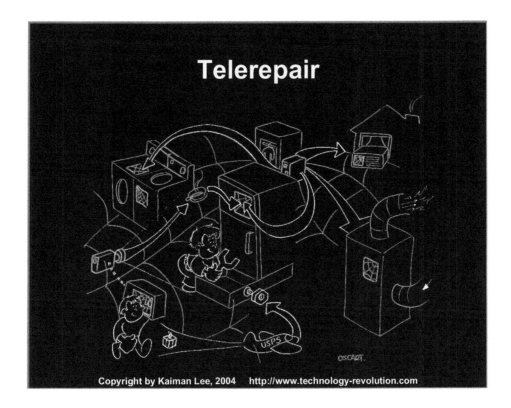

Telerepair

A repair person can <u>troubleshoot</u> your refrigerator problem remotely using a <u>Web camera</u>. You open a compartment and the repair person finds a broken bolt. The replacement bolt is on its way by express delivery. You have just <u>saved</u> the cost of a <u>physical house call</u>.

When your TV goes belly up, the repair person at your local electronics store can see how it is acting remotely. The same goes for your dishwasher, air conditioner ... all appliances.

These household devices can also be equipped with tiny, inexpensive sensors, processors, memory, and software that could transform today's <u>dumb appliances into smart machines</u>. Your Web-enabled refrigerator can diagnose itself and download a <u>fix-it Java applet</u> from its maker's Web site.

All your <u>appliances</u> can be <u>linked to your home Web server</u> in a closet. These microchip-embedded appliances can communicate with the household server via high-frequency <u>radio waves</u> similar to the way <u>cordless phones</u> work.

Your home's server can control the major household power drains such as the furnace and air conditioner. It may help the utility companies cut costs by saving energy and eliminating the need for meter reading.

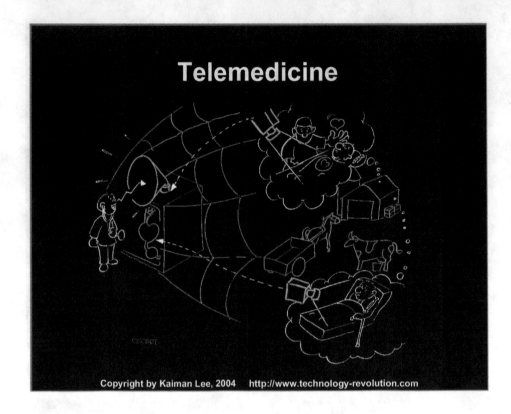

Telemedicine

Copyright by Kaiman Lee, 2004   http://www.technology-revolution.com

With Webcams, <u>rural doctors can share diagnostic tools with specialists</u> around the world.

Detailed digital X-rays, and EKGs can be examined by faraway experts in real time. Hundreds of doctors at a time, worldwide, can witness the <u>latest in surgical procedures</u>. A doctor can zoom in on a wound and start working on it while explaining the procedure.

<u>Diabetic</u> patients can <u>upload</u> data from their digital <u>glucose</u> monitoring devices at home and transmit these to caregivers. In return, the caregivers give <u>instant feedback</u> on actions to take and offer recommendations and reminders. Doctors may use wireless technology to beam instructions to <u>pacemakers</u>.

<u>Home care</u> nurses makes a video call to <u>elderly</u> homes. If there is no answer, they can see inside the house (with prior permission), and help the patient take the correct medications.

Family members can <u>visit newborns virtually</u>. Physicians and parents can review patient progress during and after treatments.

Imagine that doctors can see patients from around the world. A <u>specialist in Beijing, China may charge only $10</u> for a visit. Could medical costs be drastically reduced?

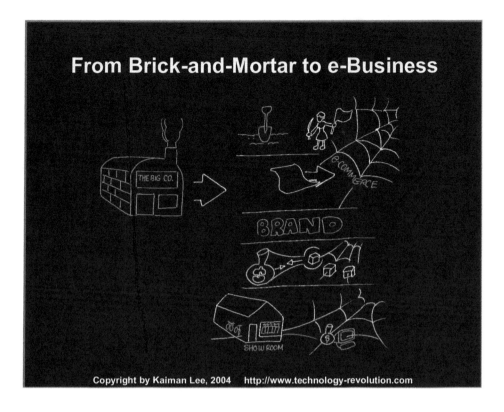

From Brick-and-Mortar to e-Business

The Web might have enabled others to take away your customers. Much money spent online are siphoned from the coffers of retailers. Look at independent bookstores, auto dealers, stockbrokers, first class mail providers, drug stores and magazine publishing. Adopt, innovate or expire.

Here are some pointers:

- Think like a start-up, but act like a leader.
- Your best weapon might be a blank sheet of paper.
- Leverage your industry position, associations, and brand -- something start-ups do not have.
- You can acquire one of the links in their value or supply chain.
- Act quickly. Experiment, and experiment.
- Leverage your company's intellectual capital. Apply idea management.
- Implement real time responses. Focus on customer service, and make it easy for your customers to do business with you.
- Make online and physical operations seamless. Brick-and-mortar stores may become showcases. Customers may want to browse or read a book at a physical bookstore – then go home to order it on the Web.
- Think of the Net expansion as an innovation business (i-business), a way to transform your enterprise.

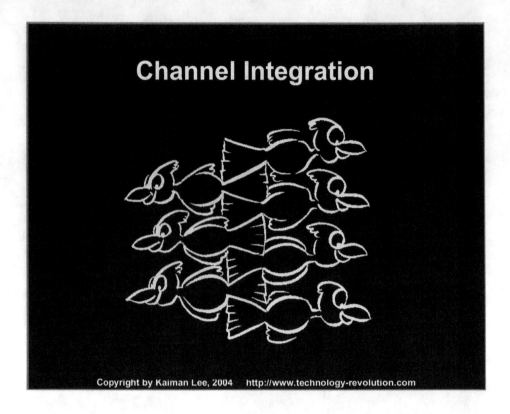

Channel Integration

Business channels include Web stores, brick-and-mortar (B&M) stores, direct sales, catalogs, TV shows, as well as e-mail, chat, toll-free numbers. Channel conflicts are such as different prices and different products of the same brand.

Consumers may want to avoid shipping costs by ordering online and picking up merchandise at the stores. They may want a physical place to return, exchange, or repair an item.

B&Ms have advantages in money and trust. While dot-coms have lower overhead and can survive on smaller margins, the B&Ms have sustainable revenue. B&Ms have customer loyalty through personal relationships with customers. While dot-coms build brand, the B&Ms did it already.

B&Ms have functional distribution systems. Dot.coms incur higher costs to stock, pick, box, wrap, ship and deliver from a warehouse, while B&Ms' customers come to the shop and do the shipping and handling themselves.

C&Bs must build only one brand for online and offline, and provide real-time information about inventory in warehouse and store, pricing, orders, shipping and customer accounts over the Web. Each channel receiving a hand-off knows what to do next. E-business is business; e-commerce is commerce.

174

Portals

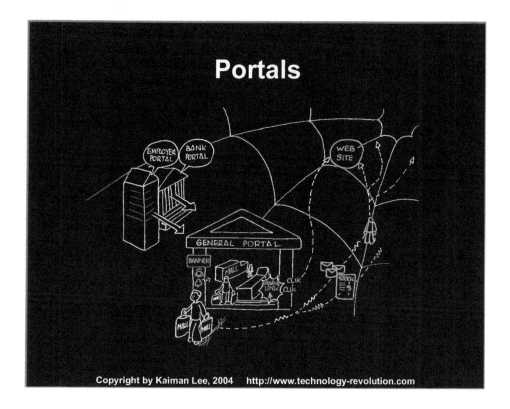

People pass through a portal on their way to someplace else. If you have many people flowing through your site, you become attractive to advertisers and commerce partners.

Many portal sites are like train stations or bus stops where people temporarily congregate on their way to work. They look at ads while they are waiting. On the Web, you do not have to wait. So, how much value is there in being a door through which you pass on your way to somewhere else?

Do people shopping for books need to go to a portal site to search for a list of online booksellers, or do they know enough to go directly to an online book retailer?

More consumers might go to their bank's portal or the one run by their employer, rather than one of the all-purpose ones.

General purpose portals seem to get virtually all their revenue from advertising. Advertising alone can not generate long-term profits.

If advertisers find portals are only used as brief rest stops, they may want to reconsider putting ads there. Portals are going to have to evolve from an information source into a truly value-added service.

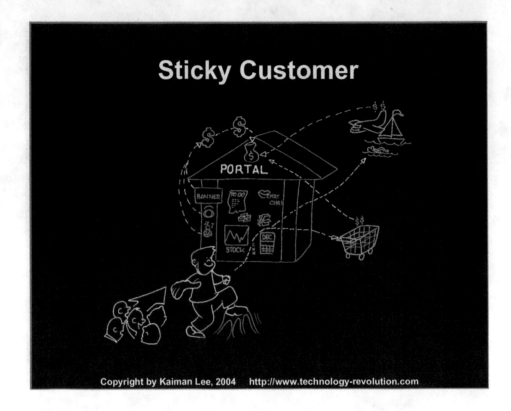

Sticky Customer

On the Web, the best customer is a sticky customer, a consumer who has developed an affection, affinity or obsession/addiction to a site that compels him or her to return there often.

Stickiness means the amount of time an average visitor spends on a Web site. Have a strategy to keep customers on a Web site as often and as long as possible. Some portal sites are adding features such as E-mail, news feeds, stock quotes/portfolios, chat, message boards, members-only areas, content, online shopping, entertainment, and personalized spaces for the customers.

Some go further by offering online Personal Information Manager (PIMs) for contacts, calendaring, scheduling and event tracking, even word processing and spreadsheet.

When portal sites succeed in their sticky strategies, they will not only collect say $.05 for every click through, but also become hot Web properties. More sticky users can mean more valuation for the Web site. And their stock prices go up.

Encourage your customers to leave something of themselves behind on your Web site, e.g., personal information to design their own clothes or filling out forms, they are less likely to want to repeat the process at other sites.

Barnacles and Butterflies

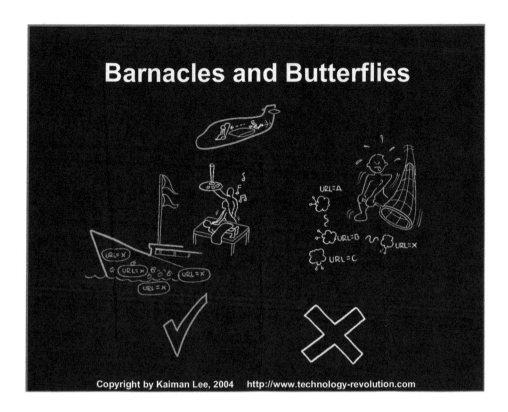

Separate your customers into groups of "barnacles," who are perpetually loyal and tend to be big spenders over time, and "butterflies," who jump from supplier to supplier at the slightest whim.

You do not want to be companies who invest precious resources in customers who are unlikely to remain faithful no matter what -- while the most loyal and highest-spending customers are neglected.

You should analyze customers and prospects -- their buying histories, attitudes, demographics -- for indicators of barnacle-like behavior, then reward them with superior service.

Several airlines now give the best seats not to passengers who book earliest, but to those paying the highest fares and those who spend the most with the airlines over time. Gate agents can do so by tapping into travelers' mileage and fare histories.

Customer Expectations

24 KARATS
LOWEST PRICE
GUARANTEED

Today's consumers want it all -- <u>convenience</u> (the ease of doing business with you), the <u>best quality</u> for the <u>lowest price</u>, <u>instant gratification</u>, and <u>customized service</u>.

They want whatever <u>information</u> fed to them to be <u>absolutely up to date</u>. They know it can be done and they expect it.

Customers come once. You have to have a strategy for <u>keep them coming back</u>. They will come back if you deliver value, e.g., free E-mail, stock quotes, etc. Another value may be a community-belonging feeling that could generate additive experience. It does not happen by accident. There has to be a guiding hand that you must provide.

Perhaps the Web has made <u>market development</u> a permanent part of any merchant's <u>daily regimen</u>, rather than a once-in-a-while initiative.

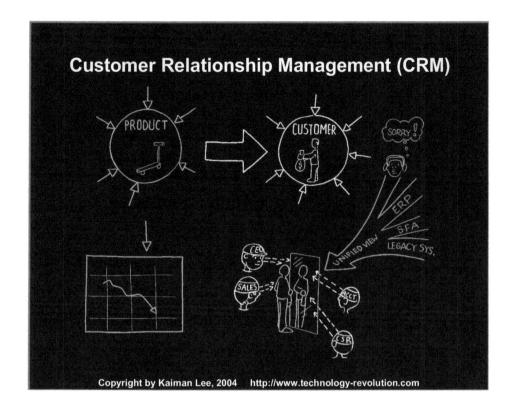

CRM is defined as building <u>customer care</u> processes that help companies expand relationships with customers to improve the <u>customer experience</u>. CRM moves a business from <u>product-centric to customer-centric</u>, providing <u>life-time value</u>.

Since the customer sees the enterprise as one, CRM must <u>integrate marketing, sales force automation, call center, customer service and back-office functions</u> to provide a <u>unified view of the customer</u> for every customer contact point.

<u>Behaving like a human</u> is a powerful CRM solution. Saying that you are <u>sorry</u> makes a difference because apologizing is a unique thing humans do. An apology can be followed by <u>forgiveness</u>. So, use high tech to achieve <u>high touch effects</u>.

<u>Respond</u> to "your site sucks!" messages, or they will tell the world through sites like epinions.com, consumerreview.com, ugripe.com or thirdvoice.com. Make all of your feedback available. Highlight required actions. Watch out for issues that come up time and again. Prioritize.

Building <u>online communities</u> is a way of building relationships. Other methods include buying loyalty with <u>reward programs</u>, and saving people time in online transactions through knowing their <u>preferences</u>.

One-to-One Relationship

Copyright by Kaiman Lee, 2004   http://www.technology-revolution.com

<u>Consider this dialogue</u>: "This is ABC Company. May I help you?" "Yes. This is Norma Koo." "Mrs. Koo. So nice to hear from you again.   How did the dress work out for your daughter on her prom day?" Wow! ABC <u>Company remembers</u>! This is what the corner grocery store used to do. This is <u>recognition</u>. This builds a <u>relationship</u>, and brings back <u>loyalty</u>.

Here is the "<u>audience of one</u>" that you want to achieve: deliver the right message, in the right context, to each individual, and based on that person's unique combination of motivations, barriers, desires and needs. Reach customer on a one-to-one level, also called "<u>1-1</u> <u>marketing</u>," through <u>personalized Web sites</u> and <u>individually tailored visual materials and E-mail</u>.

Some <u>strategies</u>:
- Notify investors via <u>E-mail</u>, Web or pager when a <u>stock</u> hits a particular <u>trigger point</u>.
- Allow your customers to select key words, categories or company names of particular interest.   All <u>stories</u> that <u>match</u> the <u>key words</u> are then saved into folders for later viewing.
- Let consumers enter the <u>contents of their refrigerator</u> into the site and receive <u>recipes</u> that incorporate all or most of the items.
- Get information about the <u>customers' height, build and hair color</u> to create a virtual model. They can then <u>try different clothing</u> on the model to get a sense of how it will look on them.

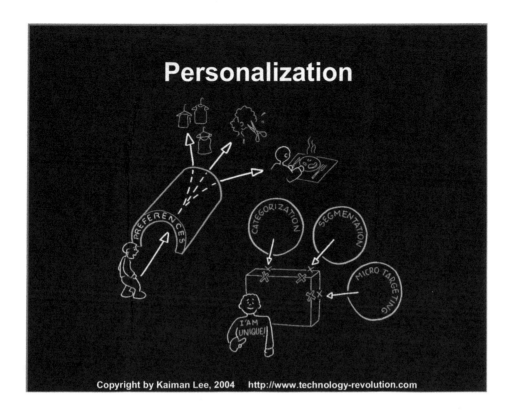

Personalization

We often go to the <u>same dry cleaner, barber or diner</u> because the servers know our <u>preferences</u>, and make us feel <u>welcome</u>. So, <u>create a relationship</u> with your customers to engender their <u>loyalty</u> that keeps them from switching to your <u>competitor</u>.

By following users' <u>movements online</u>, a marketer can send a targeted pitch to consumers for <u>cross-selling, upselling and personalized service opportunities</u>. When a Web surfer looks up Bermuda, a travel agent can offer to sell a low-price plane ticket.

Traditional <u>demographic segmentation</u> or <u>micro-targeting</u> that is based on <u>gender, age, profession, hometown</u>, etc. is giving way to personalization. <u>Personalization</u> is based on knowing the <u>customers' preferences</u> and storing them in a <u>profile database</u>.

On the Web, personalization is provided via three agents -- <u>presentation, matching and recommendation</u>. They adapt a Web site's presentation to a customer's needs at different points in the customer life cycle. They deliver the correct content and recommendation to the correct customer, based on user profiles and behavior.

To close a sale, a marketer might need to have a <u>live customer service agent on the phone</u>, or do <u>real-time Web chatting</u> with the customer.

Mass Customization

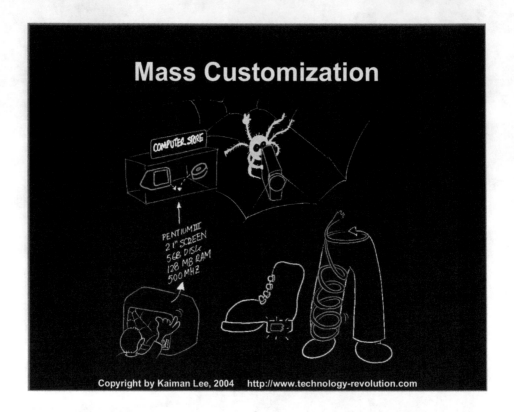

Internet-empowered consumers are now <u>telling manufacturers</u>, "<u>You make what we buy</u>." This model began with <u>building PCs to order</u>, such as size of hard drive, memory and processor speed.

It is being extended to the <u>automotive</u> industry and <u>consumer electronics</u>. A television can be configured to include options such as a digital connection, a satellite dish, and a set-top interface.

Mass customization as opposed to mass production means <u>customization on demand</u>. It is achieved at little or no extra cost because it is done automatically based on knowledge of customer and business rules.

How about golf clubs? or a bicycle? or a fishing rod? or a <u>CD with all your favorite music</u> and none you do not like.

A clothing manufacturer might customize jeans in an online fitting room with an easily-defined or scanned 3D model of the customer. You could specify custom <u>wiring</u> in the <u>pants</u> to connect the various embedded devices that you wear. You might ask a shoe manufacturer to have a <u>battery</u> charger <u>embedded in the soles</u> of a pair of sneakers which converts <u>walking energies into usable power</u>.

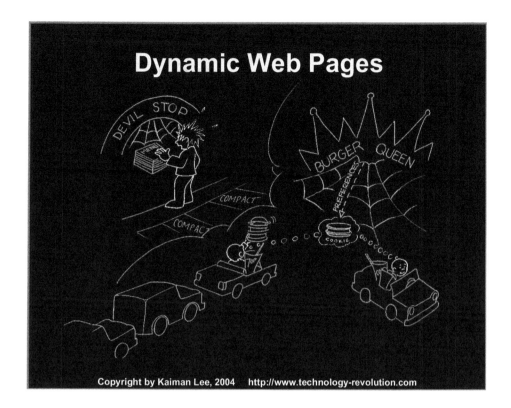

Instead of creating and linking <u>hundreds of Web pages that require customers to wade through</u> to get to where they want, companies are beginning to create <u>personalized Web pages in real-time</u> -- allowing them to establish and <u>build one-on-one relationships</u> with each Web site visitor.

It is like stopping at a <u>restaurant</u> and getting what you always get without asking. The <u>menu is tailored for you</u>. It skips all the red meat that you never order!

The Web pages are generated on the fly to tailor the links, text, graphics and layout to specific interests of a user or buyer.

The more user feedback you get, the more refined a relationship you will have with the user.

This dynamic Web is based on complex decisions made through <u>sophisticated "rule" processes</u>.

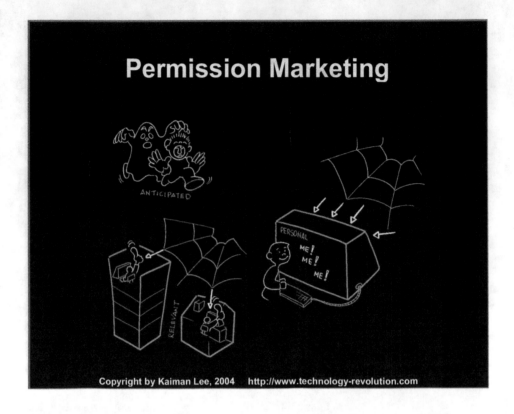

Permission Marketing

ANTICIPATED

RELEVANT

PERSONAL
ME!
ME!
ME!

Copyright by Kaiman Lee, 2004   http://www.technology-revolution.com

There are three <u>flawed assumptions</u> that most business Web sites make. One, consumers would want to <u>read their online brochure</u>. Two, consumers would <u>stumble onto their online brochure</u>. Three, once consumers got to their online brochure, <u>they would return</u>.

If consumers come to your Web site and leave, they are <u>anonymous strangers</u>. You have no idea who they are, and no idea how to contact them. But if they give you permission to correspond with them, now you have a valid lead, and an asset.

Effective marketing has to be anticipated, personal, and relevant. <u>Anticipated</u> because you <u>do not want to be surprised</u>. <u>Personal</u> because it is <u>about you</u>. And <u>relevant</u> because it is about <u>something you care</u> about right now. <u>Permission marketing encompasses all three</u>.

You go to a book seller's Web site and get a few chapters of the book you are interested in for free, and a few reviews of the book too. Because you are <u>getting something of value</u>, you give the merchant your <u>permission and your E-mail address</u>.

Most of the merchant sites are <u>one-time visit sites</u>. You go there, find out what it is about, and you do not go back. The sites that you will <u>bookmark</u> are the ones where there is going to be <u>something different there when you go back tomorrow</u>.

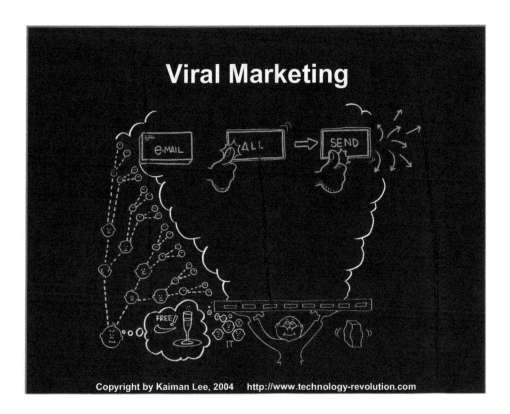

Viral Marketing

Copyright by Kaiman Lee, 2004   http://www.technology-revolution.com

Viral marketing is the ultimate word-of-mouth network marketing; you tell two friends, then they each tell two friends, and so on.

You encourage your customers to do the legwork for you by motivating them. Motivations could include the prestige of being associated with your brand, e.g., bumper stickers on cars, Nike swooshes on sweatshirts, sports teams and college logos on hats. Other motivations are: hitting your web site, registering, downloading a large file, requesting a freebie, buying something, and really valuable service or content (natural word of mouth). Do not use force, threats, dishonesty or stealth.

Viral marketing works best as a community-based event. Visitors should be spreading the word to friends with similar interests. The reward should be relevant to your market, with your message or brand all over it, and should not be so large that it motivates cheating.

Viral tactics are designed to grow exponentially. On the web, the growth is instant, as well as the reaction. A good joke can spread to thousands of people in one day because it is so easy to click "Forward," add ten addresses, and hit "Send." Is your Web server ready? Is your response staff ready? Is your budget ready?

Attention Management

Copyright by Kaiman Lee, 2004   http://www.technology-revolution.com

Time is scarce. Attention is more scarce. Do you have time to read all the books and magazines you would like to, answer all the voice messages and E-mails you are expected to, and click on all the Web pages you are tempted to? The widespread attention deficit has led to the economics of attention.

Paying attention is what an advertiser tries to make you do. In traditional marketing the more consumers are exposed to an ad, the more likely they are to buy. On the Web, if someone sees a banner four times and still has not clicked it, the odds are it will never be clicked.

Get your visitors actively involved. Entice your visitors to fill a form about themselves for some beneficial reasons, they will come back to see what happens. Build product communities.

The ads and the contents should be indistinguishable from each other. Deliver information customers want, and they will come back for more.

Advertisements/contents that are value added, relevant and interesting, offers that suit the customers, and information that matters to them will get their attention. They come not as intrusions but as attractions. If the product intrigues them, they will move step by step toward a transaction.

Customer Participation

Customer participation is a <u>critical success factor</u> in doing business on the Net.

Look at the fairy tale about <u>stone soup</u>. Two men set up a big pot full of water over a fire in a town square. They <u>drop in a stone, and start stirring</u>. The first curious passer-by asks what it is, and is told it will be a delicious stone soup. All it <u>lacks is a few carrots</u>. The passer-by fetches some carrots and drops them in. Other passers-by add <u>potatoes, onions</u> and so on until the soup really is delicious, and is served to all.

<u>Amazon.com</u> has set up the pot and dropped in the stone, the <u>Internet's town folks are contributing the ingredients to make it successful</u>, e.g., book reviews and feedbacks.

An interactive product-sponsored Web site is not always a placid scene. Sometimes members complain about the product. But that is the point. A virtual community is an ongoing focus group that provides feedback about products and services that cannot be equaled by conventional market research. It attracts a loyal membership because members generate their own excitement by sharing experiences, thoughts, and opinions.

Large publishers underestimate the <u>desire of people to simply congregate and socialize in cyberspace</u>.

Battle for Customer's Time

All businesses will compete for <u>one scarce resource</u>, their <u>customers' time</u>.

<u>Time</u> has become the <u>most sought after commodity</u> for many people. High-tech workers solve most of their problems with <u>cell phones, E-mail, pagers</u> and other devices. But how do they keep up with jobs, hobbies, and household chores?

<u>Customers</u> are recognizing the <u>supreme value of their time</u>. Computer and transmission speeds are doubling within every two years. The <u>human becomes the bottleneck</u> via the biological clock or life span limit. In the business world, life span translates into the customer's time.

During the <u>era of material scarcity</u>, the <u>customer's time</u> can be <u>exploited</u>. The entire economy is inundated with time wasting processes, e.g., TV and video games. In the information age where <u>material abundance</u> floods customer's life, <u>time</u> has become the <u>most precious resource</u>. The question for any business is: <u>are you a time enabler or a life span taker</u>?

Businesses must distribute power to the customers, i.e., <u>empower the customers</u>. There are big opportunities for companies that focus on <u>saving customers' time</u>. That is why the Internet is unstoppable. It saves the customer's time.

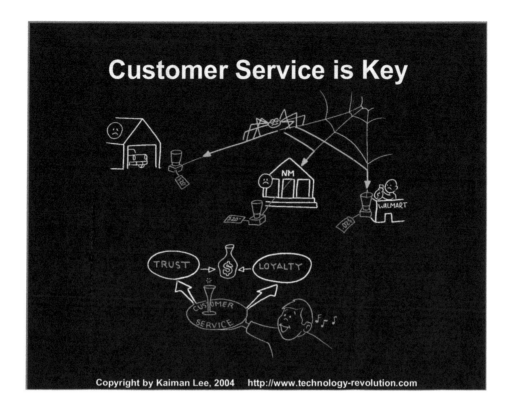

Customer Service is Key

Gone are the days when you could compete on price or a unique product alone. Using shopping bots, customers can get just about any product they want from a choice of producers at about the same price. You must use superior customer service to distinguish yourself from the competition.

Service is a process, not an event. You service customers by creating an environment of information, assurance, and comfort for them. Service is "time value" to the customers. When you deliver the right products promptly or help the customers solve their problems quickly, you are telling them that you value their time, and you earn their trust and loyalty.

"If you build it they will come," must be replaced with a new executive order, "Find out what they want and give it to them." Change from "Selling a car is the beginning of a lifelong relationship," to "Buying a car is the beginning of a life-long relationship."

When a vendor can feel instinctively that the customer's problems are its problems, it can begin to call itself a service company. A bank displays a plaque with their Rule #1 that says, "If we don't take care of the customer, somebody else will." It is impressive, easy to read, easy to remember, and it makes good sense. Make sure your corporate culture reflects it.

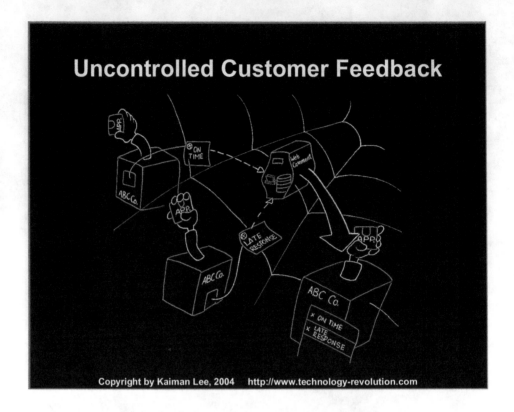

Uncontrolled Customer Feedback

A free "Web-comment" application allows you to anonymously comment on Web sites or particular portions of Web sites using. the digital equivalent of "sticky" notes.

It works when you have the same Web-comment application and you visit any particular site or page. A plug-in checks the comment server and embeds small marks into the page where other user comments have been made and displays the combined results in your browser window.

What you essentially see is a Web site with notes posted by visitors on it, or at least marks where sticky notes can be viewed by double-clicking on them.

Although most well designed sites provide an easy way to give direct feedback to the site developer or Web master, this application fulfills a need that people want to know what other people think about a Web site.

Given the veil of anonymity that many people shroud themselves behind when they go online, the number of slanderous, libelous, or rude comments that could be created by this application could outnumber the genuinely helpful critiques. It can also generate legal issues.

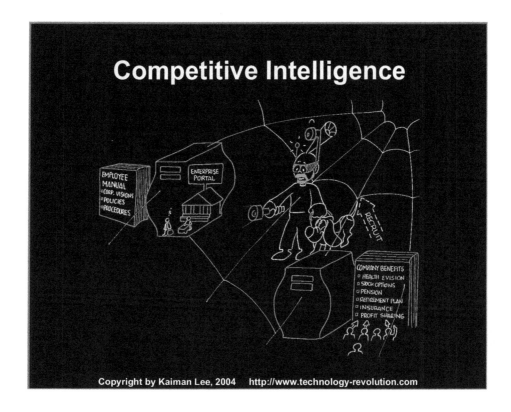

About <u>80 percent</u> of large companies have an organized competitive intelligence (CI) system. Many have dedicated CI departments, while others put the function in places such as <u>market research</u> or in the <u>CEO's office</u>. The function could also be part of the job of <u>a chief knowledge officer (CKO)</u>.

CI professionals can find competitive intelligence data from <u>financial filings, press releases, trade publications, industry analysts, conversations with industry players, and executive interviews</u>.

Some <u>company sites include their entire employee manual, and comprehensive list of company benefits</u>. That allows <u>competitors</u> to know exactly what to offer if they are <u>competing</u> with this company <u>for recruits</u>.

If you <u>post job openings on your Web site</u>, your competitors will learn about <u>your company's technical direction</u>.

Be wary about posting <u>specific product specifications, business partners or suppliers</u>. Use the <u>same standards used for print ads</u> -- if you would not print it and distribute it to a wide audience with no questions asked, do not post it. Would I like to know this about my competitors? If the answer is yes, think twice before putting it on your Web site.

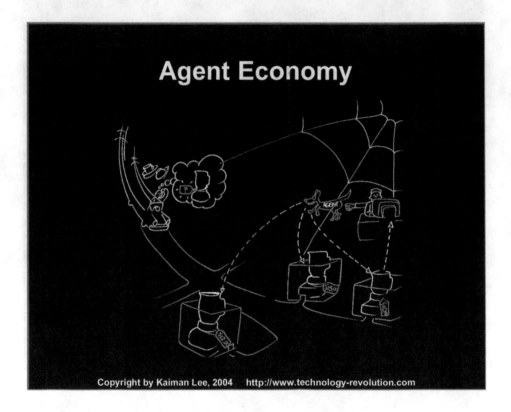

Agent Economy

Agents can trade goods, information and services among themselves.

You tell your shopping agent what you want sought out -- flowers or computers -- give a few keywords that will narrow the search, and let it loose. Your agent will compare similar products among multiple vendors and find the best deals available anywhere.

Shopping "bots" (robots) representing customers will negotiate with bots that represent your business. Your customer could give the bot specifications for features, delivery dates and price range. The bot would offer a price based on those criteria -- higher if the manufacturer could meet all of them, lower if the product could not be delivered at a specified time.

Agent technologies let vendors and customers change prices and product offerings faster than a person ever could. Rapid changes could result in price wars that drive a vendor out of business, or make a market crash.

The challenge for the agent economy is to build some friction or control into the system, and make the agents understand the likely outcome of their actions, thus keeping the automated economy from becoming a dynamic disaster.

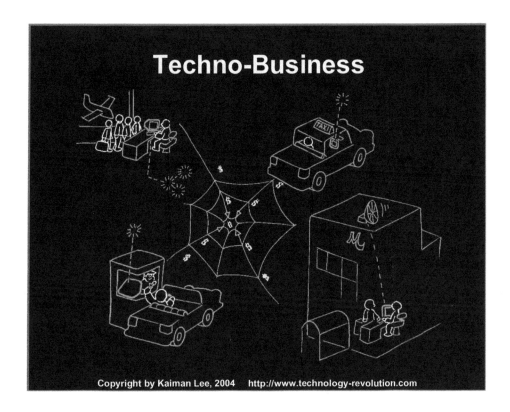

Techno-Business

Think about a time when you travel out of town. You deal with an airline, a parking lot, taxi, and hotel, etc. Say that they all use a computer in order to provide service to you. How frustrated are you when their computers are down?

It is a fact of life for most businesses these days: their computer systems are their business. Without them, they are out of business. Every business is an IT company. One happens to ship boxes, another sells them with something inside, but everyone operates an IT business.

"Business" as we know it has become "techno-business." You can not run a business or even call yourself a business person unless you understand how computer technology helps you service your customers, learn about your competitors, and deal with your suppliers.

Only those organizations that view the wave of technology revolution as part of their core business strategies can prosper. Those that tag along the wave may gain some benefits. Those that resist it will experience erosion of their business.

The message for business people contemplating their place in cyberspace is direct: get linked or get lost.

Internet Savings

Bank transaction costs:
- Teller: $1.07
- Internet: $.01

Airline ticket processing costs:
- Agent: $8.00
- Internet: $1.00

--- Source: IBM Research, 1997

These figures make it clear why almost all businesses want to do business on the Web.

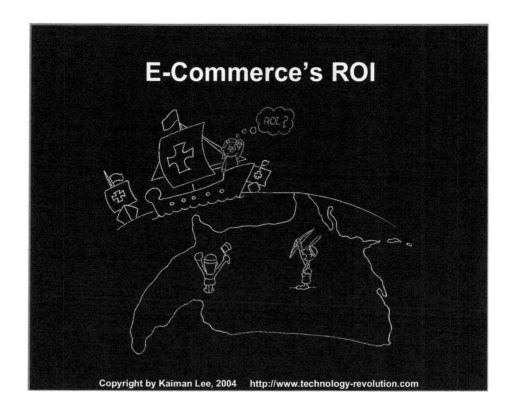

E-Commerce's ROI

Typical business investment is measured according to three dynamics: expense reduction, revenue enhancement and competitive advantage.

"What's my ROI on e-Commerce? Are you crazy? This is Columbus in the New World. What was his ROI?"
--- Andy Grove, Intel

Investing in technology that facilitates virtual relationships, a key factor for e-commerce success, rarely has as direct an ROI as technology that serves to reduce internal costs.

There is almost no time to find established benchmarks in order to calculate for return on investment (ROI).

Some immeasurable factors, such as "competitive necessity," and "customer experience" can be the most important driver to future enterprise success and thus deserves top investment in a business case.

Learn everything you can, listen to your gut, and then just do it. But watch the changing sea, and change course as much as the market and technology call for.

TRANSACTION TECHNOLOGY

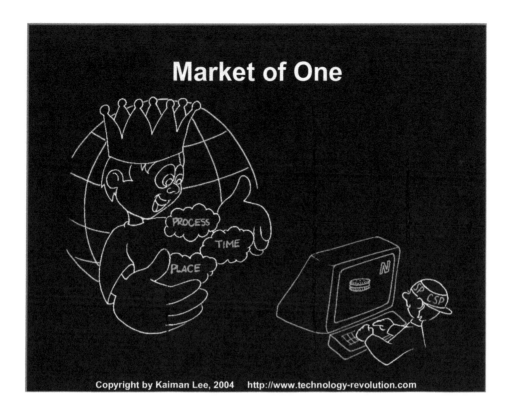

Market of One

Copyright by Kaiman Lee, 2004   http://www.technology-revolution.com

In Internet commerce, <u>customers control the time, place, and process</u>. They go to shop online when they want, where they want, and how they want. They expect 100% attention from the merchant. We are in a <u>buyer-initiated market</u>.

The <u>CSR (customer service representative)</u> has the "<u>cookie</u>" that keeps track of everything that could be known about the customer, and what s/he <u>has been doing on the Web site</u>. The <u>Web page</u> can be <u>automatically customized</u> for the customer's preferred experience.

<u>One-to-one marketing</u> involves <u>tracking</u> an individual customer's patronage over time, managing a continuing series of interactions with the customer, and measuring the customer's business across different products or groups of products and services.

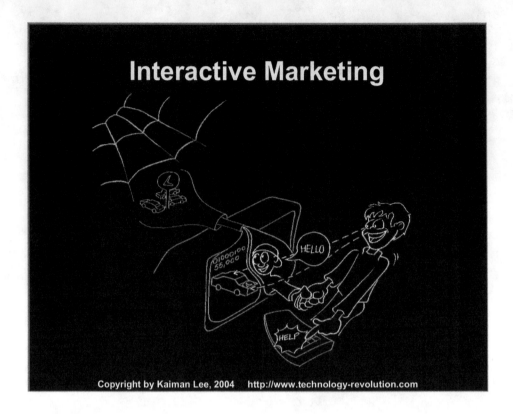

Interactive Marketing

Copyright by Kaiman Lee, 2004   http://www.technology-revolution.com

In interactive marketing, the <u>customer controls the flow of information, not the marketer</u>. You have to engage your customer in an <u>interactive dialogue</u>, i.e., you tell your customer something, your customer gives you feedback, you tell him/her more, s/he gives you more feedback, and you <u>change your Web page accordingly</u>. Most of these "dialogues" can be automated.

You must know the <u>customers' personal preferences</u> so well that you <u>know what they want almost before they ask</u>.

The customer may be doing self-service in a customer-configured experience, but, as soon as the customer wants personal <u>help</u>, and clicks the "Talk" button, your CSR (<u>customer service representative</u>) comes <u>online without the customer making a phone call</u>. Next stop: Checkout and Kaching!

Your customer may click the <u>"Chat Now" button</u> to text chat with a customer service representative who can answer questions.

The CSR already <u>knows what you have been doing</u> before you ask for assistance. Here, you are providing <u>24x7</u> (24 hours, 7 days) <u>support</u> in the world of <u>low-friction low-overhead capitalism</u>. The key is <u>convenience</u>.

A smart card can allow you to down load electronic cash directly from your bank or credit card onto your smart card via the Internet and your PC. With the protection of card identification and password, it provides a more secure alternative to petty cash and company credit cards for small businesses.

The value in your card can be used like cash for store purchases. You can use it on the Internet to purchase products and services for amounts as little as fractions of a cent.

Someone who has a debit or credit card may not want a smart card, but there are individuals who can not qualify for either of those cards, but could use a smart card with its prepaid value.

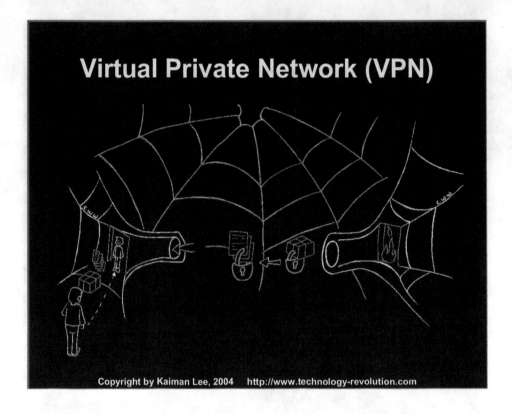

Virtual Private Network (VPN)

The basic tenet of network security has been to just keep the outsiders out. But with virtual private networks (VPN), you let the outsiders in.

VPN connects two or more Intranets together, keeping all information on those Intranets secure, but uses the Internet as the roadway to send and receive information.

VPN carves out a piece of the Internet, the "tunnel", and secures it with proxy firewalls. The tunnel is the path that a given company message or file travels over the Internet.

The basic idea of a VPN is to use the receiver's public key (128 bit) to encrypt a message as IP packets. The packets are encapsulated inside TCP/IP and then sent.

Encapsulation means the placement of data from one protocol into the protocol stream of another, a process called IP tunneling. The receiver un-encapsulates the packets, then decrypts the message with the receiver's private key.

In general, firewalls handle access control, and VPN handles authentication and encryption. Since these are complementary functions, they can be implemented on the same computer but they do not have to be.

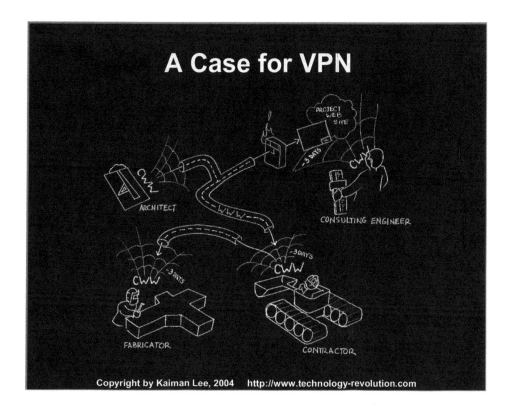

A Case for VPN

Let us look at a situation to explain how virtual private networks (VPNs, or Extranets) can be used effectively. An architect, a consulting engineer, a general contractor and a fabricator have linked their project information into a VPN through their Intranets.

They each have their own specific project information that resides on their own Intranet, but also have shared project information that resides on all the linked VPNs.

When the architect wants to see the status of a shop drawing that is being reviewed by their consulting engineer, the architect types his/her password on the project Web page on the consulting engineer's Intranet. This now gives the architect access to the project Web page to see the status.

The consulting engineer is hosting his/her own status Web page so it can be better controlled and updated in-house, but also allows others to see the information via the VPN.

The consulting engineer's status page shows that the shop drawing in question is still being reviewed with a deadline of being finished within 3 days.

Digital Signature

A digital signature vendor will install a digital certificate on an end-user's desktop or handheld. It provides the software to accompany the many different forms of personal authentication, such as a passwords, a retinal scan, a voice-recognition test, a smart card, signing pads, and digital fingerprint recorders.

A sender digitally "signs" the message or transaction with the sender's private encryption key, which lets the recipient confirm that the sender indeed sent the message, and it did not come from someone posing as the sender. The recipient verifies the origin of the message with the sender's public verification key, which typically is enclosed within the message. That confirms that the message came from the sender. This guarantees nonrepudiation after a transaction -- you cannot deny your having participated in it. Digital signature ensures that the sender is legitimate.

Signatures are legally binding when the digital signature technology used adheres to the requirements of the U.S. E-SIGN Act: user consent, permanency, privacy, audit trails, and digital authentication.

The issues facing the industry are that most signature software tools do not successfully interoperate with each other, and the tools fail to support all E-mail packages.

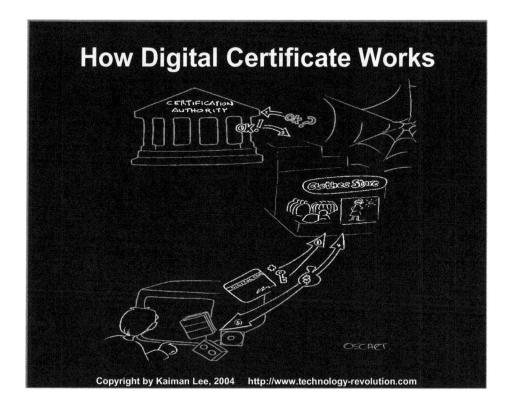

How Digital Certificate Works

Copyright by Kaiman Lee, 2004   http://www.technology-revolution.com

Here is how a digital certificate works:

1. You send your <u>digital certificate and public key to a site</u> that has asked for identification.

2. The site checks the certificate and key at the issuing <u>certificate authority (CA) for verification</u>.

3. The certificate authority checks your identity and <u>approves</u> (or disapproves) the transaction.

Here is a scenario for getting virtual credit on the Web in the early days of Web transaction:

- Merchant: advertises wares on the Internet.

- Customer: tells merchant "I want to buy your stuff. My virtual Personal Identification Number (PIN) is "my word."

- Merchant: verifies that the PIN is good, then sends E-mail to a CA's computers saying, "is 'my word' a valid PIN?"

- CA: confirms that the PIN is good. Sends E-mail to consumer saying "Do you authorize this transaction?"

- Customer: responds "Yes," "No" or "Fraud." If yes, CA sends E-mail to the merchant, authorizing the transaction. If no, CA tells the merchant the transaction has been declined. If fraud, CA marks the transaction for investigation.

Sounds a bit more complicated than using a credit card? Yes! That is why <u>credit card transaction over the Net is now a common practice</u>.

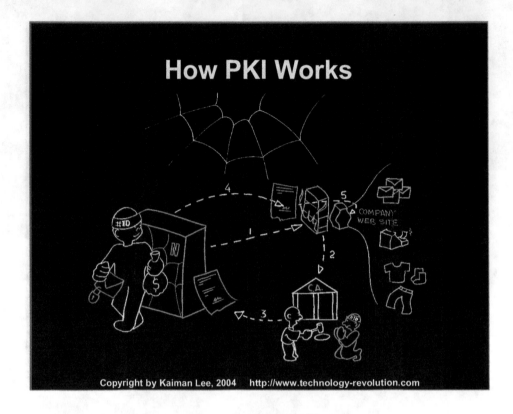

How PKI Works

Public Key Infrastructure (PKI) serves two security purposes: to confirm that <u>senders of messages are who they say they are</u> (<u>authentication</u>), and to <u>encode</u> messages so that they cannot be read by anyone who illicitly intercepts them (<u>encryption</u>).

When users first visit the company's Web site to do business (#1), they are <u>referred to a certification authority (CA)</u> (#2).

The users <u>apply</u> to the CA for <u>digital certificates</u> (#3). The digital certificate is also known as the <u>public key</u>. It carries information that positively identifies you to the party on the other end.

Assuming the users meet the CA's criteria for positive identification, the <u>CA issues certificates</u> (#4), which are then installed on users' machines.

Once a user has obtained a certificate, software on the user's computer <u>automatically sends a copy of the certificate whenever the user communicates with the company</u> (#5).

If the user's <u>signature is authentic</u> and the <u>certificate is still valid</u>, the PKI system gives the go-ahead for the user and the encrypted message to <u>pass through the company's firewall</u> (#6).

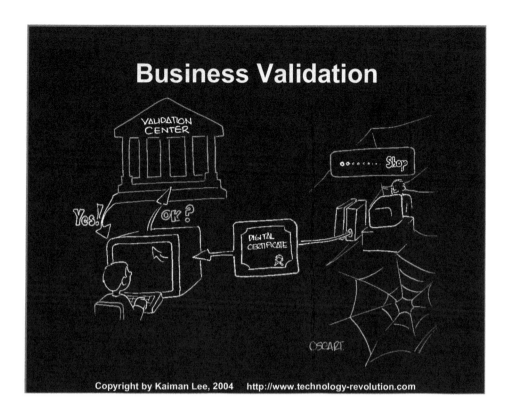

Business Validation

Before you put down your money to purchase something over the Net, you can request verification of the merchant by contacting a Validation Center (VC) such as First Virtual or Visa, who in turn confirms or denies the validity of the Web site. It is done much like stores checking credit card numbers.

A Validation Center is an independent group that will validate the identity of each Web site that has applied to the Center. The third-party Validation Center can verify that the Internet location exists and is in fact what it claims to be.

A Validation Center could potentially give you information about the business Web site, e.g., complaints and disciplinary actions.

Encrypted Containers

Copyright by Kaiman Lee, 2004   http://www.technology-revolution.com

Encrypted "containers" are used for <u>computer programs, dataware and text files</u>. They are <u>analogous to shrink wrapped</u> software boxes that can be pried open only when the user agrees to a purchase deal.

When you <u>open a container</u> you are agreeing to some contractual conditions, which can be documented should violations occur.

206

For any electronic document, information metering provides an <u>audit trail of retrieved data</u> which deters violations.

The traditional business of writing "software" application today will give way to the business of providing "<u>dataware</u>," especially user-oriented <u>objects</u>.

Everything we do will be <u>document, object or content centric</u>. You do not have to worry about applications, computer compatibility, etc.. Dataware (objects) will be <u>downloaded from the Web</u> and vendors will get paid by <u>metering their use</u>.

Delivery Assured

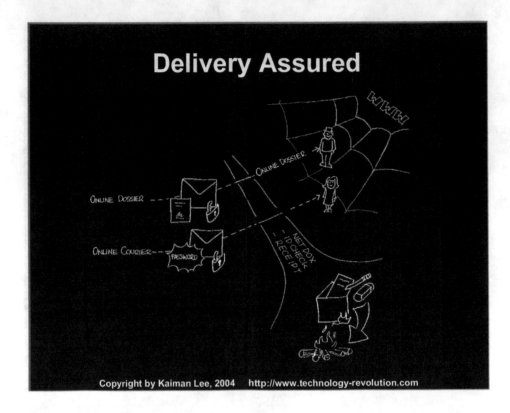

In 1999, United Parcel Service (UPS) started providing UPS Document Exchange, a service that encrypts, transmits, tracks and verifies delivery of electronic documents.

UPS offers two levels of package service. The first level, called UPS OnLine Dossier, uses two layers of encryption and digital certificates to provide secure transmission, delivery confirmation, tracking, and insurance. Both the sender and receiver need special client software, a public and private-key pair and digital certificates. If the file is altered, it is destroyed and the sender is notified.

The second service is dubbed OnLine Courier. It also offers password protection, encryption, tracking and receipts, and it is available to anybody with an E-mail address.

The process goes this way: 1. the document is encrypted at the sender's desktop using UPS client software, 2. the document is sent to the NetDox processing center, where the identity of the sender is checked, and 3. the document is presented to the recipient, and a confirmation is sent back to NetDox.

The above processes track delivery and tell you whether the intended recipient has opened the message. They are continuously being improved using public standards. You can expect a lot easier transactions in coming days.

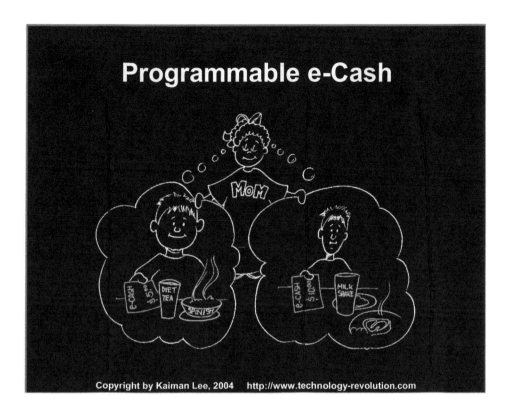

Programmable e-Cash

You make arrangement with your credit card issuer to advance digital cash or electronic cash (e-cash) to you and you pay them back later.

E-cash "is" cash and it is unlike credit card or similar payment systems where you are really moving book entries. With e-cash the numbers are the money. The moment you transfer the money, you are transferring the value.

E-cash gives you an opportunity to create an account and a relationship with your bank where your bank can download payment and debt systems to your computer and you can use this to buy things from merchants on the Web. This is much the same as taking money out of an ATM.

E-cash can be stored in an online bank account, in your PC or on a smart card.

In time, you will be able to program money. You can give Johnny a card that Johnny can use to buy school lunches, but it will be preprogrammed to prevent the purchase of soft drinks or French (or Freedom) fries.

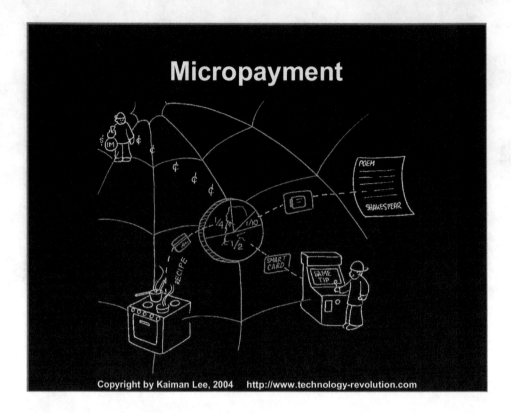

Micropayment

If you are able to <u>charge one-tenth of a penny</u> in the virtual world, you can open <u>up whole new markets</u>. For instance, if you are a <u>cook</u>, you can sell your <u>recipe</u> on the Web for <u>seven-tenth of a cent</u>.

On the Web, you could conceivably have a <u>seven-year-old</u> who is the <u>best star-war player</u>, and s/he will <u>charge a half-cent</u> to all the kids who want <u>game tips</u>. And s/he could potentially become a wealthy person.

Merchants pay about <u>two percent</u> in <u>credit card</u> transaction fees, and those fees usually have a minimum of about <u>26 cents</u>. These fees can easily <u>wipe out profit</u> margins on low cost items.

The micropayment system <u>broker</u> -- typically a <u>bank</u> -- usually simply <u>verifies</u> that the encrypted serial number on an electronic token or purchase order is valid.

Paying by micropayments allows the buyer to <u>remain anonymous</u> to the merchant because the coins do not identify the customer.

<u>Smart cards</u> support micropayments because they hold electronic funds.

**SECURITY
TECHNOLOGY**

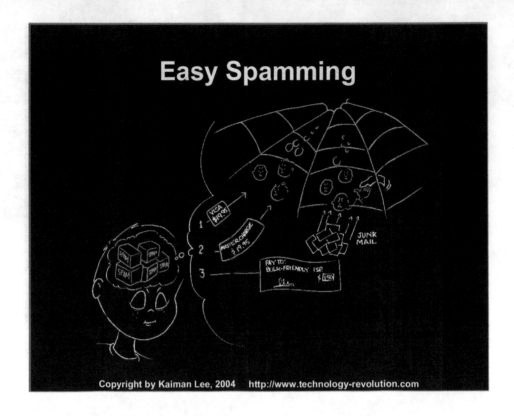

Easy Spamming

Spamming is commonly thought of as unsolicited bulk e-mail. The term "spamming" was derived from a "Monty Python" sketch in which a waitress offers diners a choice of "spam, spam, spam, spam and spam."

It costs only the price of a computer, plus about $200 for software to begin spamming. Typically, you start with a reputable Internet Service Provider (ISP) and pay about $20 per month. But within a week or two, the ISP, responding to customer complaints, shuts down your account.

After being booted out several times, you turn to the services of a "bulk-friendly" ISP and get charged $100 to $150 per month.

Anti-spam software can stop spammers from using fake Internet addresses and "promiscuous relaying" (using someone else's server to send a single E-mail to thousands of users) and block E-mail from known spammers.

States are passing anti-spamming laws, but loopholes abound. If you do a lot of online buying or frequently seek online help, you will be hit by the so-called acquaintance spam. Get one or more E-mail accounts not tied to your office server. Dedicate a dead-letter mailbox to online work that could draw spam. Messages sent to it are held only one day, then deleted automatically.

Spam Scams

Here are some of the top spam scams cited by the Federal Trade Commission (FTC):

1. You will make a lot of money for almost no money and time. They are "pyramid" schemes that offer high returns to early investors, paying them with funds from investors who join the deal later.

2. You are offered lists of e-mail addresses or software to enable your mailings. But the lists are generally poor quality. Sending bulk e-mail usually violates Internet service providers' terms of service. Some states regulate bulk e-mail.

3. Chain letters: You follow the rules and you will make $50,000 in three months. E-mail chain letters are illegal.

4. You do not usually get paid for envelope stuffing. Craft assembly promoters will refuse to buy your home-assembled crafts, contending they do not meet "quality standards."

5. "Scientific breakthroughs," "miraculous cures," "secret formulas" are among the pitches.

6. You can make $4,000 in a day by exchanging money in world currency markets. These are not legitimate enterprises.

18 Year Old Hacker

A world-known Internet hacker nicknamed "Analyzer" was a mere 18 years old. He was among the most-wanted hackers after he spawned hundreds of break-ins in February 1998. The Department of Defense described the incident as "the most organized and systematic attack the Pentagon has seen to date."

Among the damages "Analyzer" caused were tens of thousands of dollars to an Internet Service Provider (ISP). Although he did not get deep into the layers of highly sensitive information, he broke into the computer systems of Lawrence Livermore National Laboratories, UC-Berkeley, MIT, the Pentagon, the Air Force, the Navy, among others.

Pentagon computers with sensitive data or responsibilities are not accessible directly through the Internet. Those computers are separated from all other computers with networked connections to the outside world, a security concept known as an "air wall."

"Crackers" (malevolent hackers)make unauthorized visits not so much to gain access to data but to score points with fellow crackers. That is how they accumulate status in their tribe. Most low-level crackers are incapable of breaking in themselves, so they use "toolkits" -- automated software developed by elite crackers -- that can break in for them.

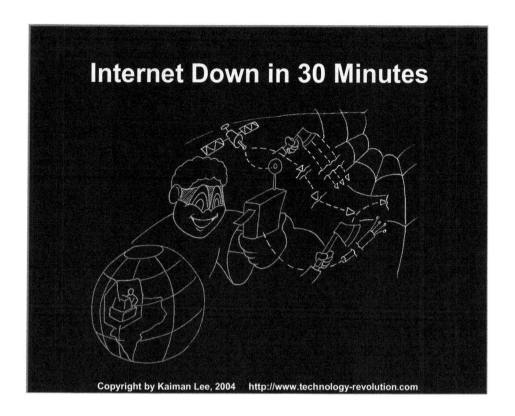

Internet Down in 30 Minutes

Copyright by Kaiman Lee, 2004   http://www.technology-revolution.com

In May 1998, seven hackers, members of an independent watchdog group, using false names, told the Senate Committee on Governmental Affairs that Internet and electronic commerce transactions are equally vulnerable from illicit intrusion.

"If you want security, the Internet is not the place to be," a man calling himself Mudge said. "In about 30 minutes, any one of us can cause serious disruption to the entire Internet, transfer funds from the Federal Reserve or reroute planes from our home PCs."

That would render the Internet unusable for the entire nation.

In fact, they asserted that the Internet infrastructure is so fragile -- the underlying network protocols are more than 20 years old -- that it would be possible to terminate communications between the United States and all other countries, and to prevent major backbone providers such as MCI and AT&T from routing network traffic to each other.

215

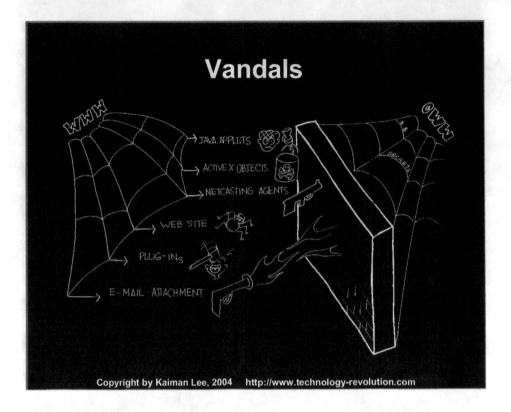

Vandals

Vandals are <u>malicious applications</u> that <u>execute automatically</u> once they have been downloaded from the Internet. They can cause damage the moment they penetrate a PC.

They can be written into <u>Java applets or ActiveX objects</u>, or <u>hidden inside plug-ins</u>.

Vandals can also be <u>embedded directly into Web sites</u>, placed <u>inside E-mail as attachments</u>, or <u>pushed via Netcasting agents</u>.

Since Vandals are executable files, they can evade many network security measures by <u>appearing to be harmless applications</u>.

<u>Anti-virus</u> products are <u>usually not able to prevent vandals</u> attacks because they rely mainly on known strings of code or "signatures" of viruses.

Vandals can have their own twists and innovations, taking advantage of the very technologies that make the Net possible and appealing. A vandal program <u>can do virtually anything a programmer can dream up</u>!

Anti-vandal solutions must work against <u>known and unknown</u> malicious auto-executables.

Security violations usually fall into just a few areas.

Violators can <u>alter or steal</u> information from the server or an attached resource, such as a database.

They can block Internet connections or bring down portions of your network by <u>flooding the Web</u>. They can drop an <u>E-Mail Bomb</u>, i.e., send multiple E-mail to the same address overloading your E-mail server.

They can <u>break into your server's operating system and tamper</u> with it.

Outside criminals and even <u>disgruntled employees</u> may be able to <u>hold critical information for extortion</u>. By <u>encrypting a file</u> -- or encrypting on top of an organization's already encrypted file -- they can create new locks and keys, thereby <u>preventing others from accessing</u> the information.

Security Attacks

Copyright by Kaiman Lee, 2004   http://www.technology-revolution.com

There is an infinite number of possibilities of security attacks. Here are some common types.

A Worm can be a destructive program that propagates itself in your system, using up resources and slowing down the network and/or your PC. It has the potential to wind its way through your entire network.

A Trojan Horse is sent with a front-end that might be an appealing program such as a cool screen saver or useful utility. It then finds its way around the company.

It will probably be stored in a folder called TEMP, FUN or PERSONAL_STUFF. As soon as you double-click on the file, the Trojan horse can proceed to extract information such as user passwords and transmit the data back to its sender.

It can corrupt data. It can lock up your system. Users are confronted with the so-called "blue screen of death," which appears with an error message when Windows crashes. The only solution is to restart the computer.

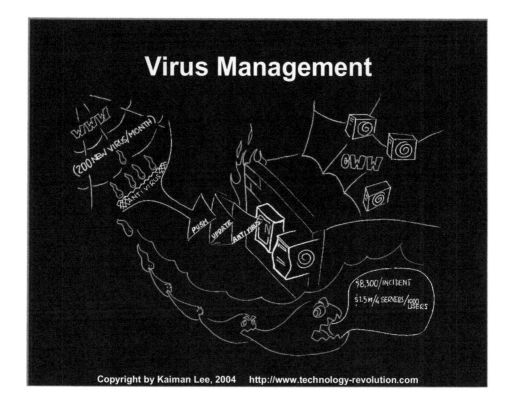

Virus Management

A survey made in 1997 showed:
- 200 new viruses per month were created.
- 99.3% of companies were infected in 1997.
- cost per incident: $8,300.
- 80% were spread by e-mail.
- cost of no virus protection in 1000 user, 4 server environment: $1.5m.

Virus scanning should be done in real-time! New virus patterns can be added as soon as they are available. Scanning is done continuously in a background mode, unnoticeable by the user. If a virus is detected, the user is notified immediately and the virus can be foiled.

A real-time scanning engine continuously scans files as they are transmitted. It helps ensure that the server is virus free, and only clean data can leave a file server, preventing the server from disseminating infected data.

Push technology can deliver anti-virus updates automatically to Web users without direct involvement by a user.

URL Filtering

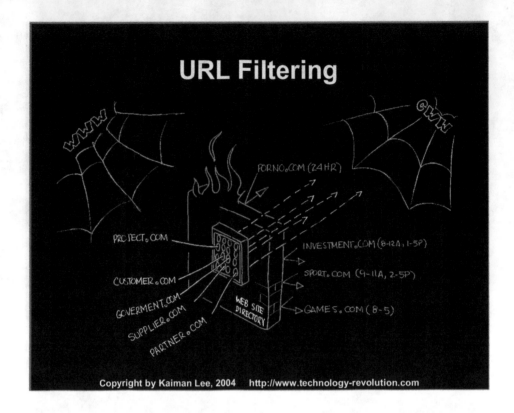

URL filtering is applied to <u>restrict access to specific types of Web sites by users from inside the company firewall</u>.

For example, URL filtering may be used to monitor or restrict employee access to Web sites with objectionable content such as <u>pornographic</u> material, or <u>business-irrelevant</u> content such as <u>games</u>. Such restrictions may also include limitation depending on the <u>date and time of day</u>.

Specialized service companies compile, maintain and market <u>URL lists categorized by Web site contents</u>.

Their database entries fall into many different categories that you can <u>selectively turn on or off</u>. You decide which areas of the Internet are acceptable during business hours and which you wish to screen.

Their databases are constantly revised and the updated information is automatically downloaded to your system each night.

A <u>rule-based editor</u> allows you to customize category criteria by individual user or groups of users.

Personal Security Objectives

There are basically three personal security objectives: Confidentiality, Privacy and Authentication.

Confidentiality. A thief does not want people to know it is him/her who is stealing things from your company. S/he wants to protect his/her identity.

Privacy. You do not want others to know about you, where you live, how much money you have, who your friends are, etc. But there is almost nowhere to hide. There are almost no secrets. Everything cybercizable will be in cyberspace including the state of people, where they are, what they are doing, and places and things.

Authentication. You want to identify and verify that it is really you who is paying for the purchase, not someone else who is using a stolen credit card. It implements the concept of nonrepudiation or proof-of-purchase.

Authentication ensures that users attempting to access your network resources are who they say they are. You can assure it if you cover all three areas: who you are (retina or fingerprint scan); what you have (smart card or token device); what you know (password and secondary password).

Internet is Made of Glass

OSCARZT

Copyright by Kaiman Lee, 2004   http://www.technology-revolution.com

Unlike television, the <u>Internet can be watching you while you are watching it</u>. The Internet is made of glass. Anyone can know what you are saying or doing with relative ease.

This is done using <u>Cookies</u>. Web Cookies can figure out <u>who the person is</u> on the other side and <u>keep track of what s/he is doing</u>. Data files called <u>cookie.txt</u> are created by Web servers and are <u>stored on the user's computer</u>. They record the trail of Web sites visited, online purchases and private information.

To the Web site owner, Cookies captures: who visited your site, what content they accessed, how they travelled through the site, and how activities of your site are distributed over time.

Your Web site may be sprinkled with <u>questions</u> throughout the pages, the <u>answers</u> to which will be stored in a <u>customer's profile</u>. The idea is to get a profile of that person -- <u>hobbies, work, income, age</u>, etc.

Cookie technology is like <u>standing behind someone at the newsstand and writing down every magazine s/he picks up</u>.

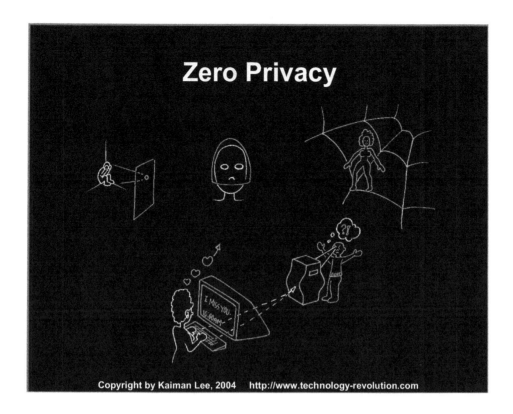

Sun Microsystems President <u>Scott McNealy</u> reportedly said at a product launch in early 1999. "<u>You have zero privacy anyway. Get over it</u>."

By following your <u>movements</u> online, a <u>marketer</u> can send you a very <u>targeted pitch</u>. Say you are looking for <u>tours in London</u>, a travel agent can offer to <u>sell</u> you a low-price <u>plane ticket</u>.

What you <u>type</u> on the <u>keyboard</u> can be <u>recorded completely</u>. If you type phrases such as, "I miss you a lot," and "I'm coming your way next week," you may get a surprise visit by your supervisor.

<u>Keystroke recorders</u> or "<u>loggers</u>" are simply programs that <u>read keystrokes, including deletions, and save them to a hidden file</u>.

They were created mainly to <u>keep tabs on the typing speed</u> (and number of backspaces) of data-entry workers. But now, you might find that the laptops of your <u>sales force</u> are used mainly for <u>Web surfing</u>. They can let <u>parents</u> see not only what <u>Web sites</u> their <u>children</u> visit, but also the content of their <u>E-mails</u>, <u>school papers</u> and <u>chat</u> sessions.

Although they can be run in a mode that is <u>visible to the user</u>, they could still be morphed into a <u>censorware</u>.

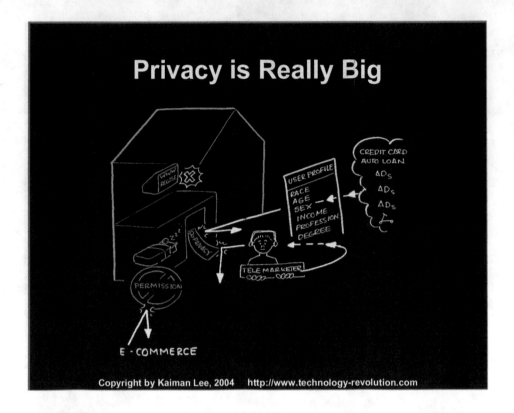

Privacy is Really Big

Privacy is one of the biggest issues of the Internet. Online retailer Toysmart, which had promised customers it would never divulge personal information, wanted to sell its customer list after filing for bankruptcy protection in June 2000. That incidence brought the subject of privacy to the fore front.

The evidence that users' wish to guard their privacy is the dominant reason why Internet users flee site registrations. With consumers increasingly worried about how companies use their personal information to track them on the Internet, many large corporations are hiring privacy officers with broad authority to protect such data.

Many Web sites create user profiles containing such data as E-mail addresses, favorite books or clothing sizes, as well as surfing habits in order to better target ads and products. Users do not complain about an Internet bookstore recommending books, but they all hate being called at home during dinner by telemarketers.

Users want control over information about themselves, but they do not know enough about computers to trust that they are in control. So, they may ask for the extreme: Don't do anything unto me unless I give you permission. Such extreme, if enacted by law will dampen e-commerce.

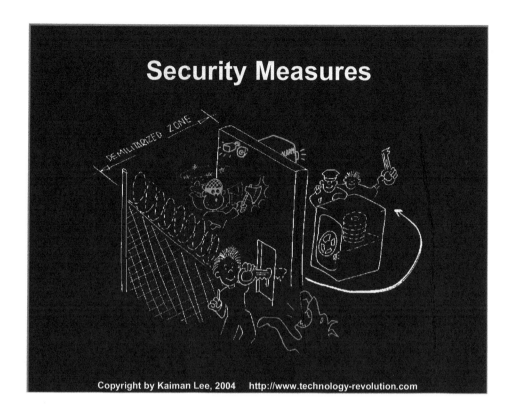

Security Measures

As basic Internet access has evolved into e-business many companies have hosted applications and services in the "demilitarized zone," or DMZ, between internal and external firewalls.

The DMZ is another boundary, constituting a neutral zone between public and private, where applications and services can live.

Instead of "public" or "private," boundaries like "employee" or "premium customer" will determine access levels regardless of where the person physically resides. These boundaries will be both logical and physical constructs, providing different classes of network access according to the sensitivity of the information exchange and the identity of the parties involved.

In today's nomenclature, boundaries will constitute multiple DMZs, each providing access mechanisms for different classes of people, groups and organizations.

Each boundary will consist of increasingly graduated levels of access, requiring higher security clearances as the entrant gets close to the center.

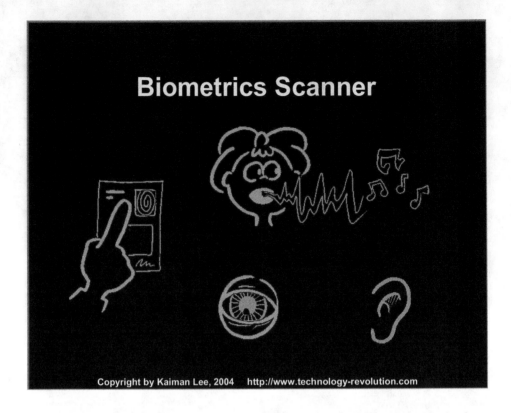

Biometrics Scanner

Each biometric form has its own qualities and drawbacks:

- ***fingerprints*** (or finger imaging): needs <u>physical contact</u> with the plate; poor quality due to <u>dirty</u> fingers and finger <u>mutilation</u>; finger prints can be <u>lifted</u>. Mouse is being embedded with a fingerprint-scanning device.

- ***Iris*** (the <u>colored</u> circle that <u>surrounds the pupil</u> of the eye): the structural pattern of the iris is digitized.

- ***retina*** (the <u>innermost</u> layer of the wall of the eyeball): maps the eye's <u>blood vessel pattern</u>.

- ***hand geometry***: takes a three-dimensional record of the length, width and height of the hand and/or fingers; any <u>injury</u> to or <u>growth</u> of the hand can cause recognition problems.

- ***facial features*** (face recognition): people can significantly <u>alter</u> their <u>appearance</u> and facial hair to try to fool the device; can also be fooled by "mission-impossible" type mask.

- ***voice*** (voice prints): requires the exact same phrase to be spoken; people's <u>voices can change and background noises</u> can interfere with system performance.

- ***hand-written signatures***: records pen/stylus speed, acceleration, pressure, direction in signature; lack accuracy due to <u>inconsistency of hand-writing</u>.

Of the above, only three characteristics currently used for biometric technologies are considered <u>truly unique</u>: the <u>retina</u>, the <u>iris</u> and <u>fingerprints</u>.

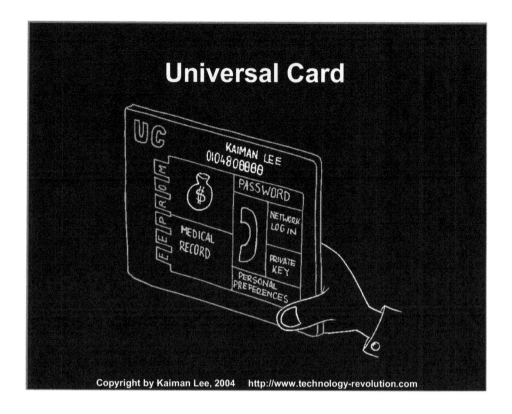

Universal Card

Private keys can be stored on a token -- computer media such as smart cards, smart keys or PCMCIA cards. Smart cards replace the magnetic strip on credit cards with an embedded microprocessor or memory chip. The card can be inserted into a reader, and PIN (personal identification number) entered.

This is similar to using your ATM card. Unless someone has your PIN and your ATM card, your account cannot be accessed. Similarly, a thief will require access to your PIN and smart card to be able to use your private key.

Smart cards can be scanned on a keyboard with an integrated smart card reader. You can access an Intranet with very specific configuration from any PC or hotel NC with just a smart card.

Soon, smart cards will become Universal Cards with all types of personal data embedded in them, e.g., medical records, cash card, phone card, personal preferences to tell Web sites that you visit, password to specific systems, network log in, and private key.

Basic Security Methods

Copyright by Kaiman Lee, 2004   http://www.technology-revolution.com

Basic security methods include encryption and firewall.

<u>Encryption</u> technology is applied to documents, objects and applications. In a nutshell, the sender <u>scrambles</u> a document and the receiver <u>unscrambles</u> it while nobody intercepting the document will be able to read it.

<u>Firewall</u> technology <u>blocks unfriendly</u> people from coming in to your network and allows the friendly ones to come in.

There are basically three types of firewalls:
- packet-filtering firewall
- proxy server firewall
- stateful inspection firewall

Public Key Cryptography

Public key cryptography is used to authenticate the signer and the document. Two keys are used. The public key is used to create the signature, and the private key is used to verify the signature.

The private key is known only to the person to whom it is assigned. Each person also has a public key, and this is published in a widely available directory.

Let us say you want to send Jane a document. It takes two steps. First, the document file is analyzed to produce a unique identifier called message digest (a hash or digital thumbprint). It can be thought of as a number on a library book. Second, the message digest is encrypted with a public key. A digital signature is associated with an electronic document, not contained in it.

The message digest, when encrypted with a public key, can only be decrypted with a private key. Only the intended recipient possesses the private key. When Jane receives the document, the software will use the corresponding private key to recalculate the message digest value for the file and make a comparison.

Private and public keys are mathematically related. You can not determine the private key with only a public key.

A certification authority such as VeriSign, Visa or USPS will associate a pair of private and public keys with a person (or a corporation). It is also responsible for publishing the public keys in a widely available directory.

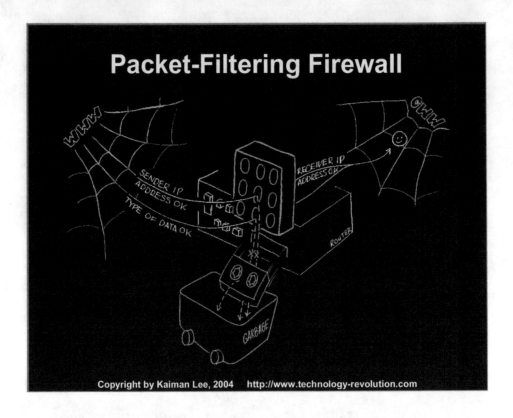

Packet-Filtering Firewall

Packet-filtering firewalls <u>examine</u> all <u>packets</u> for the <u>sender's IP address</u>, the <u>receiver's IP address</u>, and <u>type of data</u>. Then they <u>forward or drop</u> the packets based on predefined rules, such as approved IP addresses. They are generally <u>implemented on routers</u>.

They examine a packet at the <u>network layer</u> and do not depend on any application, allowing them to deliver good performance and scalability.

Packet filters provide a limited amount of protection, precisely because they are <u>not application aware.</u>   They cannot understand the context of a given communication.

They can easily be <u>spoofed (tricked into thinking that incoming data is valid when its source is in fact an intruder)</u> by a hacker who changes the IP address in a packet header to be acceptable to the firewall.

230

Proxy Server Firewall

The proxy server firewall (also called proxy firewall, application layer gateway, or gateway firewall) acts as an intermediary or buffer for user requests. It uses application proxies written for such Internet services as Hypertext Transfer Protocol (HTTP) and File Transfer Protocol (FTP).

With a proxy server, internal users never directly interact with any external server. The proxy server acts as a stand-in for client requests. That means internal IP addresses can be hidden and protected from outside prying altogether.

The security comes with a sacrifice. Proxy server breaks the client/server model, the direct connection between sender and receiver, by routing the traffic through a separate port, thereby eliminating a hacker's ability to read internal addresses and, as a result, gain access to network components.

Every client/server communication requires two connections: one from the client to the firewall and one from the firewall to the server. Each proxy requires a different application process, making scalability and support for new applications a problem.

Proxy firewalls are recognized as the most ironclad, but a major shortcoming is that they must include support for every TCP/IP application that you want to use through the firewall.

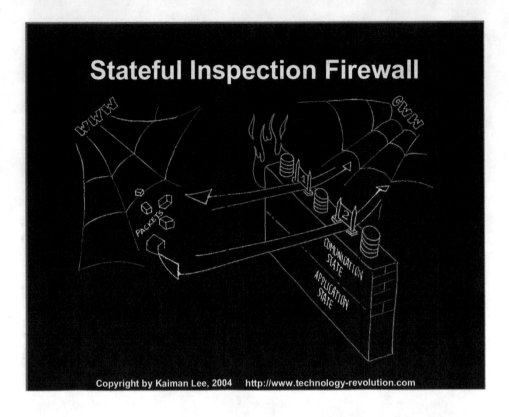

Stateful Inspection Firewall

A stateful inspection firewall analyzes the nature of the traffic and allows direct sender-to-receiver connections. It not only examines the packets, it also compares incoming packets against known states of packets. It only allows authorized traffic to enter and engages protective measures to restrict access once transfers are complete.

There are two states of information: communication state (derived from past communications) and application state (derived from other applications).

They are stored and updated dynamically.

A stateful inspection firewall tracks the state of an internal user's request so that when the data is returned, the firewall can verify that the information is what was specifically requested. The firewall remembers which connections use which port numbers and shuts down access to those ports after the connection closes.

A stateful inspection firewall overcomes many limitations of the packet filter and proxy server approaches. It provides application-layer awareness without requiring a separate proxy for every service to be secured, and without breaking the client/server model.

Layers of Security

Security approaches based solely on firewalls will soon be out of date. Today's firewall-ringed enterprise networks are reminiscent of the castle walls and gated cities of the Middle Ages.

When bad folks arrived, good folks retreated behind the walls, i.e., good guys inside, bad guys outside.

But today, a city's health is measured by the amount of commerce it conducts with other cities. People traverse the streets freely.

Security measures like door locks, theft alarms and safe deposit boxes, i.e., layers of security, protect the good guys from the bad guys.

Onion Rings

Security measures such as <u>encryption, firewall, authentication, and digital signatures</u> will protect your system from intruders. You can have as many levels of security as you want.

The market for standalone firewalls is slowing. What you mostly need is not one <u>giant wall</u> to keep out hackers but a number of <u>lesser walls</u> or security layers to keep trouble out.

You should treat security solutions in the future <u>not as walls but as layers of security like layers of an onion ring</u> interwoven throughout your network. Every time a would-be invader breaks through one barrier, s/he is <u>confronted by another</u>.

You need an overall solution in which <u>different people are granted different levels of access</u> to different applications and different data. You should go <u>from perimeter-based-only solutions to security in depth</u>.

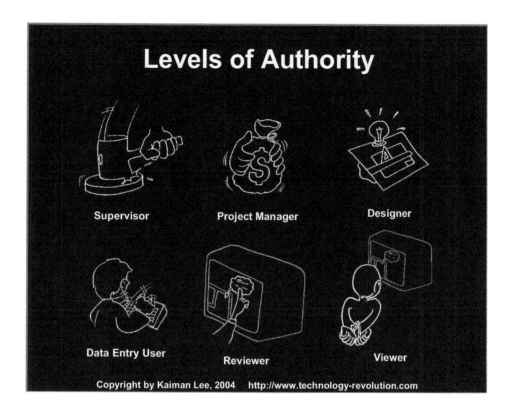

People with different roles have different authorities as to what they can do with documents. For example,

- <u>Supervisor (Administrator)</u>: can create, <u>can edit</u>, <u>can delete</u>, can set up commands & customize applications.

- <u>Project Manager</u>: can create, can edit, can delete.

- <u>Designer</u>: can create, can edit, can not delete.

- <u>Data Entry User (Operator)</u>: can create, can edit, can not delete.

- <u>Reviewer</u>: can annotate, <u>can not edit</u>, can not delete.

- <u>Viewer</u>: can view, can copy, can not annotate, can not edit, can not delete.

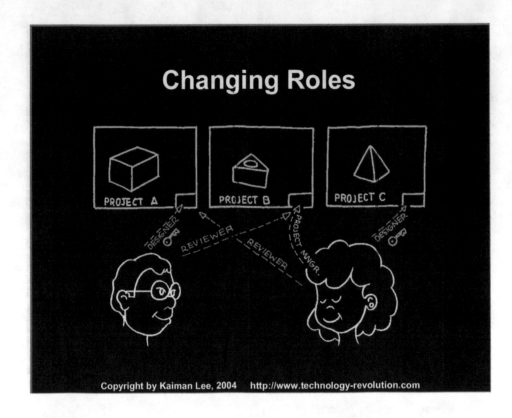

Changing Roles

PROJECT A   PROJECT B   PROJECT C

DESIGNER   REVIEWER   REVIEWER   PROJECT MNGR.   DESIGNER

People can be assigned or can volunteer for <u>different roles in different projects</u>.

A person can be any one of these job types for different projects: <u>designer, reviewer, or project manager</u>.

Document access rights must allow for this variation.

Access Rights by Classes of Documents

Document security is critical for a large-scale system, as a sensitive document should be accessible only to authorized personnel.

Documents are grouped into <u>classes such as specific projects, correspondences, personnel files, and financial statements</u>, and each new application may have its own class. Users are granted access to document classes by the system administrator.

<u>Supplemental network access rights</u> imply that the system can be configured to create (not remove) <u>further restrictions</u>.

For example, if a user is assigned to project A, then <u>access</u> is only available to documents associated with <u>that project</u>, although <u>network rights</u> for that user are <u>broader</u>.

237

Future of Security

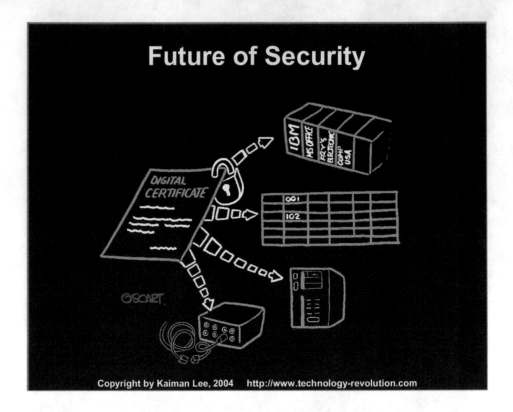

Enterprises that continue hiding behind strong walls could find themselves cut off from the vibrant and growing world of Net commerce.

Layered security technologies that protect individual servers, databases and even objects are needed as the enterprise becomes more porous and available to the outside world.

One way of achieving layered security is to embed security mechanisms into products, applications, databases, servers, and networking equipment. This would make security transparent to the end user.

However, you do not want to tediously log into each product or application separately, therefore, if a smart card can be swiped once ("single sign-on") in the morning and it makes all your applications secure, rather than if it just makes one application secure, that would make a lot of people happy.

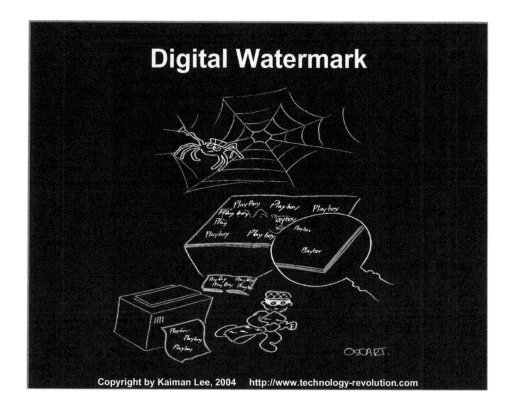

Digital Watermark

Holographic (or digital) signatures or digital (or electronic) watermarks can be embedded within a video clip, sound recording, graphics image or movie. They help prevent theft of proprietary work.

Individual bits can not be seen, heard or removed. They are randomly sprinkled throughout the document. They are virtually impossible to remove even when the image is edited or its format is changed.

There are so many hidden bits that they will survive even after repeated digital to analog conversions, re-recording the sounds and digitizing the copy. Copying over copies will not eliminate the "hidden tags" or "digital watermarks."

Companies producing this kind of product can also offer a service where a Web spider travels the Web continuously looking for pirated images. They can trace the illicit copies back to the source. Playboy's Web site uses this technology. They found pirates, sued them and won.

Another product called Content Protector safeguards images, audio, video and Java applets. They are transformed into a protected format when a Web pirate saves a file. The browser then displays a broken image.

239

Security Consultants are Expensive

Copyright by Kaiman Lee, 2004   http://www.technology-revolution.com

Professional security help comes at a high cost. The average <u>network security consultant</u> earns about <u>$1,600 a day</u>.

S/he carries technical security credentials, such as <u>Certified Information System Security Professional (CISSP)</u>, and a lot of relevant experience. Becoming a CISSP requires passing a rigorous technical examination.

Another method is to <u>hire hackers</u> to find out flaws in your security. <u>They do the so-called "ethical" hacking</u>! They break into corporate computer systems and networks with a <u>company's permission</u>.

You may even turn teenage hackers into <u>safeguards</u>.

Geoff Mulligan, a high-profile hacker in the 1970s, became senior security engineer at Sun Microsystems.

True Site Security

Copyright by Kaiman Lee, 2004   http://www.technology-revolution.com

True site security must go <u>beyond encrypting data, network access</u>, physical access to the machine, and levels of access you allow internally.

<u>This basic principle is to make it harder for vandals to break in</u>, thus encouraging them to move to an easier target elsewhere. When they do get in, you want to <u>ensure that the damage is limited</u>.

The <u>weakest point</u> in security today is <u>you</u>. World-class encryption will not help any if you <u>post your passwords</u> on your computer or leave the workplace <u>without logging off</u>. So, do not give your password to anyone, … yes, anyone.

Most firewalls are hacked or destroyed by in-house hackers or by what security experts call "<u>social engineering</u>," the subverting of security measures by <u>subterfuge</u>.

Recognize that when you work from home, you may have dial-up modems unprotected by firewalls or even passwords. Also, the <u>data inside the notebook is more valuable</u> than the hardware.

CYBERLIVING

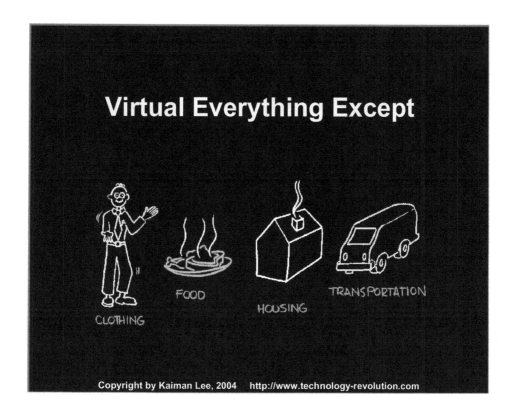

There is a Chinese saying that says that there are only <u>four (physical) necessities: clothing, food, housing and transportation</u>.

Does that mean everything else can potentially be virtual?

"<u>Virtual Lover</u>" came after the "<u>Virtual Pet</u>" that you attach on a key ring.

The gadget requires the owner to court his or her "virtual partner" with gifts such as flowers and chocolates, karaoke dates and love letters to win affection and earn "<u>affinity points</u>."

A player can win a "<u>virtual kiss</u>" and a "<u>virtual marriage</u>" if s/he scores enough points.

But if s/he misses giving enough affection, the partner may snub him or her <u>in favor of others</u>!

Things that can be virtual are just up to your imagination.

Intolerable Annoyances

Are you not annoyed by all the waiting you do every day ... buying tickets, traffic jams, waiting for the doctor ...? Do you feel bombarded with unwelcomed advertisements ... TV commercials, highway billboards ...? How about all the time you spent on travel that you would rather have spent at home?

Enter the world of Internet living or cyberliving, and you will be relieved from most of those annoyances.

Imagine coming home after work. The Web-based TV turns itself on. You order a loaded pizza with your remote control and schedule a movie to start later in the evening.

While you are waiting for the pizza delivery, you flip to the banking channel to pay a few bills, check on your balance and transfer some money into a mutual fund.

Then you shop from an electronic mall which is tailored to your specific tastes. After dinner, you visit some friends on the other side of the globe using the video camera on top of the TV.

Then, just before the movie, you jazzercise with a virtual group of people in a spa.

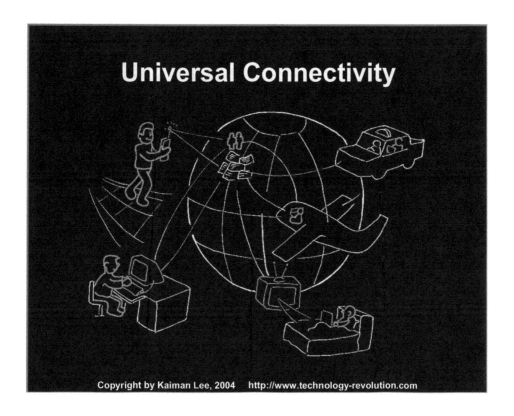

Internet brings technology's biggest impact: connectivity. The connectivity is based on universal network access to knowledge and people.

No matter where you go, you will have access to a computer of some kind that will allow you to tap into your personal space and your personal information. So if you are working on a document in your office and then in a plane later, there will be a keyboard on the plane that will let you keep working on it. The same holds true in a hotel room, in a taxi ride, and in the next office or store you visit.

You can have virtual meetings. When you can truly feel a presence with somebody over a high-speed network, it will transform community. Next, imagine if you can be there electronically as a living holograph.

You can always be connected to the Net wherever you are. If people want to contact you, they will be able to, if you let them. You may be more efficient, but perhaps not more effective because of distractions.

Connectivity will change the way we work and live. It will have an effect on culture that is really hard to estimate.

Global Yellow Page

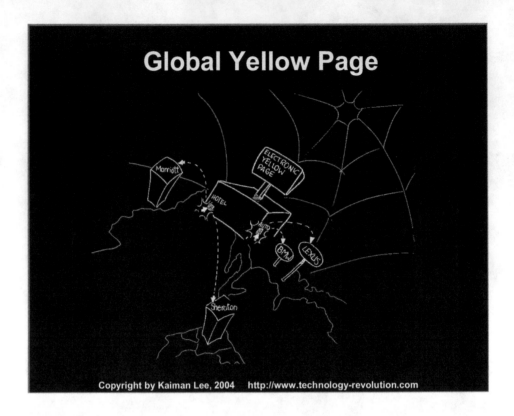

Online city guides such as Microsoft's Sidewalk, America Online's Digital Cities, and City Search all have the potential to fill the same need as that formerly filled only by the Yellow Pages. And Bell Atlantic's Big Yellow is an example of a phone company developing a product where one's computer mouse can do the "walking."

Electronic Yellow Pages or directories are all over the Web to facilitate anyone in e-commerce. It is conceivable that you can do almost all your buying and selling over the Web.

Similarly, finding and contacting relatives and friends gets easier and easier.

Yahoo! People Search, Yahoo! 's white pages directory service, for instance, is providing users the ability to call any phone number around the world.

Hi, Grandma

Copyright by Kaiman Lee, 2004   http://www.technology-revolution.com

People <u>above fifty years old</u> make up the "<u>mature market</u>."

Internet allows them to <u>decrease their isolation</u>, and <u>improve their overall quality of life</u>. They can be <u>connected</u> to all their children and friends.

With WebTV type of devices affordable to most families, Americans will suddenly realize that they are <u>all being Web-enabled</u>.

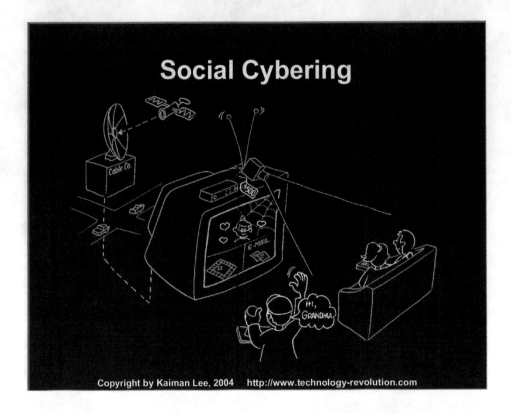

Social Cybering

The whole family can gather around a large color monitor (TV) just like the family of the 1930s huddled around the radio, or its counterpart in the 1950s gathered around the TV set.

The <u>TV and the computer screen will be synonymous</u>. The computer will be running all the time. The TV display may be on our desk and/or in our living room.

Not only can you plug in your surround-sound speakers and play movies off your cable connection, you also have this message center for telephone and E-mail. A video camera on top of the TV will let <u>grandma see and talk with her grandchildren every night</u>.

Wireless devices, like keyboards and joysticks will let groups of people watch TV, and surf the Web.

Your family members and friends in other locations can role-play a game where you can battle each other, form mystery questing parties, or chat in a tavern over a goblet of virtual wine.

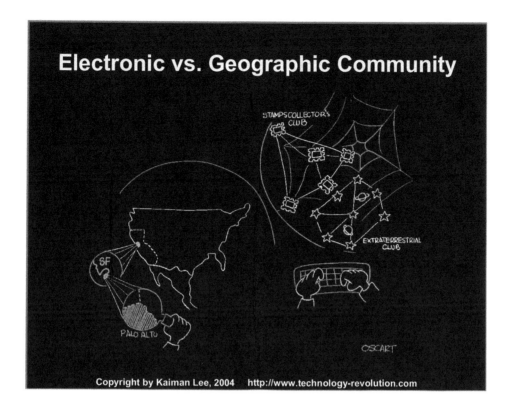

Electronic vs. Geographic Community

Geographic communities limit participation of those who can physically reach each other, while electronic, network or virtual communities have <u>no limit in terms of time and space</u>.

A virtual community is a huge, ongoing focus group, providing feedback of experiences, thoughts and opinions about mutual interests, products and services. It empowers people with <u>political, social, and educational interests and ambitions</u>.

Members located anywhere can work on common interests in real time. They do not have physical handshakes, but they can see and talk with each other using <u>desktop video conferencing</u> technology.

There is a potential for an infinite number of electronic communities, e.g., <u>product communities, affinity communities, industry communities, professional communities, and media communities</u> on any topic of interest.

Unlike a passive Web site, where all information traffic flows outward to visitors, a community site <u>engages its members in dialogs</u> among themselves and with the site sponsor, in real time or at any time.

Closing The Gaps

If you can not get the name of the person when you are having a text chat on the Internet, or if you can not recognize a name as to its gender, you will not know whether it is a male or female.

Indeed, over the Internet, everybody seems to be generic. You can not tell the age, color, sex, nationality and/or disabilities.

That may be one reason why Internet grows so fast. There are presumably more introverts than extroverts in this world.

Internet is non-abrasive and non-threatening. No used-car salesman! When you find it objectionable, just push the off button.

As such, people can ignore others they do not like very easily on the Net, but not as easily in the physical world. Therefore, the Internet, like other inventions such as the automobile, designed to bring us closer together could actually create a more isolated society.

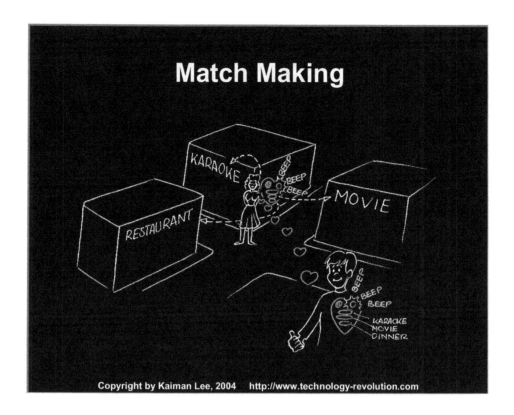

Match Making

A "love beeper" may be the ultimate matchmaking tool of the electronic age. People carrying this embedded device are hoping it will open the door to romance.

The gadget sends out different signals, depending on the setting. When someone of the opposite sex carrying the same device comes into range, the two devices beep or flash.

Then, it is up to the would-be lovers to seek each other out -- or run the other way.

The device could have numerous settings for favorite activities, e.g., karaoke, chat, movie, drink, dinner, and friends, etc.

A flashing green light means a match in interests. Red means there is a same device next to you, but you have got the wrong setting. The settings can be changed any time, and the timid can turn the beeper off so only the light will flash.

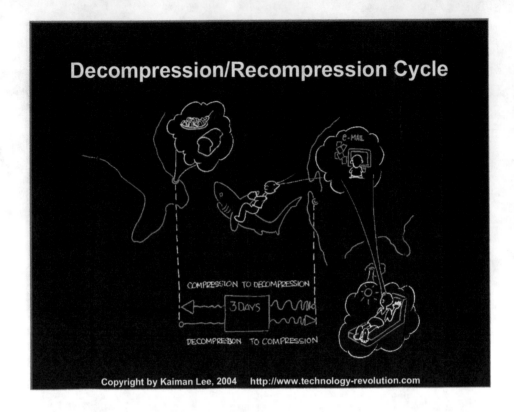

Decompression/Recompression Cycle

Copyright by Kaiman Lee, 2004   http://www.technology-revolution.com

Once you have cruised cyberspace in the fast lane, there may be <u>no slowing down</u>. <u>Instant gratification</u> will make the Web even more <u>addictive</u>, pushing you to becoming a <u>Webaholic</u>.

A couple left on a <u>four day weekend to Italy</u> in 1996. They spent most of it on planes. Only one day was spent on location. It almost was not worth it if the pasta puttanesca and Tuscan bread did not make up for it. For many, work and play have fused to the point that <u>multiple weeks in the Bahamas would be torturous</u>.

Some dismiss the <u>"I live for the weekend" attitude</u> found on Garfield posters as "<u>pathetic</u>." To them, long vacations mean <u>more work (E-mail pile up) when they come back</u>.

The cyber world is no longer about capitalists vs. communists, or rich vs. poor, but <u>fast vs. slow</u>. There is a limit as to how much people can handle. If they go beyond that point, they will begin to <u>deteriorate, feel stressed and harassed</u>.

<u>Time- and labor-saving devices</u> could actually <u>create more work</u> for us. We allow technology "improvements" to be pushed on us that have no inherent value. Therefore, the real problem is our willingness to give up ourselves to technology without thought. How to have <u>self control over technology and the Net</u> will become an essential <u>skill for a better life</u> in this networked world.

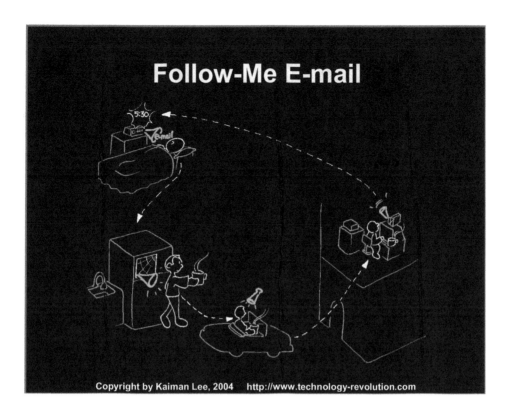

Follow-Me E-mail

Imagine beginning your day waken up by an <u>alarm clock</u> reading off <u>high-priority E-mail</u> messages. They have been automatically forwarded from your company's server to your home during the night. Text-to-speech technology turns <u>E-Mail to voice mail</u>.

As you walk towards your kitchen to pour yourself a cup of coffee, an unobtrusive sensor on a radio type device would spot your presence there. It signals the bedroom alarm clock to transfer the remaining messages to the kitchen.

You speak freely to <u>answer or delete any E-mail</u>. Those E-mails that you do not get to before finishing your breakfast would find you in your <u>car</u>.

Then, you arrive at your office, and you have been <u>working since you woke up</u>.

Next, you will be getting your E-mail on the touch-screen terminal located where the <u>control panel</u> of the stair-climbing exercise machine usually sits. There you have it: <u>working while working out</u>.

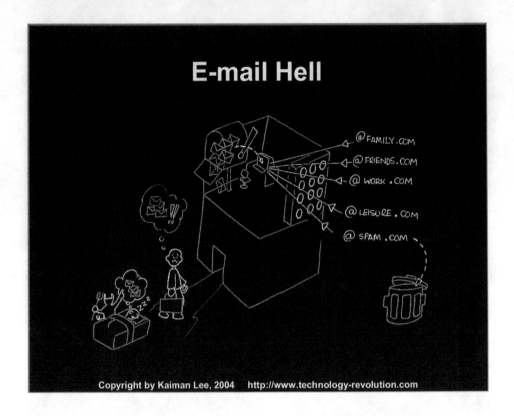

E-mail Hell

@ FAMILY.COM
@ FRIENDS.COM
@ WORK.COM
@ LEISURE.COM
@ SPAM.COM

Copyright by Kaiman Lee, 2004   http://www.technology-revolution.com

E-mail, you cannot live with it, but cannot live without it. Your employer will refrain from calling you at 11:00 at night, but not from sending you E-mail that needs reply. E-mail does not just collapse distance, it demolishes all boundaries. That can be a blessing or a curse depending on when it is used.

E-mail has saturated your desktop. If it has not done so, it will. Sane business people wade into it with dread, since finding from that mountain of electronic paper something you actually need or want can be a futile if not demeaning task.

You want filtering technologies that screen out messages from all unknown senders. It might become common for people to reserve secret E-mail addresses for the exclusive use of family, friends and close colleagues; and to have E-mail addresses for spammers; or to change addresses often to keep the spammers one step behind.

Knowledgeable people will use smart filtering to distinguish what they really want to know from the sea of E-mails that they hope never to see.

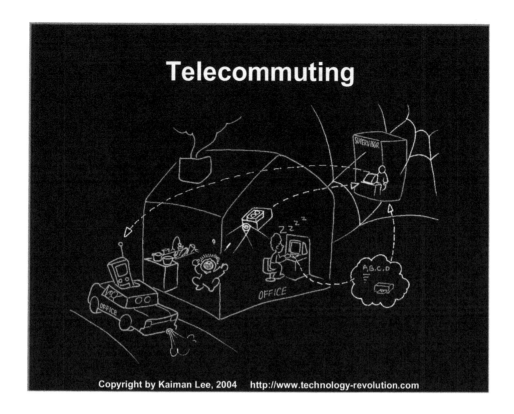

Telecommuting

Copyright by Kaiman Lee, 2004   http://www.technology-revolution.com

With the advancement of <u>connecting technologies</u>, such <u>as E-mail, fax, WebCam, and videoconferencing</u>, an increasing number of people are <u>working at home</u>. They have a "<u>telepresence</u>" to the office via those devices. <u>The "office" is where the worker is</u>.

<u>Telecommuting</u> or <u>virtual work</u> could <u>connect rural and urban areas</u> through "<u>electronic migration</u>," a virtual phenomenon wherein qualified teleworkers can roam the planet.

There seems to be a <u>downside</u> to telecommuting. Some people have tried telecommuting and found that it does, indeed, make home seem just like the office -- with the result that <u>non-work activities are crowded out</u>.

Especially when telecommuting is viewed as an <u>experiment</u>, a worker may <u>feel under constant pressure</u> to make up for the <u>perceived lack of commitment</u> to the job by <u>out-performing coworkers</u>. There does not seem to be a boundary on this process. <u>Even eating and sleeping are often sacrificed</u>.

Related to telecommuting, a growing amount of a company's work is performed by "<u>e-lance</u>" (re: <u>freelance</u>) <u>contractors</u> in virtual departments. Not every manager can handle a group of this kind, and not every worker can function in this mode.

255

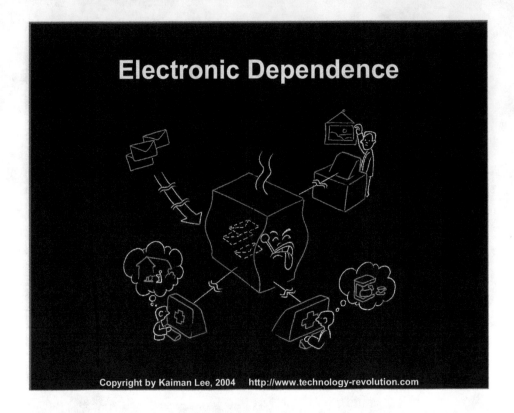

Electronic Dependence

E-mails and Web surfing have become as second nature to many people as dial tone and tap water. You will be amazed how quickly you could become so dependent on E-mail that you feel it is indispensable in your life, both work and social.

With the Internet and Web-enabled appliances, you could use the Web browser on an office computer to program your VCRs, turn on your porch lights, even activate cameras to check on the baby sitter. You are now even more hooked.

When your E-mail system or network goes dark, you might not even know what to do with yourself. You could see people keeping themselves busy by cleaning their desks and making coffee. They gather at the water cooler and gossip. Employees go home early and facilities are being closed.

Have a strategy in place before that happens so your productivity will not suffer significantly, and perhaps you could gain something from the adversity because of it.

On-line Trading

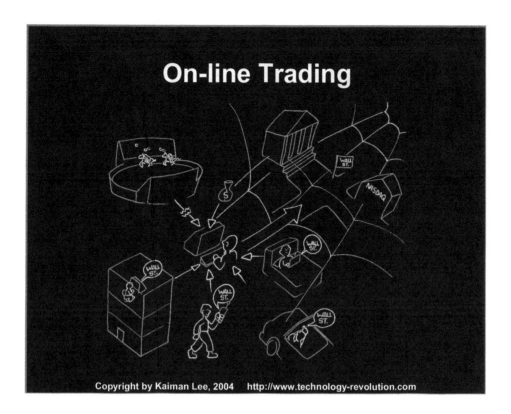

Day trading has replaced off-track betting as USA's favorite sport. It bears all the similarities of gambling: easy credit and the conviction that the house can be beaten. Online investing, however, can be profitable if you can control yourself.

There are basically three kinds of Internet-related stocks.

1. Pure Internet stock. Their whole business model is built around the Internet, and all their revenues derive from transactions on the Internet.

2. Traditional brick-and-mortar companies that are successfully changing their business model to seize the opportunities offered by the Internet.

3. Companies that make the switches, routers, modems, satellites, and/or software for the Internet's infrastructure.

When the steam engine came along, most people wanted to stick with horses. The visionaries invested in railroads, in companies that built locomotives, made products shipped by rail, and new communities that would be built in the new territories.

Investing in emerging Internet-related stocks can make some big winners, and many losers. It is your responsibility to differentiate value from just potential and hype no matter how fast its growth or how high its technology. Knowledge is key.

Internet Addiction

Copyright by Kaiman Lee, 2004   http://www.technology-revolution.com

People are becoming more and more <u>impatient</u> because there is <u>too much information and everything is changing too fast</u>. People do not have time for the <u>normal human pace</u> anymore.

<u>Technostress</u> is due to <u>our over-reliance on technological devices, a panicky feeling when those devices fail, and a state of near-constant stimulation, or of feeling continually "plugged in."</u>

You will feel <u>unable to slow down, impatient or overwhelmed</u>. <u>You can not concentrate, relax or sleep</u> like you used to. You may <u>overeat or drink</u> too much to sedate yourself.

The continual build-up of stress chemicals can eventually lead to serious health problems, both mental and physical. You could acquire <u>Internet Addiction Disorder</u>, also called <u>Pathological Internet Use</u>. It is just as hard to shake as cigarette smoking. That <u>addiction represents compulsive use, loss of control, and continued use despite problems it is causing</u>.

You should get back down to a <u>human rhythm</u>. Ask yourself "Do I want to know this now?" If not, <u>resist</u> the urge to open your <u>E-mail</u>. Do not feel you have to immediately respond. <u>Doing things asynchronously is okay</u>. Make technology serve you.

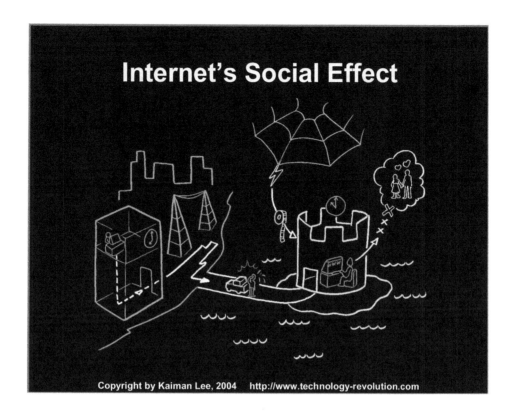

Underline connectivity via telephone, e-mail, and the Web causes us to see less of our friends and families, and also spend less time stuck in traffic, shopping in malls, and watching television. The Internet could be an isolation technology that further reduces our participation in communities even more than television did. We work more hours at home without cutting back at the office.

The Internet may not make us more productive if it is not used judiciously. It could give us more new and inventive ways to waste time anytime, anywhere. Bandwidth will increase which will cause the Internet to move from an information medium to an entertainment medium, and you could download a new movie easily.

A recent survey finds the keywords that describe people's mood about the future are: upheaval, change, frightening, confused, chaotic, traumatic, insular, dangerous, technology oriented, and decadent. Key words for the preferred future are: family values, order, discipline, simple, happy, peace, community based, tolerant, safe, and ordered.

In the post-material economy, also known as the dream society, experience economy, and leisure society, businesses will offer products and services that feed people's hunger for nostalgia, stories, memories, meaning, spirituality, and adventures.

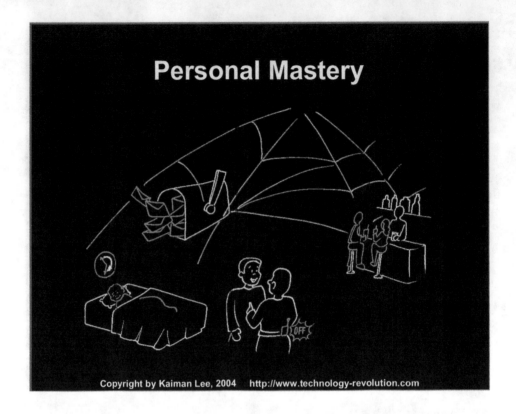

Personal Mastery

Copyright by Kaiman Lee, 2004   http://www.technology-revolution.com

We are working in a world where <u>fast enough is not enough</u>.

Set <u>priorities</u>. If you are going to <u>exceed</u> your limits, or decide to <u>break</u> a decision, do so <u>consciously</u>.

<u>Say no</u>. Do not feel like you have to do every last thing or the world will fall apart.

Negotiate about what you <u>can do</u> and what you <u>cannot</u>, at work and at home.

Schedule <u>family time</u>. <u>Make dates</u> with your spouse, and your other family members.

Take <u>total downtime</u> each day for working out or reading, etc.

Arrange to <u>work less than full time</u>.

Be realistic. <u>Choices</u> are <u>okay</u>.

Find a <u>job you love</u>. Figure out what you like.

Use the <u>weekend</u> to <u>refresh</u> yourself -- <u>turn off the cell phone</u>. Go <u>someplace</u> where you <u>can not be reached</u>.

Warp Speed

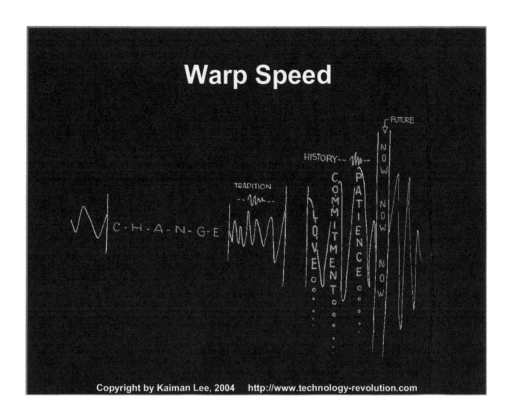

The more we <u>depend on electronic</u> information flow and entertainment, the more our everyday lives need to <u>keep up</u> with its lightning pace. We fight between <u>the slower pace our minds and bodies crave</u> and the faster tempo our technology demands.

We are in "<u>warp speed</u>," a velocity that can warp our <u>behavior and our most basic values</u>.

Warp speed disengages us from the <u>past</u>. <u>Traditions</u> become incomprehensible and <u>history</u> becomes <u>irrelevant</u>. Warp speed plunges us toward the <u>future</u>. Brilliant <u>inventions</u>, glittering <u>products</u>, and luminous <u>celebrities</u> swarm past us in <u>accelerating waves</u>.

Nullifying the past and negating a true view of the future, warp speed is transforming our society at large into a <u>speed-driven hyper culture</u>. The <u>power of now</u> tells you to <u>get as much as you can as fast as you can</u>. It obscures the need to cultivate <u>life-sustaining skills and virtues -- patience, commitment, self-denial, and even self-sacrifice</u>.

In the realm of technology, we must <u>define the kind of life we want</u> -- personally and communally -- and <u>then select the technologies</u> that truly serve those ends.

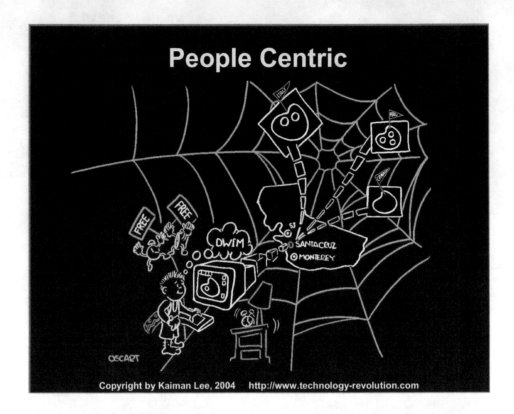

People Centric

The information technology environment will be people-centric, i.e., hightech hightouch, else it will not be ubiquitous. It will be taken for granted just like telephones and fax machines.

Bathrobe warriors are taking advantage of the many possibilities of cyber-living, working at home most of the time, i.e., teleworking.

There will be more and more independent contract workers. They can live anywhere, work any time on their own schedule, work with anyone around the world, and work as much or as little as they want. There is no doubt that the teleworking community is growing rapidly. Telecommuters will be the stay-at-home work force of the future.

Work teams no longer must be co-located. They can transcend distance, time zones, and organizational boundaries. Most people will work in virtual teams for at least some part of their jobs. The face-to-face aspect of normal working relationships is changing dramatically.

Combining with the increase in "do what I mean" (DWIM) intelligence of the computer, there is a quick shift from technology-centric to people-centric paradigm.

Future Office

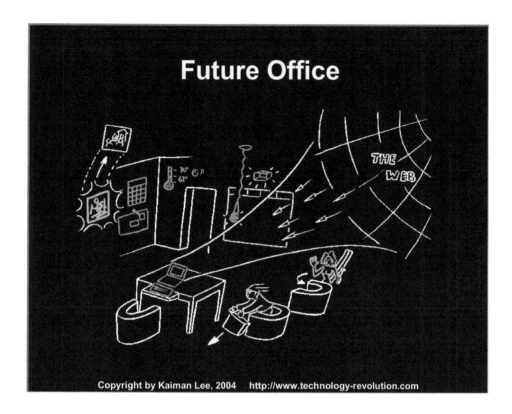

The future office may not have an engraved name plaque at the door. You might be sharing the office with others.

When you walk through the door, the computer changes the pictures on the wall, and sets your preferred temperature and lighting level.

You insert your smart card, and now you have access to the world.

In a very competitive business environment where price and quality of competing products are very close, customer service is becoming the differentiator. So executives are eliminating phone tag, pagers and public address "carpet bombing" in favor of employee tracking.

Your identification badge emits infrared signals that are picked up by receivers on the ceiling, which in turn report your whereabouts to your company's personnel directory on the Intranet.

If a customer needs you in a hurry, the receptionist merely clicks on your name in the company's personnel directory, finds your location -- which can be updated every five seconds -- and sends you a targeted audio message from an overhead speaker.

Future Work

The future work environment will be <u>intellectual-based</u>. <u>Farmers</u> could become <u>farm managers</u>. They will primarily work <u>indoors</u>, and <u>oversee automated smart farms</u>. Sensing technologies will feed data into computers, which will analyze soil conditions, plant health, fertilizer mix, and moisture content, etc.

<u>Pilots</u> could become <u>flight supervisors</u>. Their chief functions will be to <u>coordinate</u> the <u>plane's on-board technologies with air-traffic control</u> to assure safety.

<u>Teachers</u> could become <u>learning facilitators</u>. They will rarely lecture, but will be primarily a <u>helper and coach</u>, helping students draw on resources.

Jobs that once required a high level of training or education (including <u>architecture, accounting, and property appraising</u>) are threatened by computer programs and expert systems.

The future will be based on the continuing expansion of how the natural <u>cleverness</u> of human beings can be <u>enhanced</u> by <u>automated tools and assistants</u>.

There will be many positive changes, making many jobs more challenging and rewarding, but they may also lead to <u>depersonalization or boredom</u>.

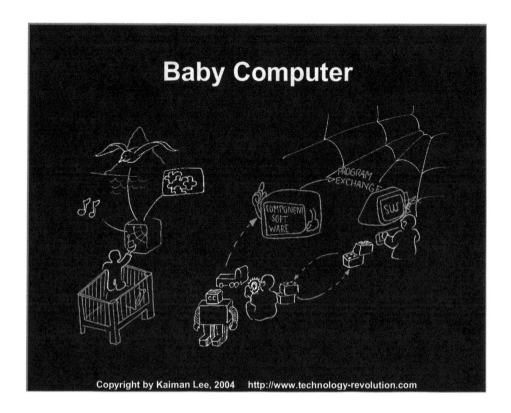

Baby Computer

A <u>baby computer</u> is used to <u>stimulate</u> babies' natural <u>curiosity and imagination</u>. It offers babies an <u>interactive</u> combination of <u>activities, animation and sounds</u>.

Guided by an animal, say an onscreen teddy bear, youngsters can choose from among many activities: <u>connect-the-stars, puzzle time, picture fun, where's Teddy?, dress Teddy, down on the farm, color train and let's make music</u>, etc. Any keyboard touch or mouse-click does the job. It provides an abundance of images/photographs, and words in several languages.

A baby computer is <u>not about games</u>; it is <u>about stimulation</u>.

We must recognize that <u>children learn best </u>when they play with <u>real objects</u> like puzzles and teddy bears and with adults or other children. Such contacts provide <u>social context and tactile experience</u> crucial to child development. Using the computer as an <u>add-on educational tool</u> is okay.

We need to be vigilant as to how new technologies like <u>voice recognition, deep computing, pervasive computing and ever-faster, smaller microprocessors</u> will revolutionize the way we bring up children, live and work.

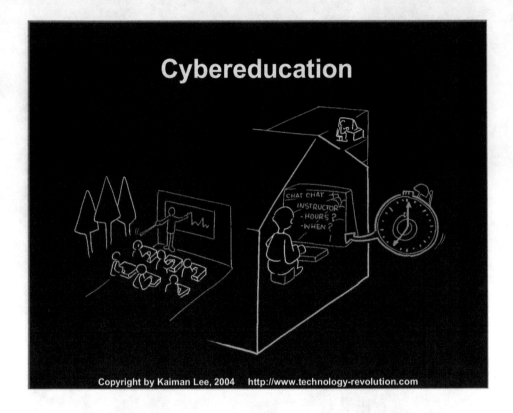

Cybereducation

Classroom education works well for young adults preparing themselves for the career world, but online education could be enormously beneficial for working adults.

An online class is not for you if you have always chosen to sit at the back of the classroom, because more responsibility is put on the learner.

Ask how many hours the online instructor is available. When? Is there an online chat facility so students can help each other?

Synchronous classes usually require students to attend online chats and turn in homework at designated times. Asynchronous classes let students work at their own pace. Synchronous classes cause some peer pressure that is not present in asynchronous classes.

If a topic is hard to grasp, the instructor can slow down in a synchronous class. But in an asynchronous online class, most of the communications are static.

Understand that schools are not buildings, but communities of instructors and learners. Whether to go to a physical school or go online depends mainly on the quality of the instructors and the desires and conditions of the students.

Learning a skill can be done anywhere.

A person in a <u>convalescent home</u> or in <u>prison</u> can access the same channels to learn.

Some prisons are offering training in everything from computer aided design (CAD) and programming to PC help desk skills in an effort to reverse a 62% (1998) national rate of ex-cons who wind up back behind bars.

For people with Web access, it is truly <u>equal opportunity</u>, and "it's all up to you."

TECHNOLOGY CHANGES

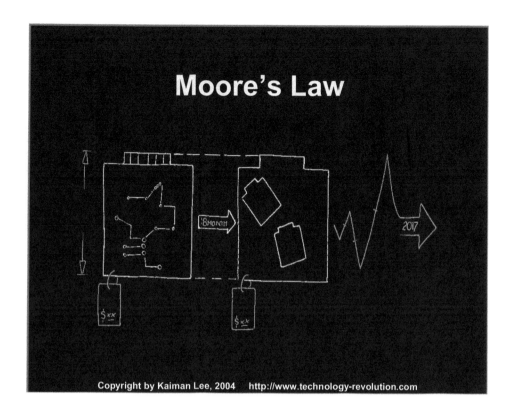

Moore's Law

Gordon Moore is an engineer who cofounded Intel. In 1965, the number of transistors on a chip doubled from 60 to 120. Moore then developed the rule of thumb in predicting computer powers. Roughly every 18 months, the number of circuits that fits on a chip doubles, while the price remains the same. Facts:

- 1979: 8088 (286); 29k transistors; 5MHz clock speed; 8-bit processing
- 1985: 80386; 275k, 16 MHz; 16 bit
- 1993: Pentium: 3.2m, 66 MHz; 32 bit
- 1999: Merced: 40m, 900 MHz; 64 bit

If you imagine the amount of addressable memory area that a 32-bit processor can access as equal to the size of a business card, then a 64-bit processor's addressable memory area would be roughly equal to the earth's surface.

Gordon Moore believed in 1998 that his law could hold true until about 2017.

"System on a chip" (SOC) or "system-level integration" is allowing the guts of an entire PC to be put on one piece of silicon. If you can do everything on a single chip vs. three, you get a faster, cooler, better, and cheaper chip.

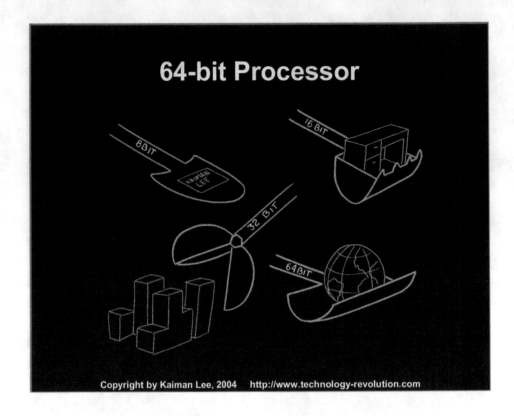

64-bit Processor

The term 64-bit refers to the size of "words" or chunks of data that a computer processes at one time. Most computers today are 32-bit, so common sense says 64-bit computing must be twice as good. Not necessarily.

To fully exploit a 64-bit computer, the software applications must be written for 64-bit processing, or it will process data in 32-bit chunks. Applications that can especially benefit from 64-bit architecture are digital signal processing, image processing, real-time Internet content creation and very high-precision calculation.

The processor's number of bits determines how much information a computer can keep track of in RAM. You prefer to hold data in RAM because data there is retrieved at a rate that is 10,000 times faster than data from disk drives.

32-bit computers can address 2 to the 32nd power -- 4 gigabytes (GB). 64-bit computers can address 2 to the 64th power -- 18 exabytes.

Visualize the difference in addressable memory. 8-bit word systems represent an area the size of a business card, 16-bit systems the size of a desktop, 32-bit systems a city block, and 64-bit systems the earth's surface. The Genome Project uses 64-bit systems to address 80,000 GB.

Future Portable Computer

Today, a business person can carry an <u>entire office in a briefcase</u>: a laptop computer, a Jaz drive, a cellular phone, and a portable printer. It makes any hotel room a complete and productive work area.

Also today, you can reach your database or Web site in your office or home from any remote network computer or kiosk.

Tomorrow, your <u>whole life's database could be on a card</u>. Go anywhere and push it in any computer that has a keyboard and a screen, and you are in business!

The <u>world's smallest computer</u> was an aspirin-size computer that, embedded in household appliances, could let you on the road or at your office use the Internet to cool your homes, heat coffee and tape TV shows. Mr. Shrikumar, a student at the University of Massachusetts, built it in 1999 for less than one dollar. It has a tiny 4-megahertz processor he bought for 49 cents and a 32-kilobyte memory chip that stores Web pages and other data. The <u>PC has gone on a chip</u>.

The PC becomes an appliance behind the dashboard of your car, or behind a flat-panel display in your kitchen. The <u>PC could disappear</u> just the way electric motors are <u>invisible</u> in our lives.

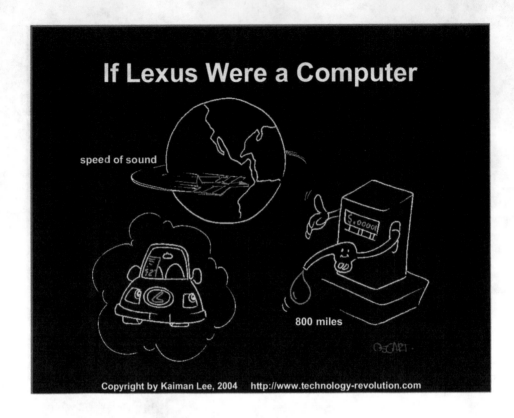

If Lexus Were a Computer

speed of sound

800 miles

In about 1994, computer power was about 8,000 times less expensive than it was 30 years ago.

Imagine the following when you explain the astounding rate of advancement in computing power.

If we had similar progress in automotive technology, we could buy a Lexus LS400 for about $2 today. It would travel at the speed of sound, and go about 800 miles on a drop of gas.

You might argue that Lexus does not crash by itself, unlike the PC.

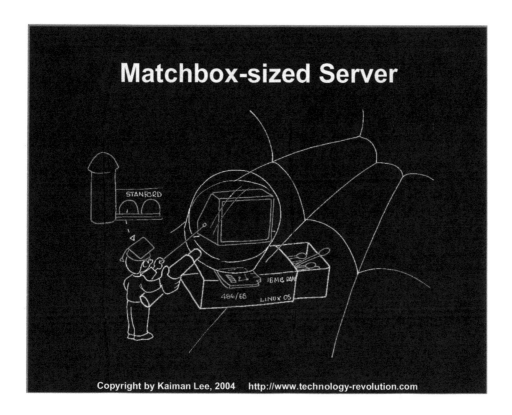

Matchbox-sized Server

In earlier 1999, Stanford University computer science professor Vaughan Pratt created the world's smallest operational Web server the size of a matchbox. It means we could potentially run Web sites out of our shirt pockets.

It uses off-the-shelf components. It has a wireless modem to connect to the Internet and to a display that is viewed using special glasses.

The device consists of a 486-66 processor, 16 MB each of RAM and flash ROM, and a slightly tweaked Linux operating system.

How did this come about? Professor Pratt said, "It was just a matter of hacking away one morning." He specializes in concurrency and miniaturized "wearable" computers. He is interested in seamlessly integrating computers into everyday life.

"The boundary between embedded systems and desktop computers is blurring," Professor Pratt said.   He thinks that as desktop machines get smaller, it makes less sense to depend on limited-function embedded systems that require specialized software and offer limited connectivity. "The regular desktop-capable machines are now presenting a more credible threat to embedded systems."

PC's Magic Moment

Copyright by Kaiman Lee, 2004   http://www.technology-revolution.com

A PC is <u>analogous to a car</u>.

The car, <u>by itself</u> can be used for many things. You can listen to the radio or CDs. You can be warmed or cooled. You can be protected from intruders.

But, the car's <u>real performance</u> comes only when the <u>rubber meets the road</u>.

The <u>PC's real performance</u> comes when it is <u>connected to the Web</u>.

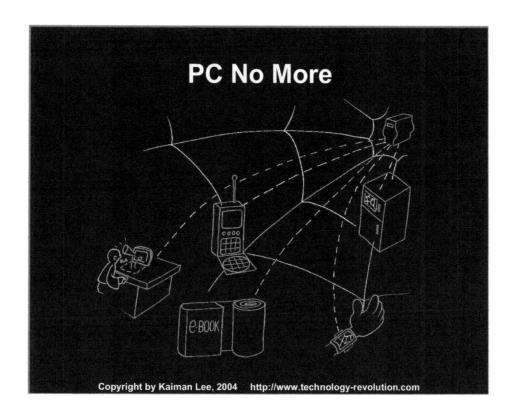

You will not see <u>computers</u> because they will be <u>tiny and tucked out of sight</u>. You will <u>be wearing your computer with keyboards on your T-shirt</u>.

In Comdex (Computer Dealer Exposition) 1998, leading PC manufacturers such as <u>Compaq, Dell, Apple and IBM did not exhibit their PCs</u>. <u>The PC has lost its respect</u>. PCs are far too complex than task-specific, unobtrusive, pervasive devices that communicate with each other across a vast wireless network.

Now it is the <u>connection speed and Internet services</u> that differentiate the vendors. <u>Connection</u> has <u>won over</u> <u>crunch</u>. The handhelds, palmtops and <u>network appliances</u> are championed as <u>smarter, cheaper, faster</u> connection alternatives to the <u>one size fits all</u> approach of the <u>PC</u>.

When <u>Java</u> becomes <u>dominant on the Web</u>, <u>network appliances can replace PCs</u> on commercial networks. The PC as we know it will be surrounded and overwhelmed by <u>big-server computing</u> based on Java and tiny client computing devices.

In the near future, a lot of people who do not already have a PC will buy a <u>simple browser-enabled terminal costing perhaps less than $100.</u>

David vs. Goliath

ABM MS

Copyright by Kaiman Lee, 2004   http://www.technology-revolution.com

There was a movement in the Silicon Valley that was dubbed "Anyone But Microsoft" (ABM). It means that some companies are willing to do business with anyone but Microsoft no matter how much money it costs them.

Another interpretation of ABM is "anything to bash Microsoft," a community that wants an alternative to Windows.

The battle between Silicon Valley and Microsoft is like a "Jihad," or holy war. ABM would like to make Microsoft the Philistine. The stone is Java.

In early 1998, Project to Promote Competition & Innovation in the Digital Age (ProComp) was formed. Among the members are: American Airlines, American Society of Travel Agents, Computer & Communications Industry Association, Corel, Knight Ridder New Media, Netscape Communications, Oracle Corp., Preview Travel, Software Publishers Association, Sun Microsystems Inc., Air Transport Association, The SABRE Group, and Sybase. One of the distinguished members is the past U.S. Senator Bob Dole.

It is important to remember: Goliath can squish David; David can slay Goliath. By 2003, most of the hostilities have reduced to the reality that Microsoft can not be beaten.

Attacks on Windows

"If we are not careful, the <u>Browser will quickly be an operating system</u>."
--- Bill Gates, Chairman & CEO Microsoft Corp., Internet World, April 30, 1996

Bill Gates was <u>right</u>.

<u>Internet standards</u> will chip away the dominance of proprietary operating systems.

<u>Java</u> (small one-time executable programs over the Web), <u>Jini</u> (allows all devices to talk to each other), <u>network computers</u> (where all applications come over the Net), <u>Linux</u> (an open-source competing operating system of Microsoft's Windows), and various forms of <u>operating systems for handheld devices</u> are threats to Windows.

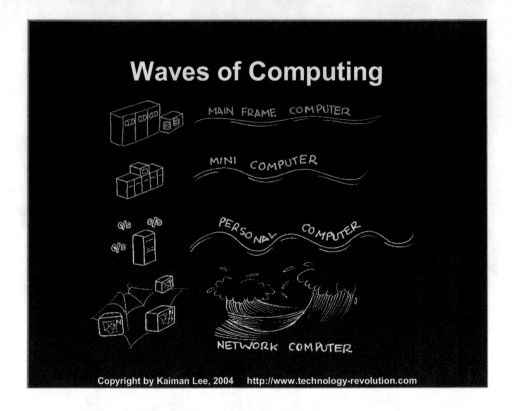

Waves of Computing

MAIN FRAME COMPUTER

MINI COMPUTER

PERSONAL COMPUTER

NETWORK COMPUTER

First Wave: Mainframes.
They contain centrally-managed or host-centric IS functions, e.g., calculating, counting, recording, and reporting.

Second Wave: Mini-computers.
They provide added applications like process management, laboratory measurement, and departmental operations to their IS activities. They remain largely host centric.

Third Wave: Personal Computers.
PCs have locally stored applications and data. LAN-based client/server systems are used to tie these islands of automation to legacy mainframe and mini-computer systems. Application functions can be split between the server and the PC. It is a desktop-centric computing environment. Computer maintenance is a chore.

Fourth Wave: Network Computing.
This is about information content, data distribution and personal communication in a dynamic network-centric environment. Applications are executed on the network. The user no longer needs to care about its technology, or maintenance.

The trend of computing in the last thirty years has been towards being smaller, lighter and more powerful computers, and bigger computer programs. The next seismic shift is towards net-centric (or Web-centric) applications, e.g., object-based Java programs dynamically assembled and optimized on the fly.

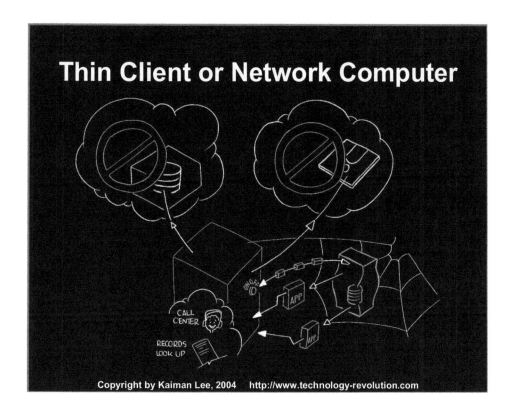

Thin Client or Network Computer

A thin client, network computer or Internet appliance has no hard or floppy drives. Application processing and data storage are shifted from desktops to centralized servers. The network-based architecture could reduce per user costs, and increase uptime. Set-up time can be sliced dramatically because new software is installed on the server only, instead of on every desktop. Because thin clients have no local storage and no moving parts, you save on purchase, installation, maintenance, administration, even on energy costs.

Thin-client networks could cut support-staff costs by 80 percent compared with their bloated PC-based counterparts. The main obstacle could be employee resistance. Users may worry that network performance will suffer or that network computers offer them less control than their PCs do.

Thin-client technology are particularly well suited for certain environments, including customer service, call centers, point of sale, patient records and factory floors.

If you think of the computer as less of a computing device and more of a communication device (Web and E-mail), then thin clients architecture makes sense.

Peer-to-Peer (P2P) Networking

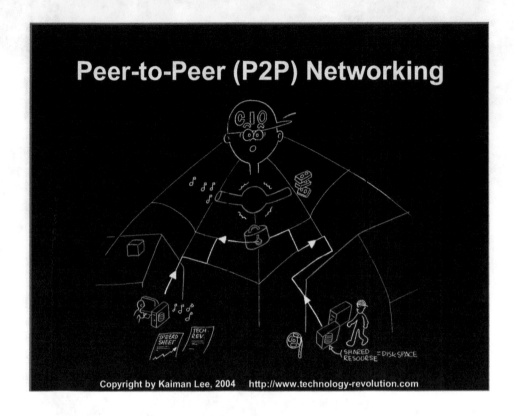

Copyright by Kaiman Lee, 2004   http://www.technology-revolution.com

P2P began with <u>Napster</u> and <u>Gnutella</u>. They provide software and host <u>indices of files such as MP3-formatted songs</u> that PC users want to share with others. PC users keep their music files in their desktop <u>PCs</u> which act <u>as servers</u>.

P2P lets users <u>search</u> for personally created or collected <u>content on other people's PC hard drives</u>, e.g., recipes, photographs, videos, research papers, corporate documents, as well as systems resources such as disk storage, and processing power.

<u>Users</u> can be employees, family members, or friends with <u>common interests</u>. The P2P file sharing technology can be <u>applied to Extranets, B2B exchanges, and portals</u> of all industries. The idea is to <u>keep</u> their <u>content within their own premises</u>, and <u>not at the Internet Service Provider</u> (ISP).

<u>Intellectual rights</u> concern involving <u>pirating copyright material</u> is being tested in federal courts. <u>CIOs worry</u> that contents at the employees' PCs are being exchanged vs. contents residing on the <u>Intranet</u>. <u>Bandwidth</u> consumption for P2P traffic multiplies similar to <u>"chat" traffic</u>. <u>Security</u> concern is such that if you can get access to information at a PC level without much security protection, you can potentially get access to change it. <u>Privacy</u> concern will play itself out when sharers experience the consequences of P2P file sharing.

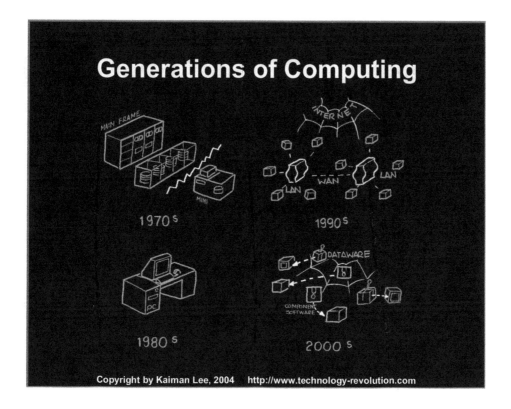

Generations of Computing

1970ˢ

1990ˢ

1980ˢ

2000ˢ

Through three generations of computing -- mainframes, PCs, networking/Internet -- we are entering the fourth: the pervasive computing, using devices such as Web-enabled cell phones and handheld computers (a.k.a. personal digital assistants). Each generation of computers does not necessarily drive the previous one out of existence but could actually increase demand for it. Each generation becomes an information supply source for the next -- a base that allows you to exploit the capabilities of the new generation of computers.

The fourth generation of computing is based on objects mostly done on the Web. Object technology can be broken down into two distinct set of objects: Dataware and component software.

Dataware are those that represent physical objects, e.g., a chair in 3-D with all its characteristics and attributes. Component software are the software objects, e.g., zoom and print functions, that when put together with other unique functions can form larger programs or applications.

A new paradigm of selling and buying dataware over the Web will evolve. Dataware will usually come for free. The manufacturer of the physical objects that dataware represent will make money from selling the physical products (e.g., chairs, partitions) when customers such as architects and engineers specify them.

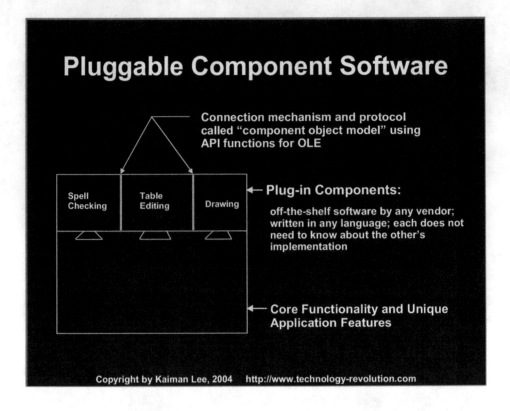

Pluggable Component Software

Connection mechanism and protocol called "component object model" using API functions for OLE

Spell Checking

Table Editing

Drawing

◄— Plug-in Components:

off-the-shelf software by any vendor; written in any language; each does not need to know about the other's implementation

◄— Core Functionality and Unique Application Features

The applications of the future will be <u>browser-based, multi-tiered, and distributed across multiple platforms</u>. Component technology will fuel its progress.

<u>Components</u> are the natural evolution of <u>object technology</u> to include the processes, technology, and standards we need to create plug-and-play, low-cost, and quickly deployable applications. The objective is <u>component-based code reuse</u>.

Just write <u>codes for your core functionality</u>, then <u>add off-the-shelf common components</u>, and you have a finished application.

Good components are good objects. Building with objects is not always as easy as it could be. When you try to merge homegrown objects with those from other teams or outside vendors, you will often find yourself fighting a host of <u>incompatibilities</u>.

<u>Components</u> address that problem by providing objects with technology and <u>standards</u> that reduce these incompatibilities and ease the integration of objects, regardless of their source.

Components will be the <u>most important technology</u> for building software in the years to come.

Reusable Objects

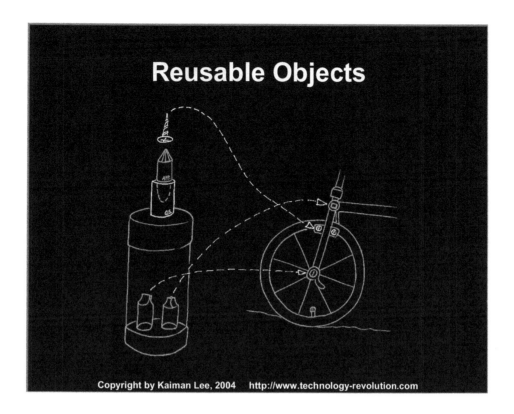

Object technology employs reusable code, and these self-sufficient modules contain both data and the instructions for manipulating the data's behavior.

You can compare object codes to a screwdriver with a fixed head and one with replaceable heads. The former can be used for only one kind of screw, but the latter can be used with different screws because the head can be changed. The application objects (kinds of heads) can be used with differing underlying operating systems (kinds of handles).

An object has methods that may be active or passive. In an example of a wheel which carries information concerning its type, size, manufacturer, and tread, etc. One passive method is that the wheel understands that it has connectivity to other objects such as an axle or a road, and will seek to maintain that.

An active method may be in the form of the behavior of the object when it is given an outside stimulus. For example, when the wheel is given an outside stimulus to roll, it's active method understands that if it is rolling, its side walls are being impacted by an external load, and the air within it is being compressed.

It has a friction coefficient that if a braking message is sent to it, it will stop rotating.

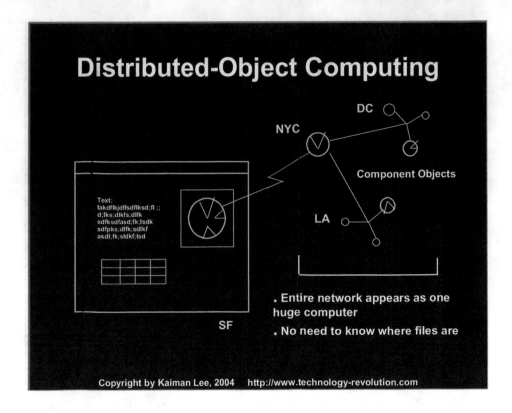

Distributed-Object Computing

DC

NYC

Component Objects

LA

Text:
lakdflkjdlfsdflksd;fl ;;
d;fks;dlkfs;dlfk
sdfksdfasd;fk;lsdk
sdfpks;dlfk;sdlkf
asdl;fk;sldkf;lsd

. Entire network appears as one huge computer

SF

. No need to know where files are

Distributed-object computing is the wave of the future. With it, the entire network appears to be a large computer.

It hides the boundaries between physical objects such as computers and disk drives, allowing you to easily and confidently locate or access any information anywhere in your organization.

Distributed computing allows the utilization of the spare time of computers on the network to be used by other computers needing more processing cycles, and allows faster application.

Distributed-object computing connects objects by passing packets from one of those objects to another object, regardless of their location.

The Internet has taken distributed object computing further. Now that you can connect with any computer worldwide anytime, there is no need to duplicate objects as is required in a client/server environment. The objects stay at one place and are being updated at the same place. Anybody who needs to see that object or extract information from it can do so with the right access code.

It's ---, Stupid

Sun Microsystems CEO Scott McNealy was quoted as saying, "It's Java, stupid," at SCO Forum '96.

There are many of such sayings. Here is a bundle.

- "It's the Web browser, stupid."
- "It's the Intranet, stupid."
- "It's the E-mail, stupid."
- "It's the server, stupid."
- "It's the application, stupid."
- "It's the Internet, stupid."
- "It's scalability, stupid."
- "It's the software, stupid."
- "It's the content, stupid."
- "It's the people, stupid."
- "It's the bottleneck, stupid."
- "It's the caching, stupid."
- "It's the bandwidth, stupid."
- "It's the latency, stupid."

These were executives speaking. Each one signaled a possible change in paradigm.

Eyeball War
Battle for the Electric Outlet

PCs now in addition to playing 3D video games that rival console systems, can be used to watch television and listen to music. TVs are hooked up to the Internet using set-top boxes that sit on top of TVs.

Cassette tape players, VCRs, TVs are analog technologies. The signals that represent music or video are converted into electrical pulses that can then be re-created on a stereo or TV.

A cable set-top box connects a TV to the Internet via a modem attached to a phone line. Now, you can surf shows and sites. With its wireless keyboard and remote control, you can type E-mail and chat with friends.

The monumental eyeball war to capture audience viewing is being waged between the massive computer and television industries. It is a battle for the electrical outlets in the living rooms.

This battle may mean that digital advances will come faster and cheaper. More companies are going to make cheap products that consumers want. Customers do not care what a product is called, a PC, a TV, or a Web-enabled TV ... they only care what it does and how convenient and easy it is to use.

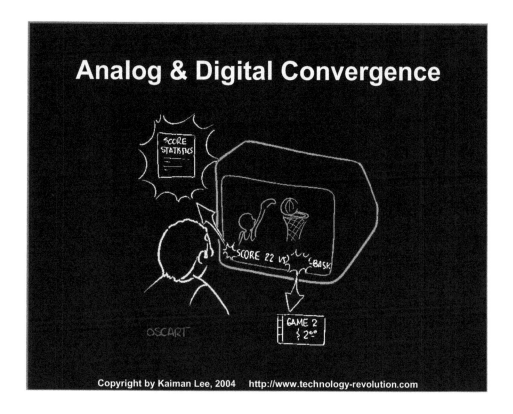

The TV screen of the future will not consist of a video image of a sports event alone. You can surf the Web while watching TV. Sitting on the bottom of the screen might be a set of icons you could click to bring up digital information.

If you are watching a basketball game, you can see statistics of players, or order tickets. You can get a different view of the field by choosing different camera angles. You can obtain more information from an advertiser or buy merchandise by clicking a button on the screen during a commercial.

Some information would come as a broadcast signal. And some might be accessed from the Web via "channel hyperlinking." When you hit the button, it sends a signal to the cable head end that tells what channel you are watching. A database table will know what the show is and sends you the Web page.

We are now at a point of convergence for both industries -- analog and digital. Convergence, or integrated communications services (ICS), is inevitable. Distinctions between voice and data will no longer exist. Services will be provided on a single network where streams of data are differentiated for delivery within specified time requirements.

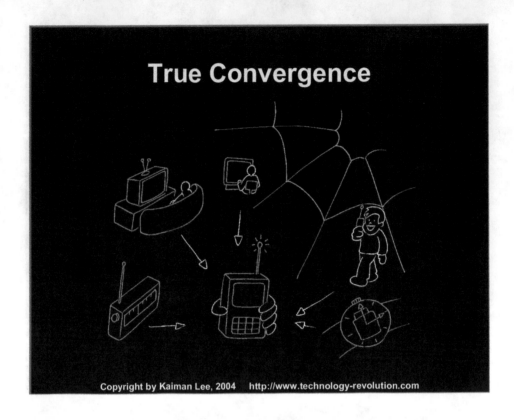

True Convergence

Marrying voice and data networks will generate all kinds of new applications. For instance, while you are shopping on the Web, a real live person can talk with you on the same line to close the deal.

That can also mean chatting and sharing electronic snapshots between buddies as they surf the Net together.

Integrating voice and data on a "single pipe" network can be perfect for small-office or home-office (SOHO) environment, because those workers are mostly telephone-based. It will let them manage contacts and make calls from that contact list from their PCs, and keep track of all their messages -- voice, data or fax -- from a single device on a single network.

The true convergence is when you look at virtually everything as digital packets that will include computer, voice, video, radio, TV, and all types of information appliances. Then ATM would not play as important a role and you might go directly to IP over optical fiber using Wavelength Division Multiplexing for literally unlimited bandwidth at blinding speed.

Digital Video Recorder

Digital Video Recorders (DVRs) are set-top boxes that use <u>hard drives to store and replay television programming</u>. DVRs will allow you to <u>pause</u> and <u>replay</u> in-progress shows, and automatically record programs for later viewing, thus dubbed "personal television."

A <u>television signal</u> from cable and satellite is fed into a DVR with a <u>standard PC hard drive</u>. When you are watching TV, the hard drive <u>automatically records</u> the signals and feeds it back <u>a second later</u>.

A <u>modem connection</u> automatically retrieves updated, <u>searchable program guide</u> data, giving you an easy way to sort through the growing glut of programs. DVR is expected to finally bring "<u>time shifting</u>" -- watching programs on your schedule rather than a network's -- to fruition.

You can quickly <u>zap through commercials</u> using the remote control's "quick skip" button that automatically advances the program by 30 seconds.

DVRs could cause commercial viewing to be cut drastically and advertising-supported networks be supplanted by pay TV. DVRs could eventually <u>replace VCRs</u>.

289

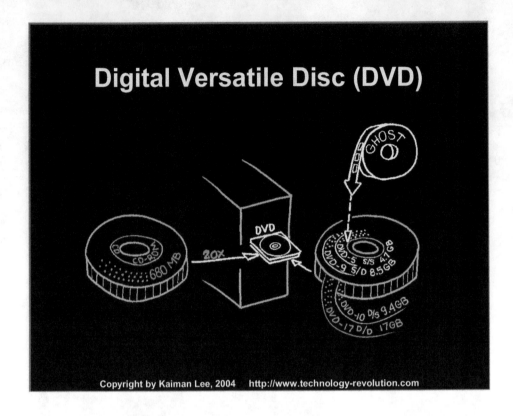

Conventional <u>CD & CD-ROM</u> drives use an invisible <u>infrared laser</u> to read the pits which reflect back the digitized sound, video or data. The discs contain <u>680 MB</u> of data.

Digital Versatile Disc (DVD) drives read smaller pits which are spaced closer together. The discs may contain two layers on each side. The laser reads the deeper reflective layer, then refocuses to read the semi-transmissive layer.

DVDs can hold from 4.7 GB to 17 GB of data depending on how they are made. There are four types:
- single-sided, single-layer = <u>4.7 GB</u> (DVD-5)
- single-sided, double-layer = 8.5 GB (DVD-9)
- double-sided, single-layer = 9.4 GB (DVD-10)
- double-sided, double-layer = <u>17 GB</u> (DVD-17)

The most popular DVD drive handles the current generation of <u>4.7 GB discs</u>. It can produce <u>full-screen, high-resolution MPEG-2 video</u> that you can view on your PC monitor. You can also view it on an external TV monitor for better quality.

DVD drives can <u>read CD-ROMs</u> at speeds up to twenty times (<u>20X</u>) and work with discs made by <u>CD-Recordable</u> drives.

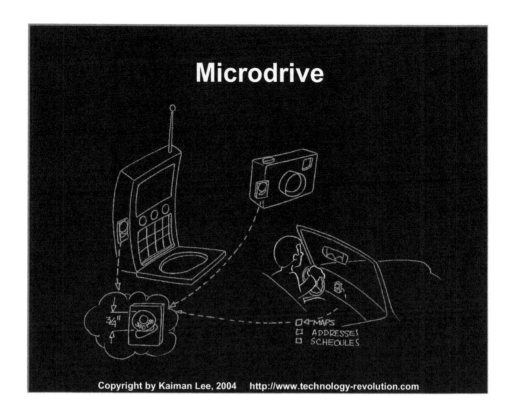

Storage is never a problem!

Look at a hard disk drive with a disk platter about as big as a large coin.

Unlike other portable storage options such as flash memory where data is stored as electric charge on transistors, and is not considered a permanent storage, this is a hard drive!

The "microdrive" weighs 0.56 ounce (16 grams), less than an AA battery, and measures 1.68 inches by 1.43 inches by 0.19 inches. It can hold up to 340 MB. It is intended for portable electronic devices, including digital cameras and handheld PCs. Less than two years later in mid-2000, IBM increased the Microdrive capacity to 1 GB.

The drive could be used in car-navigation systems to store maps and addresses.

All-in-one Handheld

The do-it-all digital <u>cellular phone is part computer, Web terminal, and phone</u>. You can peck <u>memos, e-mail messages, or faxes</u> from its tiny keyboard. Its <u>electronic organizer</u> can store many megabytes of information, including contacts and their phone numbers.

It can come with a subscriber identity <u>smart card</u>, that when placed in <u>another digital cellular phone</u> will take calls there. You can program it to allow it to place calls only to certain numbers.

Today the <u>pager</u> is more than a device that displays the phone number of callers. It relays <u>names and messages</u>. A paging system can be considered a <u>form of E-mail</u>.

Messages can be <u>dictated</u> to an electronic phone operator or sent as E-mail from most Internet-connected computers. Some carry <u>voice</u>. They have gone <u>two-way</u>. Before they could only receive. Now some can also <u>send numbers and words back</u>.

The missing piece is here. A <u>foldable</u>, <u>portable full-size keyboard</u> can <u>connect</u> to any hand-held device such as <u>two-way pagers and smart phones</u>.

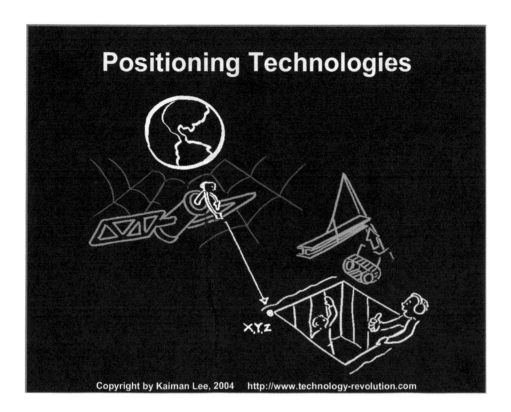

Positioning Technologies

Global Position System (GPS) is a technology revolution.

It will <u>impact everything</u> that requires <u>location identification</u>.
Examples are:
- identifying where you are on the <u>highway</u>,
- identifying where you are when you have gone astray in the <u>mountains</u>, and
- exploring and mapping the land and sea.

It can generate city-to-city routing instructions and provide audio updates on where you are heading with real-time GPS tracking. Its can also locate local restaurants, ATMs and hotels.

Federal Communications Commission has ruled that by <u>2001</u>, <u>all cellular phones</u> must be equipped with <u>GPS receivers</u>, or other location devices. That will enable police to locate the user of the phone if the police deem it necessary.

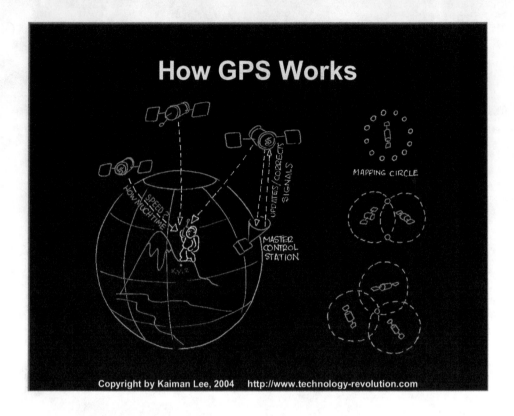

How GPS Works

The Global Positioning System (GPS) uses radio signals sent by 24 satellites to show the people carrying a GPS receiver where in the world they are and where they are going.

The satellite's radio signal is stamped with the time as it is sent. The GPS receiver measures how long it took for the signal to reach it and calculates the distance from the satellite. Ground stations can correct some of the errors in these calculations. Based on that measurement, the GPS receiver could be anywhere along a circle.

When the receiver gets a signal from another satellite, the possible locations of the receiver on the ground are narrowed down to the two points where the arcs intersect.

When the receiver locks onto a third satellite signal, it can determine its single location. But because most GPS receivers give a reading within 100 meters, additional satellite signals received will improve the accuracy of the reading.

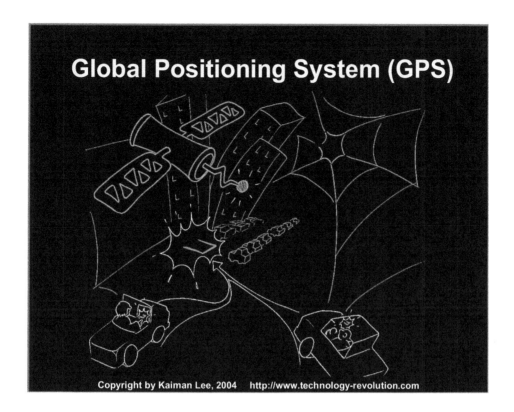

Global Positioning System (GPS)

Global Positioning Systems (GPS) will play a big role in the cyber world. There are 24 GPS satellites.

Using GPS to <u>find a parking space</u> in any parking lot in a major city, and to beat the others to it, may be a fad, or necessity.

A GPS device that is <u>embedded</u> in your <u>daughter's shoe</u> could signal the home server to tell you that she is at her <u>study</u> pal's place -- or, at least, <u>her shoes are there</u>.

Positioning technology using GPS and Geographic Information Systems (GIS) can be very useful to oil and utility companies, in fact any organization that requires positioning management.

A GPS device can be used to <u>track Alzheimer patients</u> with receivers embedded in their <u>clothing or shoes</u>.

When your <u>car's "check engine" light flashes</u>, you can be guided to the nearest, least busy service station.

In an emergency <u>fire trucks</u> can head for the problem as soon as they receive the call. Because they know from GPS where they are going, they have already downloaded information while <u>en route</u> about exactly where to <u>turn off the electricity and gas</u>.

The use of GPS is up to your imagination. It can be used as a trip calculator, compass, speedometer or scientific measuring device, etc.

Hand-held GPS devices used by backpackers could cost less than <u>$100</u>. Electronic parts needed for GPS will become as <u>cheap</u> as small solar-powered calculators are today. It is at that point that "<u>geo-coding</u>" -- <u>telling a computer exactly where an object or person is</u> -- will become commonplace.

<u>CNN</u>'s lower right corner of screen <u>shows a map with geo-coding</u> XYZ of the world where news is occurring which can be used for searching and finding location.

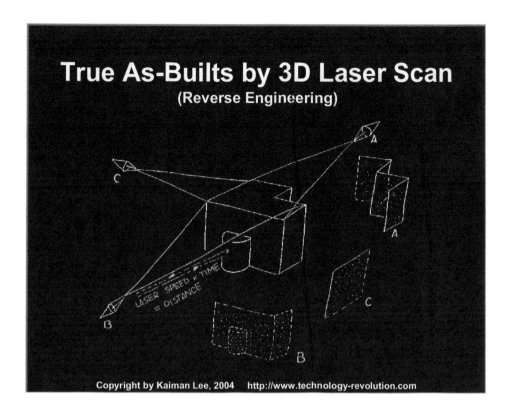

True As-Builts by 3D Laser Scan
(Reverse Engineering)

3D scanning is done by using a laser digitizer. It is based on triangulation: if light arrives on a surface from one direction, and if the light is seen from another direction, the location of a point can be inferred. Or, it measures the time taken by each laser pulse to travel from its source in the unit to an object's surface and back to the unit. The shape and size of odd-shaped objects can be captured.

The digitizing produces a fabric of points or 3D point clouds, a point map or a voxel map. A voxel is a 3D or volumetric pixel in space. It creates x,y,z coordinates of points on the surface of an object.

Adjacent scans taken from different scanner viewpoints can be "stitched" together to create 3D models of complex structures.

Post-interpretation is done by either replacing the point map with surfaces and shapes or replacing the voxel map with specific physical entities from a master catalog, such as valves, pipes, etc.

Once the 3D model is created in the computer, you can use "rapid prototyping" to re-construct it automatically.

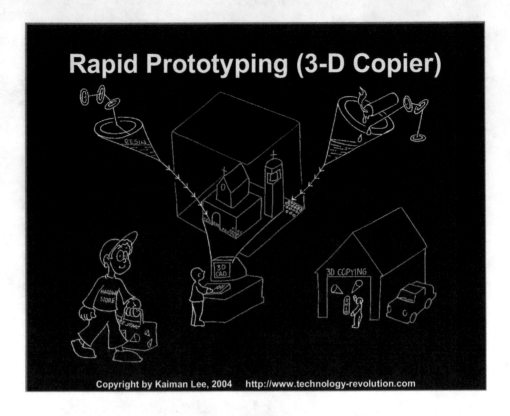

Rapid Prototyping (3-D Copier)

In layman's term, rapid prototyping (or <u>autofabrication</u> technology) <u>slices a 3-D solid model</u> into horizontal cross-sections down to <u>1/6000th</u> inch in thickness.

One method uses photopolymerization, a chemical process in which <u>liquid resin is converted to a solid polymer after exposure to ultraviolet (UV) radiation</u> or visible light. The solid part of a layer is <u>sprayed dot by dot</u> with resin and the <u>remainder</u> is sprayed with <u>wax</u>. Layers on top of layers, the resin will glue together forming the solid. When all the layers are sprayed, <u>melt away the wax</u>, and the object with even moving parts emerges!!

Another method uses <u>a platform that is lowered into a vat of photopolymer resin</u>. An ultraviolet laser traces the shape of the first layer on the surface of the photopolymer. The intrusion of the <u>laser hardens the liquid polymer</u>. The platform then <u>goes down an increment</u> and the <u>laser traces the next layer</u>. This continues until the model is complete.

When it is time to send an official request for a quotation, you can enclose an inexpensive <u>3-D "printed" model of the design</u>.

Think about a <u>hardware store in a briefcase</u>. Have a couple of 6-inch bolts <u>"autofabbed" right in your garage or basement</u>. What about an "autofabber" on board of an <u>aircraft carrier</u>?

298

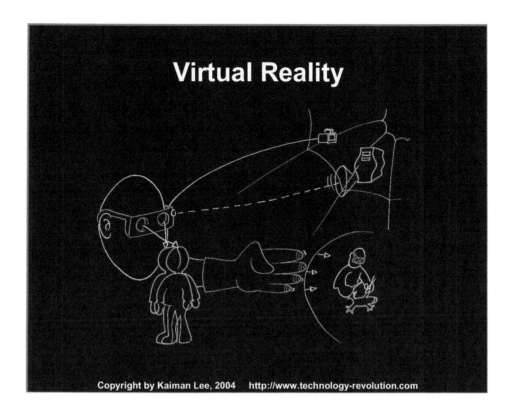

Virtual reality involves putting on a <u>head-mounted display with tracking sensors, data gloves</u> or other <u>sensing devices</u>. A pair of <u>glasses alternates between covering and showing a scene</u>. The flip over happens so fast that you can not see it. Each lens alternately shows you a slightly different perspective on a scene, so that you feel you are viewing it in <u>3D</u>.

When you move your head, your views shift and the <u>sound is adjusted</u>. You can <u>move around and through the objects</u> you see. You can also <u>pick things up, manipulate them</u> with the sensation of <u>feeling</u> the object in your hands.

Stanford University developed the "<u>virtual frog</u>." Students can view it from any angle, turn its skin transparent to see the internal organs and skeletons, and peel back the muscles for more anatomy.

Virtual Reality gives human freedom from <u>real limitations</u> -- <u>size, location, motion, weather, varying conditions, strength, and time</u>.

In a <u>remote surgery</u> situation, you put on a glove that is full of sensors and hooked up by wire or radio to another glove somewhere else. The <u>other glove then mimics your movements</u> exactly.

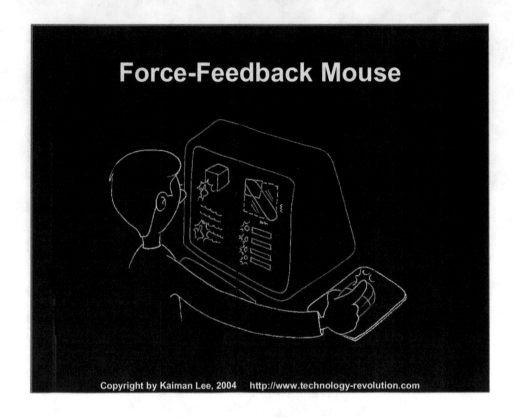

Force-Feedback Mouse

A force-feedback mouse applies <u>physical forces to your hand</u>.

As you move the mouse across Web pages, you can feel yourself <u>bump into the edges of an object</u>. You can <u>feel the</u> <u>texture</u> as you move across it. Resizing a desktop window feels like <u>stretching a</u> <u>rubber band</u>. As you move over menu items, you can feel the cursor move in <u>discrete clicks</u>.

Click on a <u>car engine</u> and you can feel the engine <u>shake</u> as it turns over. The <u>visually impaired</u> can <u>feel boxes and images</u> of the computer screen. You can call the new tools the <u>ultimate</u> <u>prosthetic</u>. And the uses by <u>game players and students</u> are obvious.

A force-feedback <u>fishing rod</u> uses motion sensors and reduction gears to give the feel of casting a line, getting a nibble, and hauling a big one onto the dock. Specialized controllers for <u>golf, tennis</u> <u>and baseball</u>, as well as a stand-on platform for <u>snowboarding or</u> <u>skateboarding</u>. The mouse slaps back in your hand when a <u>gun</u> <u>shot</u> is fired, or feel a machine-gun rapid-fire vibration.

E-Book

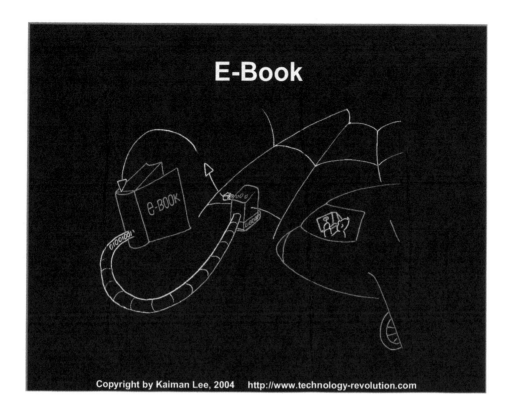

Instead of carrying a bunch of heavy books, you can carry the contents of a whole bookshelf in one slim e-book. When you want more, just use the wire in the book's spine or the infrared eye at an Internet kiosk.

A publisher grants an e-book retailer the right to make an electronic manuscript available in a protected format.

You can not give the electronic manuscripts you buy to anybody else, nor can you print them. The purpose of the box is to protect publishers. This might be the reason why e-books are using proprietary hardware running proprietary software.

You can annotate, highlight text, and do key word search. The portrait orientation of the screen shows a whole page.

E-books can let you access a single chapter or even a single page. The ability to provide regular updates will enable an ongoing relationship with the reader. An author could make more money selling e-books for $5 than a paper book for $30.

Ultimately, e-book as a separate device will give way to other existing devices, e.g., PC, laptop, cell phone, PDA, etc.

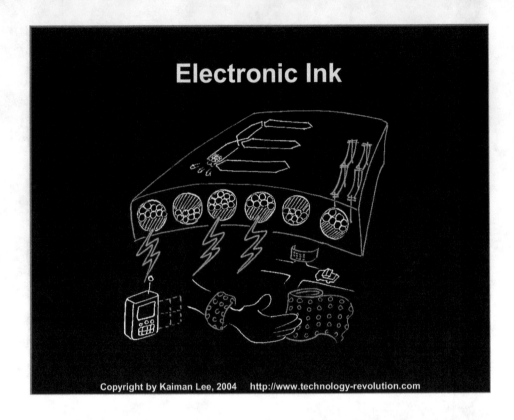

Electronic Ink

Electronic ink consists of a <u>fluid</u> with <u>microscopic spheres</u> suspended in it, about 100,000 spheres per square inch. Each sphere contains a <u>dark-colored liquid dye</u> <u>with light-colored pigment chips</u> in it. When the <u>pigment chips settle on the bottom</u> of the spheres, only the dye is visible, and the ink appears <u>dark</u>. An <u>electric charge</u> brings the <u>pigment chip to the upper surface</u> of each sphere, making the sphere appear that color. By controlling which spheres get the charge, you can make high-resolution images.

Imagine millions of these sphere sandwiched between <u>two clear, flexible pieces of film</u>. Each micro capsule contains a dark fluid and hundreds of white paint chips. A grid of electrical circuits printed onto the back of the display controls the movements of the chips, attracting or repelling them. Where the electricity <u>repels</u> them and pushes them to the <u>front</u> of the display, it looks white. Where it <u>attracts</u> them toward the <u>back</u> of the display, you see the <u>dark</u> fluid instead.

And once a pattern forms, it <u>persists indefinitely</u>, without any need for additional power. Applications are such as <u>freeway signs, wallpaper, electronic books, and a wristband</u>. What about <u>newspaper with paper-like pages</u>? A very good use might be a <u>large folded screen for a personal digital assistant (PDA)</u>.

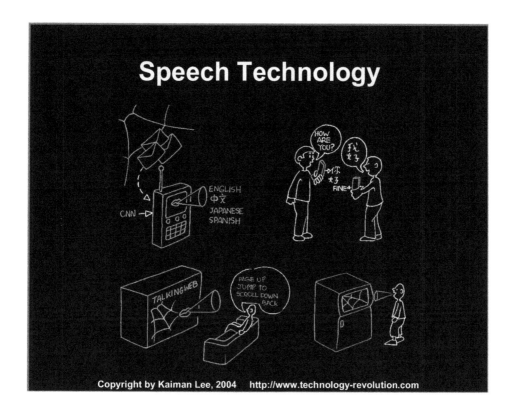

Speech Technology

Reading e-mail out loud in any language to the mobile user, and making a transcript of a meeting are not big deals anymore.

Text-to-speech technology in a talking Web browser gives blind and visually impaired computer users access to the Internet. It navigates users by reading aloud the information on a Web site. A male voice reads text and a female voice reads links. It can speak the information in forms and tables, and describe graphics. Functions such as fast-forward, bookmarks, and integrated e-mail are included. You can tell the computer to "jump" to a site, "page up," "scroll down," or "back."

The use of translation, speech recognition and speech synthesis technologies would allow an American and a Chinese to hear a real-time translation via their mobile phones. The impact of machine-based language translation for regular phones, video phones and for videoconferences, etc. could be enormous.

Using speech technology now can be a competitive business advantage. Instead of using a phone keypad, your customer can read in an account number, or use phrases such as "I want to fly from Boston to San Francisco tomorrow." Natural language processing rather than "directed speech," or carefully articulated single words will switch a caller to the appliance department when a caller says "I want to get a price on a refrigerator."

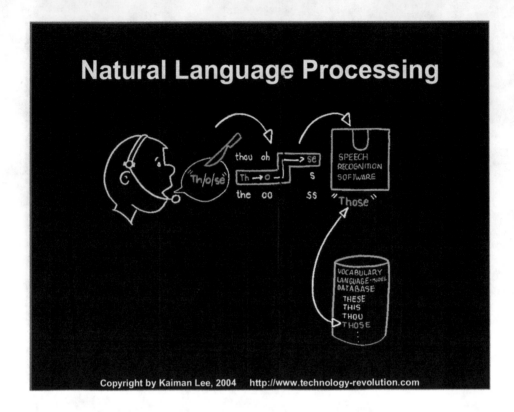

Extremely large databases are used to turn spoken input into commands or words on-screen. They are tremendously complex pieces of software that work by <u>disassembling spoken input</u> into <u>component sounds</u> and then <u>piecing these sounds together to form words</u>.

The process goes as follows:

First, as the user speaks into the microphone, the speech-recognition software continuously <u>breaks down</u> the flow of sounds into foundational units called <u>phonemes</u> -- pronounced "foe-neem."

Second, with the phonemes, the software does a hypothesis <u>search</u> of the database of <u>phonetic word spellings, seeking possible interpretations</u>.

Third, the speech-recognition software then <u>compares</u> the possible phonetic interpretations to its <u>vocabulary- and language-model databases</u>, using techniques such as context and incidence to <u>select the correct word</u>.

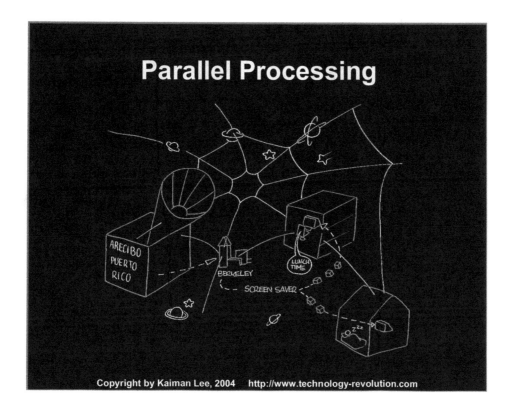

Parallel Processing

Parallel processing is defined as lots of processors -- either in one computer or inside several linked machines -- gang up to work on a single problem at one time. It works by assigning <u>rule-based operations to each processor and orchestrating its actions to the whole</u>.

A simple example of <u>Internet-based parallel processing</u> comes from the Search for Extra-Terrestrial Intelligence (SETI) Institute in Mountain View, CA. The SETI@home project makes use <u>of volunteer computers (2 million in mid-2000) to analyze radio signals</u> collected by the Arecibo radio telescope in Puerto Rico. These signals from space <u>might indicate alien life</u>.

<u>During idle time, a volunteer's screen saver downloads a chunk of data and works on it</u>. It then uploads the results and downloads a new piece.

SETI data is perfect for this type of background computation, because there <u>is no rush</u>. What about other data collected by satellites -- <u>waves, temperatures, animal migrations</u>?

If your objective is to <u>use all your processing power</u> as opposed to letting it sit idle, why not let your computer go to <u>work on what you are likely to ask it next</u>, e.g., hyperlinks that are most likely to be hit.

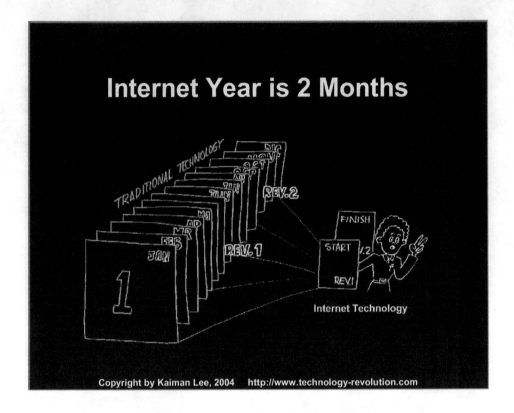

Internet Year is 2 Months

While <u>traditional software upgrades</u> at best have had <u>two revisions per year</u>, <u>Internet applications</u> are being <u>upgraded every month if not continuously</u>, faster than users could absorb them.

Internet applications and upgrades are <u>not shrink-wrapped anymore</u>. Their <u>distribution</u> over the net incurs <u>almost no marginal cost</u>.

The Web has <u>compressed</u> the time for <u>product cycles, distribution channels and vendor/customer interaction</u>.

Other <u>metaphors</u> in Silicon Valley:
- Living on <u>Internet time (at warp speed)</u>,
- Progress is measured in <u>Web weeks</u>,
- <u>Stop for lunch and you are lunch</u>.

Internet time has removed the border <u>between home and work life</u>. The compression of time has made some people rethink the meaning of life, and move back to basics.

To extend the two-month metaphor further, some equate the Internet year to <u>dog years (seven to one), to hamster years (26 to one), or even mosquito years (462 to one)</u>.

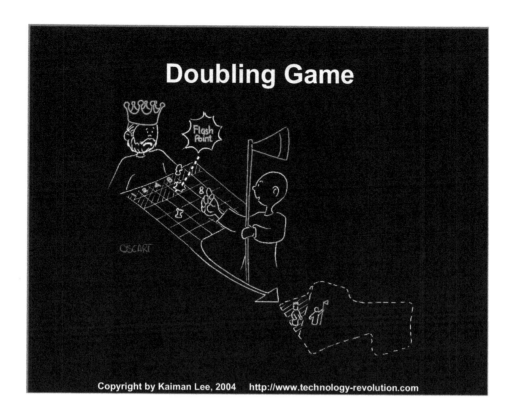

Doubling Game

Recall the <u>Chinese</u> fable of the mighty <u>emperor</u> who agreed to give a commoner <u>one grain of rice</u> for the first square on a chess board, <u>double that for the second square</u>, double again for the third and so on. He gave away almost his whole kingdom's supply before the board was <u>half finished</u>.

Doubling games are <u>boring</u> for the <u>first quarter</u> of the board. Then all of a sudden, you get very big numbers.

The <u>Internet</u> itself has been around for more than a <u>quarter of a century</u>, quietly <u>doubling in size each year while few people had been looking</u>. In <u>1994</u>, it suddenly <u>burst into view</u>.

In <u>electronic commerce</u>, <u>too</u>, many of the trends have been gathering force for years, but are only now becoming obvious as they are harnessed to the <u>breathless runaway growth</u> and global reach of the Internet.

The <u>Information Superhighway is one of those rare technologies that are actually far more powerful and promising than the hype surrounding them</u>.

Internet's Growth

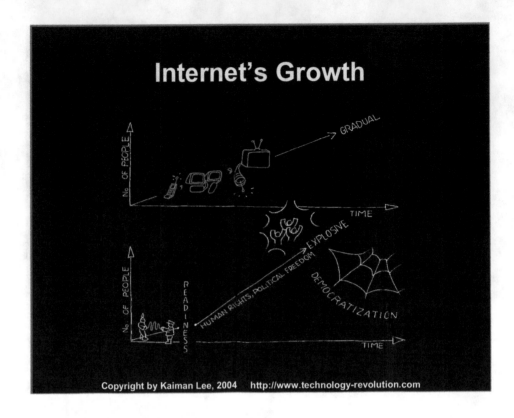

Internet's growth is <u>not gradual</u>, it <u>is a phase change</u>. The traditional <u>gradual growth</u> are in products such as <u>cell phones, PCs and cable TV</u>.

When a country crosses the <u>threshold of readiness</u>, demand from its citizens <u>explodes in a hurry</u>. <u>Below</u> that threshold, trying to introduce the Internet is like <u>pushing string</u>.

Dictators will not be convinced of the Internet's tremendous potential for human development. That idea is contrary to dictatorship. <u>Internet is the most democratizing medium</u>.

<u>Governments can not really trace or control the telephone system or the Internet</u>. <u>Low earth orbit satellites</u> can give you direct phone service and Internet access.

Massive Internet adoption will require a massive increase in <u>political freedom including human rights</u>. What a democratic country has more of than a dictator county is not necessarily infrastructure, or money, but the <u>right of the citizens to get information from anywhere</u>.

Among nations of relatively equal development, it will be the <u>freer nations and not the richer ones that adopt the Internet fastest</u>.

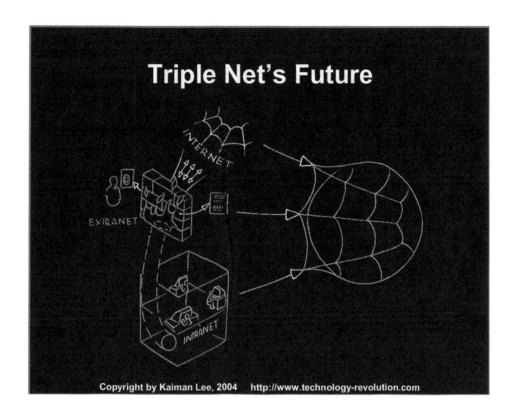

Triple Net's Future

Internet, Intranet and Extranet will disappear into just <u>one big communications network</u>, with <u>different groups having access to different parts</u> of it. The <u>distinction between Internet, Intranet and Extranet will blur</u> as network carriers increasingly offer secure and reliable connections over the native Internet.

<u>Intranet-based applications</u> will increasingly <u>merge</u> with <u>Internet-based business-to-business transactions</u>. Intranets will become the local area network you always wanted. They will be the answer to all those promises Novell Inc. and Microsoft Corp. made during the mid-1980s and early 1990s.

However, creating an Intranet and <u>Extranet</u> that is "information and procedure-friendly" is <u>no small task</u> -- especially when the <u>customers</u> who access the Extranet <u>keep changing</u>, as they are likely to do over time.

It is <u>not</u> just a matter of <u>adding layers over existing systems</u>. For some companies, it means <u>rethinking all of the systems</u> in terms of facilitating information flow and ruthlessly replacing any part that impedes this.

Companies must make a mind shift from an "<u>island</u>" perspective to dealing with the <u>world</u> at large.

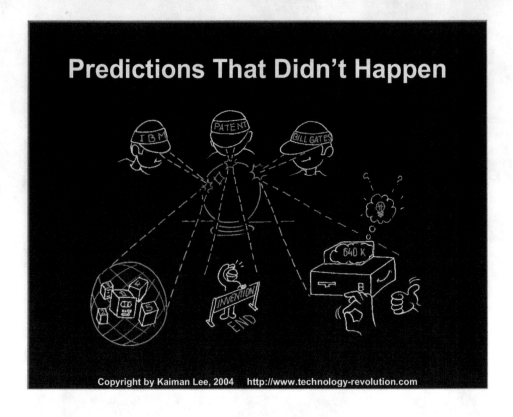

Predictions That Didn't Happen

Copyright by Kaiman Lee, 2004   http://www.technology-revolution.com

"640K ought to be enough for anybody."
-- Bill Gates, 1981

"Everything that can be invented has been invented."
-- Charles H. Duell, Commissioner, U.S. Office of Patents, 1899.

"I think there is a world market for maybe 5 computers."
-- Thomas Watson, Chairman of IBM, 1943

"Computers in the future may weigh no more than 1.5 tons."
-- Popular Mechanics, forecasting the relentless march of science,
1949 (It is true in the literal sense!)

"There is no reason anyone would want a computer in their home."
-- Ken Olson, president, chairman, and founder of Digital
Equipment Corp., 1977

Don't make linear predictions that anyone can see, e.g., the
demise of music stores and video rental businesses. Make
discontinuous predictions. Ask how different the future needs to
be from today before it disrupts your business model and requires
you to move aggressively. Then make a judgment call about how
likely that future state will be.

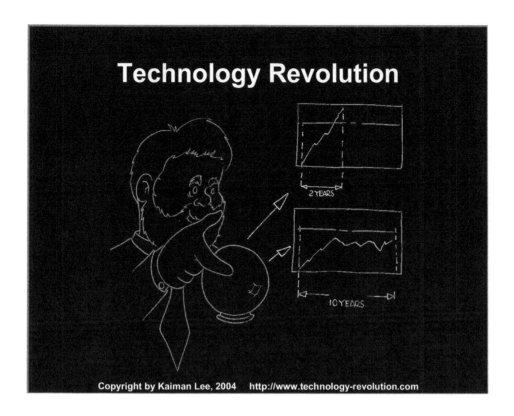

Technology Revolution

2 YEARS

10 YEARS

Copyright by Kaiman Lee, 2004   http://www.technology-revolution.com

"A <u>new paradigm</u> is emerging that will transform the industry and the economy just as sharply as the Moore's Law Paradigm did, when it wreaked a plunge of <u>mainframe</u> market share <u>from 100% to below 1%</u> between 1977 and 1987."
--- George Gilder, Editor, Gilder Technology Report, December 1997

What George Gilder is talking about is <u>Telecosm</u> where <u>unlimited bandwidth</u> will become available.

<u>Connecting</u> to everywhere and everybody will be just like <u>a telephone call away</u>.

Here is an aphorism from Bill Gates, *"People often <u>overestimate</u> what will happen in the next <u>two years</u> and <u>underestimate</u> what will happen in <u>10</u>."*

Innovations are happening everyday and they are accelerating. One day you read about a <u>vertical keyboard</u>, next day a <u>smart pen</u>.

However, you must learn to be able to discern what is important and what is not.

Disruptive Technologies

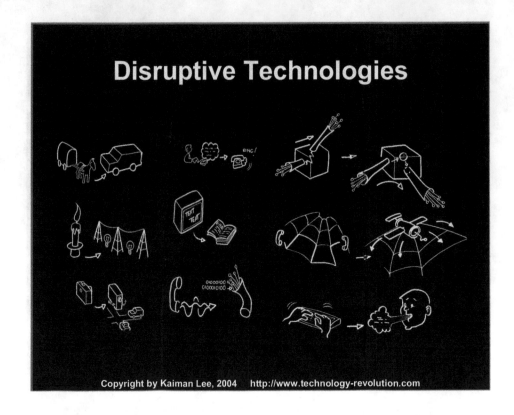

Examples of disruptive or pivotal technologies are cars, electricity and telephones. They were large enough in scope and promise to have the capacity to redefine an entire industry. They changed the pace and fabric of life for a country and later the world. The sense of possibility they engendered seized the imagination of the markets.

Although the price/performance improvements in microprocessors, disk drives, semiconductor memory and network connections continue to race along exponential growth curves, they are no longer disruptive technologies. However, putting certain components of them together could yield an impact so great as if they were multiplied, not added.

Ascending disruptive technologies are such as Voice over Internet Protocol (VoIP), all optical Internet, satellite wireless, natural speech recognition, Webcam, electronic ink, etc. If you wait until a disruptive technology matches the quality of the preceding technology to act, e.g., digital camera, it is often too late to take advantage of it as a competitive advantage.

Since it is much easier to put together an Internet company than set up a car factory or computer manufacturing plant, the end of new companies could come all the faster, evidenced in dot.coms.

Fubini's Law

People initially <u>use technology to do what they are already doing --
but faster</u>. They then gradually begin to use technology to <u>do new
things, in new ways</u>. That is Fubini's Law.

These new things <u>change life-styles and work-practices</u>. The new
life-styles and work-styles <u>change society</u>, and eventually <u>change
technology</u>.

Let us use TV as an illustration. In the initial stages of <u>TV</u>, quiz
shows that were done in <u>radio</u> were done on TV. In the later
stages, different uses such as <u>video games</u> were discovered.

Likewise, <u>Virtual Reality</u> (VR) may eventually be used to do things
only made possible through the "new" technology.

And it is not difficult to imagine that VR will change life-styles,
work-styles, and society in general.

Another example of Fubini's Law is <u>automation</u>. People used computers and robots to automate the mass production process, cranking them out at ever faster pace.

With affordable <u>automobiles</u>, a lot of people moved from the cities to the <u>suburbs</u>. With the <u>Web</u>, you could connect with anybody, at anytime, and from anywhere. Now you could <u>telecommute</u> and work from home.

With airplanes, you could take a round trip between San Francisco and New York City in the same day if you want to. You could be <u>working</u> on the airplane as if you were in your office by using a <u>laptop</u> computer.

These technologies are changing our life-styles and work practices.

With all the information and connections at your finger tips, will you be <u>less mobile and social</u>? There is almost nothing in your life that could not be found out by others. But you want your privacy. <u>Privacy</u> may well be the <u>key social element that will change technology</u>.

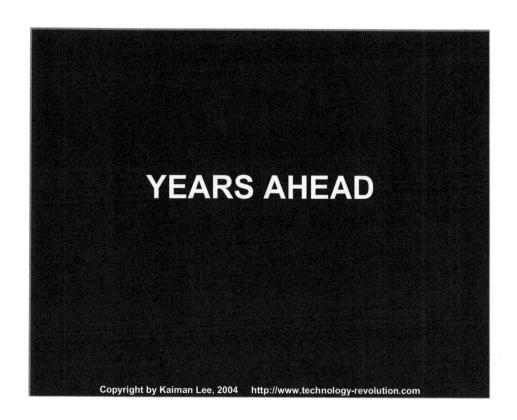

YEARS AHEAD

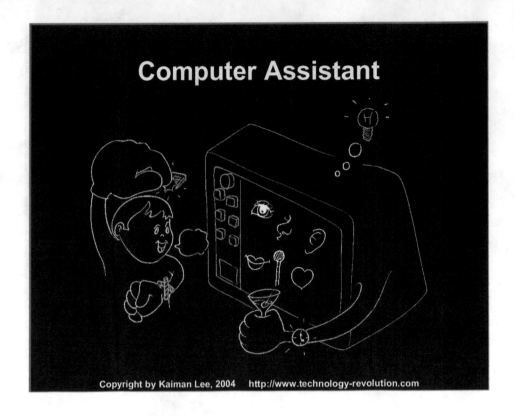

Computer Assistant

The computer of the future will be more human, driven by softer software. It will be more intelligent because it will learn and adapt. Bill Gates predicted in the CA-World 1998 technology conference, "10 years from now every personal computer will have seeing, listening and learning capabilities." The computer will be simpler to use because it will communicate using all media. It will be as mundane as a telephone but just as obvious to use.

The one-desk-one-general-purpose-computer model is on its way out. Computers will be ubiquitous. We will always be surrounded by "information wilderness."

The computer will be a human assistant with common sense, not just a tool. It will do not only what you say, but what you want.

The computer can perceive because it will see, talk, feel the temperature, be ware of your presence, and recognize your gestures. These are "human interfaces," not just graphical user interfaces (GUI). It will know what you are looking for.

We all need others. We all want some belonging. We all would like to have companionship. We can have a computer that could give us those feelings. Can we make the computer accountable?!

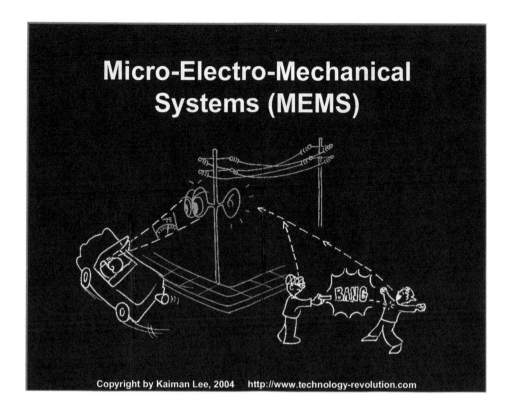

Micro-Electro-Mechanical Systems (MEMS)

Copyright by Kaiman Lee, 2004   http://www.technology-revolution.com

Today, people and computers inhabit parallel universes: people live in a sensory-rich, physical, analog world; computers live in a deaf, dumb and blind digital world. Soon, cheap sensors, e.g., eyes, ears, and sensory organs will give computers and networks an awareness of the analog world around them.

They are called micro-electro-mechanical systems (MEMS). They allow you to create analog sensors spanning from video sensors, motors and gears, to accelerometers and pressure-temperature sensors.

They can recognize light, sound and motion. They work in concert with microchips, e.g., sensor in an airbag, blood-pressure kit and carbon-monoxide detector for use at home.

Utility poles can be equipped with sensors that can "hear" gunfire and pinpoint locations; they may even recognize specific voices.

MEMS will allow networks to collect all kinds of information. Imagine the fryer at a burger shop has sensors that monitor how well the French (freedom) fries are being cooked and report back to a central server dedicated to quality assurance.

Electronic Post-it notes, electronic paper clips, and a computer in every piece of paper are possible in the next 20 years.

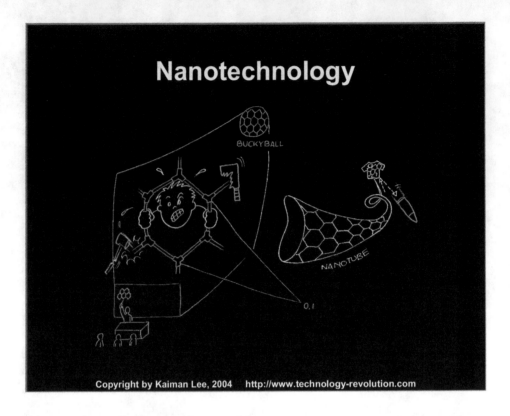

Nanotechnology

When carbon, as in soot, is vaporized in an inert gas such as helium and allowed to cool slowly, it spontaneously forms a buckyball, formally named buckminsterfullerenes for the late American architect and geodesic dome expert Buckminster Fuller. The buckyball carbon molecule is shaped like a soccer ball, and consists of 60 hexagonal carbon atoms arranged in a symmetric pattern.

Buckyballs are chemically inert, much stronger than steel, highly efficient at emitting electrons, and in some cases electrically and thermally conductive.

Nanotubes (also called buckytubes) are made by adding millions of extra sets of carbon atoms to the middle of the soccer-ball molecule so that it stretches out to form a tubular fiber. Nanotubes are thin, elongated versions of buckyballs.

Nanotubes grow at less than 650 degrees C (1,202 F). This makes it possible to grow them on glass, which melts at higher temperatures. Nanotubes can grow on a thickness of about a millimeter (0.04 inch).

Nanotechnology will have a wide variety of applications: any size flat screens, teeth as hard as diamonds, bullet-proof clothes that also heat and cool.

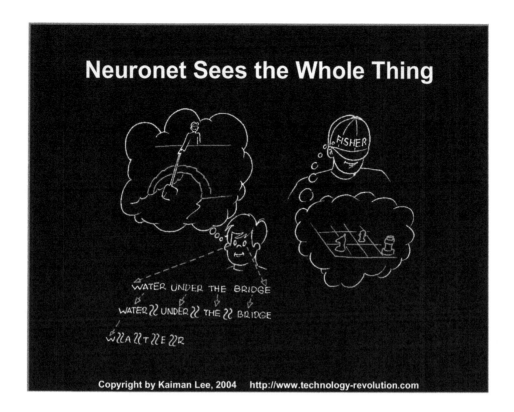

Neuronet Sees the Whole Thing

WATER UNDER THE BRIDGE

Copyright by Kaiman Lee, 2004   http://www.technology-revolution.com

Neural network (Neuronet) software learns by observing patterns in the real world and learning to do different tasks in response to different patterns. It allows computers to work in three dimensions, as the human brain does, instead of a single line.

A chess expert sees the board as a unit, not the pieces. Neuronet also sees patterns in human tasks. It sees a purpose and a direction -- in the same way that we learn to recognize a whole printed word rather than having to spell it out.

Neuronet uses cognitive processing to solve problems, which means it can understand ordinary phrases, engage in a dialogue to arrive at a solution and remember what transpired.

You type in a phrase like "My computer freezes up a lot," or "My modem disconnects too often," or "How do I split screen?" Neuronet will come up with answers to fix the problem.

Neuronet can be most valuable in situations where tasks are continually redefined, e.g., it can use pattern-oriented monitoring of news and advertising media to assess your company's business environment; by tracking the moves of Web site visitors, neuronet can determine which ads are most relevant to individual surfers, thus boosting the likelihood that the ads will get visitors to respond.

In human relationships and endeavors, the <u>answer to a question</u> or <u>solution to a problem</u> is often <u>not yes or no, but maybe</u>; <u>not good or bad, but okay</u>; <u>not hot or cold, but temperate</u>.

Where math and science have "hard lines" describing what is and is not true, fuzzy logic is "reasoning with vague concepts." Instead of the black and white truths that we associate with traditional logic, our concepts are fuzzy and our reasoning is <u>approximate</u>.

Essentially, fuzzy logic is a method of imposing scientific theory on the organic way we think. It is adding <u>subjective thought</u> to the process of recognizing fact then arriving at a final answer based on that fact.

<u>Fuzzy sets</u> and <u>fuzzy logic</u> reject the binary notion that the world is entirely discrete. They operate on a <u>continuum of values</u>. As a result, fuzzy logic will enable <u>computers to think more like people</u> do and to create real-world simulations. A fuzzy system acts like a human expert who has a lot of if-then rules of thumb in his head.

Fuzzy logic already allows camcorders to more accurately focus lenses and cars to more efficiently shift gears.

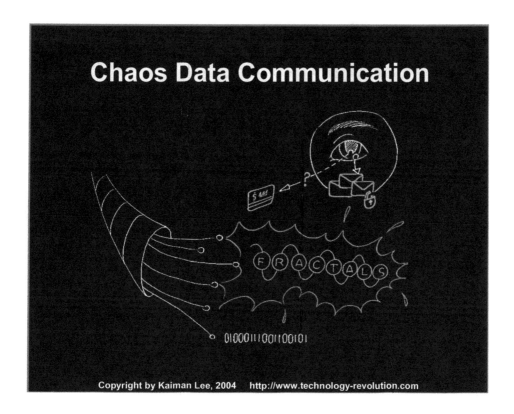

Chaos theory, also known as the study of fractals, is being used to develop communications and computing protocols. Chaos theory emerged as a way to mathematically study the infinitely complex systems of the natural world. Where chaos begins, classical science stops. The theory grew out of MIT computer science Professor Ed Lorenz's discovery in the 1960s of equations with solutions that appear to be random. The mathematical techniques are applicable to simple systems that appear to be complex.

Georgia Tech's Professor Rajarshi Roy is trying to apply chaos theory to practical applications. He claimed that Chaos communication could be much faster than binary means, and the use of irregular wave forms might prevent prying eyes from discerning the contents of a transmission.

He uses a laser to generate chaotic waveforms -- signals that are highly irregular and never repeated. The waves are sent over optical fiber lines. You do not know whether any information is being transmitted when you look at the chaotic waveform, so it could offer enhanced privacy. This could provide a secure way of sending credit card information over the Internet.

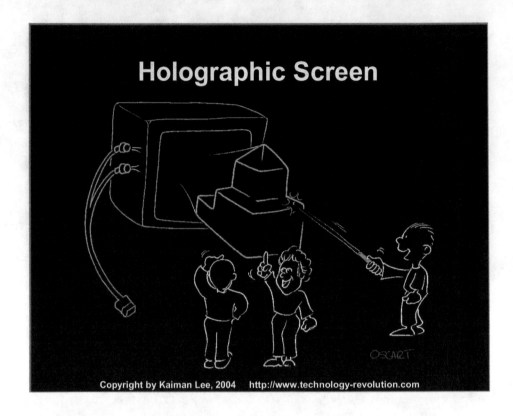

In the distant future, a computer may create its own <u>display screen out of thin air</u>.

Using <u>holograph</u> techniques, or <u>light-projection</u> systems, the computer will be able to project the display in the air in front of the users.

Users can then <u>walk around</u> the holograph, and use a <u>laser pointer</u> to point at features during a collaborative work session.

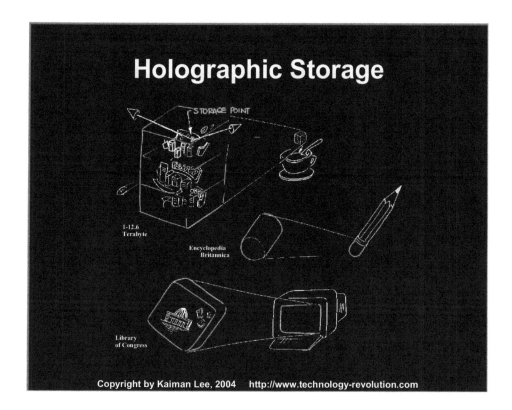

Imagine the Encyclopedia Britannica fitting into a space the size of a pencil eraser. And data could be transported in and out of the crystals at a rate of 1 billion bits per second.

Holographic storage could contain 12.6 terabytes in a space the size of a sugar cube, equivalent to 3 football fields of filing cabinets.

The entire Library of Congress could eventually fit onto a 3-D holographic memory system the size of a PC's monitor.

Mind boggling!

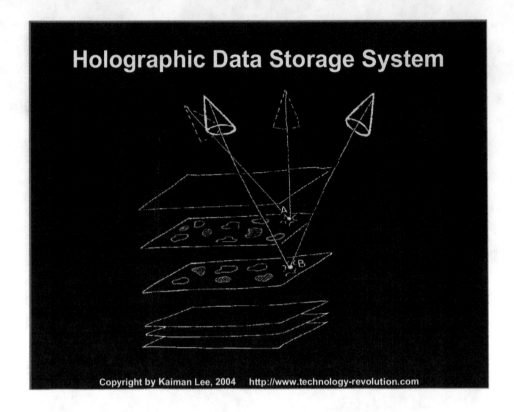

Holographic Data Storage System

Holographic data storage system (HDSS) uses lasers and other electro-optic components to create two-dimensional patterns called "pages," of light and dark regions representing digital bits.

These are recorded in light-sensitive crystals as holograms. Thousands of pages representing billions of bits can be stored in the crystal. The bits are stored and accessed with 2 or more lasers pointed at the storage point in 3-D.

Each page can be recovered by illuminating the crystal with the unique reference beam that was used to record that page.

You may assume that computer storage will not be an issue. Relatively infinite storage will be available using holograms.

What is the thickness or diameter of a laser or light element? Almost nothing. So, how many layers and dots can be incorporated in a 3.5" disk with 1/4" liquid crystal on it?

324

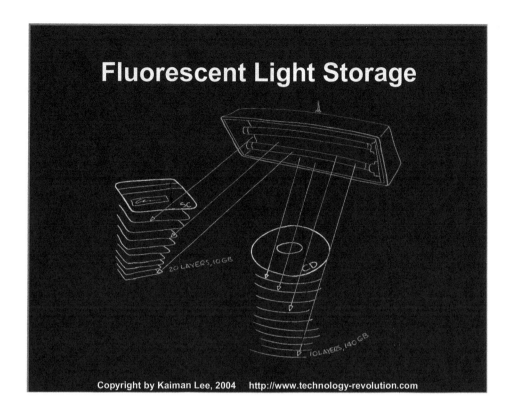

Through <u>fluorescent multi-layering</u>, data is stored on numerous layers on the devices. It will allow an increase of data storage capacity by up to <u>2500 times</u> that of current systems, e.g., <u>10GB</u> of data on <u>credit card-sized disks</u> (<u>currently 4MB</u> capacity).

Using <u>fluorescent light</u> rather than the reflective optical devices currently employed, the technology allows data to be stored on <u>multiple layers</u> of smart cards or disks. Currently, data is stored on only <u>one layer on smart cards and CD-ROMs</u> (650MB), or <u>two layers on DVDs</u> (17.5GB).

A vendor has demonstrated an <u>FMD (Fluorescent Multilayer Disk)</u> that plays <u>music</u> with the <u>quality</u> of a traditional <u>CD</u>.

<u>Pilot productions</u> will be for a <u>10-layer FMD-ROM disk</u> (in the standard 120mm disk format) which will store up to <u>140GB</u>, and a <u>20-layer smart card</u> with <u>10GB</u> capacity.

<u>Future</u> cards and disks will have capacities exceeding one <u>terabyte</u>, or 1,000GB. Existing CDs and DVDs and drive equipment can be adapted to accommodate the new technology. The expanded memory capacity would enable people to store up to <u>20 hours of high definition television-quality video on one small card or disk</u>.

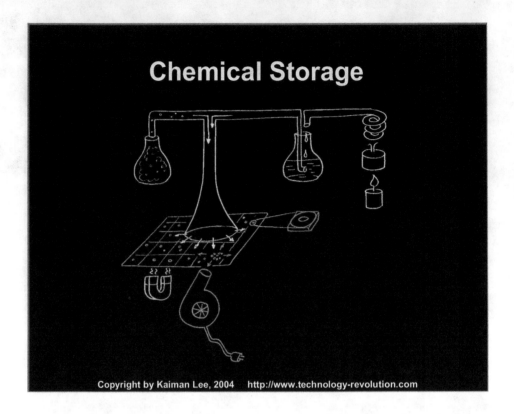

Chemical Storage

IBM scientists have discovered that a <u>chemical reaction</u> could cause tiny <u>magnetic materials</u> to automatically arrange themselves into <u>well-ordered arrays</u>. They put molecules containing iron and platinum into a heated solution. The molecules reacted with each other, forming into iron-platinum nanoparticles that are coated in a substance similar to olive oil.

The <u>nanoparticles</u> were put on a surface and allowed to <u>dry</u>, which caused them to <u>spread out in even rows automatically</u>. The particles were then heated in an oven for a half hour. The heat fixed the particles in place, <u>coated them with carbon</u> and made them <u>magnetic</u> which could possibly <u>hold data</u>.

The nanoparticles are about <u>half</u> the average <u>size</u> of the <u>grains</u> IBM used to store its record density of <u>35.3 billion bits per square inch</u> in 1999. They are also <u>10 times more uniform</u> in size. The smaller size allows smaller data bits, and uniform particle size permits smaller data bits to be detected easily and accurately.

Eventually, IBM hopes the technology will allow one data bit to be stored on one grain of magnetic material, instead of the 1,000 grains needed today. This will allow for <u>100 times</u> more <u>data</u> than current products.

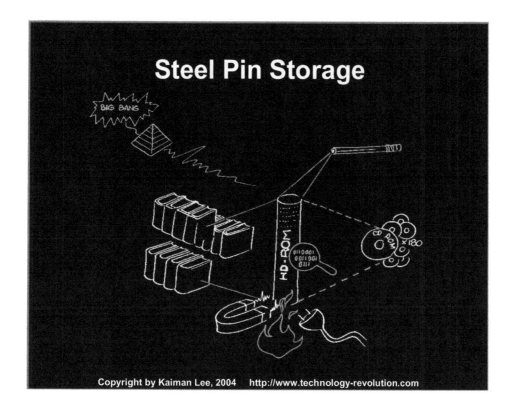

Steel Pin Storage

The new non-magnetic, high-density read only memory (HD-ROM) developed at Los Alamos National Laboratory can store the equivalent of four sets of encyclopedias on the surface of an inch-long steel pin that is about as thick as a pencil lead. That is about 180 times the storage capacity of today's CD-ROMs. It stores about 23 GB (gigabyte)of data per square inch.

The data is written using a focused ion beam micromill operating in an ultra-high vacuum. Current writing speed is about 1 GB per day.

Data can also be written as three dimensional graphical images, alphanumeric characters or binary formats. These different formats all can co-exist on the same HD-ROM to form a computer Rosetta stone. So, even if the binary codes of the American Standard Code for Information Interchange (ASCII) are lost during ensuing centuries, the data still may be read with magnifying equipment.

Data can be written on such enduring materials as steel or iridium that will last thousands of years despite fires, floods, and electromagnetic bursts that would destroy magnetic and holographic media. The only danger is abrasion and corrosion of the metal.

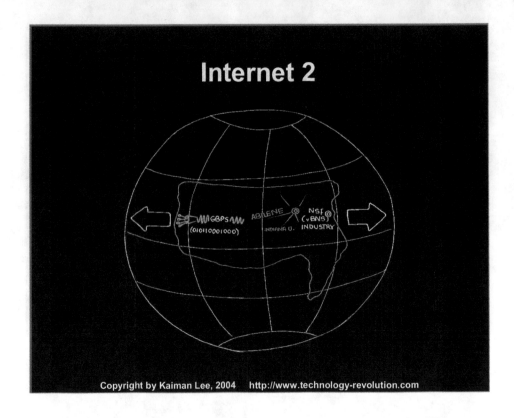

Internet 2

Internet2 (I2 in short) which began in 1996 was officially launched on Feb 24, 1999. I2 is supported by over 150 U.S. universities, nonprofit research centers, government agencies and industry corporations. In October 1997 they formed a consortium called the University Corporation for Advanced Internet Development (UCAID).

I2 will connect the university campuses with Abilene, which is made up of over 16,000 miles of donated fiber networks. It will operate at 2.4 Gigabits per second by 2000, eventually at 10 GBPS. Abilene links these networks via GigaPoPs (gigabit-capacity points of presence). Abilene's network operations center is at Indiana University.

I2 makes use of vBNS (very-high-performance Backbone Network Service), a project of the National Science Foundation and MCI Telecommunications, and a closed nationwide network available only to about 92 academic and research communities. It runs at 622 MBPS, towards 2.400 GBPS by 2000.

I2 will change IP addressing from 32 bits to 128 bits that allows for exponentially more IP addresses.

I2 is focused upon the needs of academia first, but is expected to eventually make their way into the rest of society.

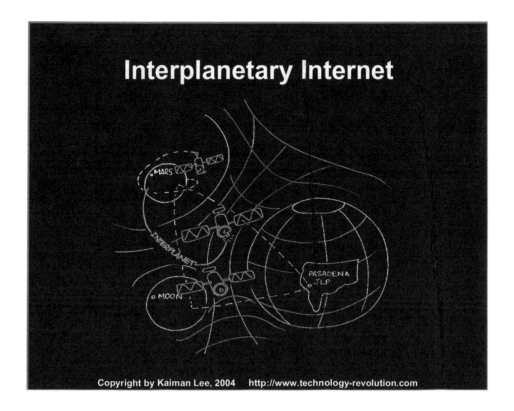

Interplanetary Internet

NASA's Jet Propulsion Lab (JPL) in Pasadena, California is working on "Interplanetary Internet." It will establish gateways in outer space to help send and receive data to and from the planets and their satellites. Included in this vision are mobile vehicles that operate between the planets, and satellites.

The Interplanetary Internet networks will look like the ones we use on earth today. There will be a series of interplanetary gateways for bouncing communications between planets without first sending them back to earth. The Interplanetary Internet (InterPlaNet, or Interplanet as commonly called) protocol will be used for transmitting data between them. Each planet will have a network similar to the earth Internet of today.

Interplanet manages the long transmission delays and intermittent data links that plague deep-space communications. A standard communication to Pluto could take 6 hours.

With domain names such as ".Earth" or ".Mars" it will be possible to send scientific data from a space mission orbiting another planet such as Mars via Interplanet.

A satellite device will be left on Mars first, which will act as one of these Internet gateways. It is expected that by 2020-2040 the Interplanet will become a reality.

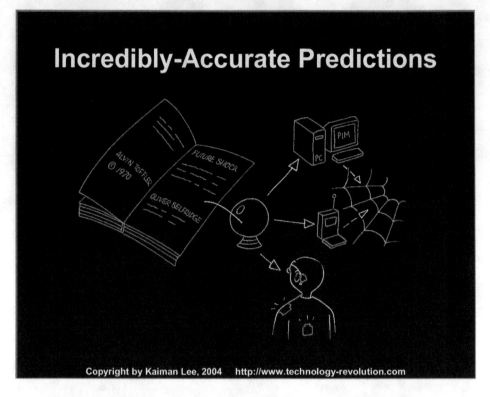

Incredibly-Accurate Predictions

In 1970, Alvin Toffler in his book "Future Shock," wrote the following text about OLIVER (On-Line Interactive Vicarious Expeditor and Responder, to honor Oliver Selfridge, originator of the concept).

All the predictions have occurred, or are now being realized. Do not underestimate predictions!

"In its simplest form, OLIVER would merely be a personal computer programmed to provide the individual with information and to make minor decisions for him. At this level, it could store information about his friends' preferences for Manhattans or martinis, data about traffic routes, the weather, stock prices, etc. The device could be set to remind him of his wife's birthday -- or to order flowers automatically. It could renew his magazine subscriptions, pay the rent on time, order razor blade and the like.

As computerized information systems ramify, moreover, it would tap into a worldwide pool of data stored in libraries, corporate files, hospitals, retails stores, banks, government agencies and universities. OLIVER would thus become a kind of universal question-answerer for him.

However, some computer scientists see much beyond this. It is theoretically possible to construct an OLIVER that would analyze the content of its owner's words, scrutinize his choices, deduce his value system, update its own program to reflect changes in his values, and ultimately handle larger and larger decisions for him.

Thus OLIVER would know how its owner would, in all likelihood, react to various suggestions made at a committee meeting. (meetings could take place among groups of OLIVERs representing their respective owners, without the owners themselves being present. ..."

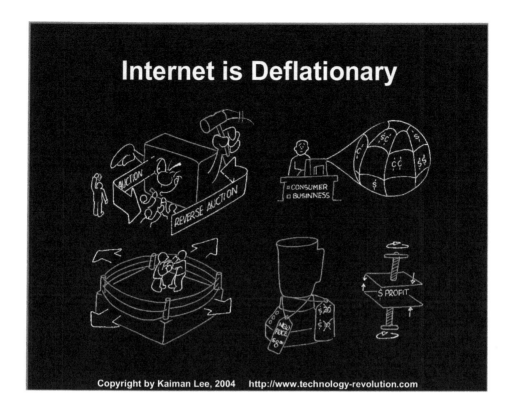

Internet is Deflationary

Internet has a tremendous deflationary implication. It could significantly reduce the costs of doing business, increase competition, and lower prices and squeeze profits.

Internet creates a near textbook model of perfect competition, with buyers easily gaining access to information on the pricing and other characteristics of competing products. For example, when you are ready to buy a book online, a subversive software asks you if you are sure, and presents to you better deals offered by others. This forces retailers to cut their profit margin.

In January 1999, Orange County, California, launched a Web-based purchasing system that requires companies to sell basic commodities to the county online. The lowest bid from anywhere usually makes the sale.

Internet could turn suppliers into "price takers," a situation in which every supplier must sell at almost the same price.

The book business vividly illustrates what happens to pricing in a market that features commodity products and near-perfect information. No wonder amazon.com has moved aggressively into online auctions, where no two items are exactly the same. Some companies have refused to sell through Web-only retailers, striving to avoid the Internet's deflationary kiss.

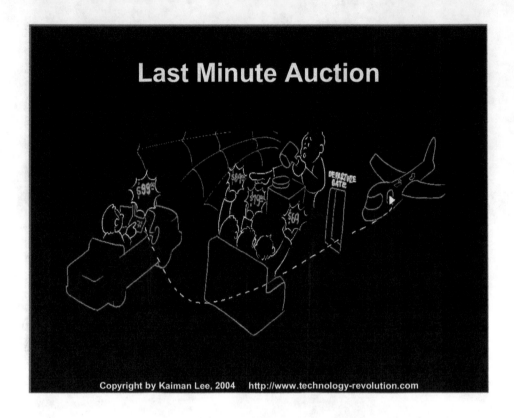

If your automobile has Internet access, you can get on your airline's Web site, and participate in a ticket <u>auction</u>. Wait until just before takeoff, and your ticket price will most likely delight you. <u>You get a cheap ticket</u>, and the <u>airline fills the seat</u>.

Once businesses are able to offer customers <u>up-to-the-second data</u>, <u>prices</u> will <u>fall</u>. Net prices will begin to create new niche markets.

Instead of buying gas at the closest gas station, for instance, you will be able to find the best price on the Internet and drive a little out of your way to get it, if it is worth your time.

A Place to Stay

Connect yourself to a <u>hotel Web site</u> just after <u>6 p.m.</u> when the hotel has a final count of the <u>no-shows</u>. You can then bid for a night's stay in an auction. "The rich pay less."

A hotel reservation service can offer a big block of rooms at half price when a group cancels. It raises rates when the hotel is oversubscribed.

This is <u>dynamic pricing</u>. Prices are fixed entirely by <u>supply and demand</u>.

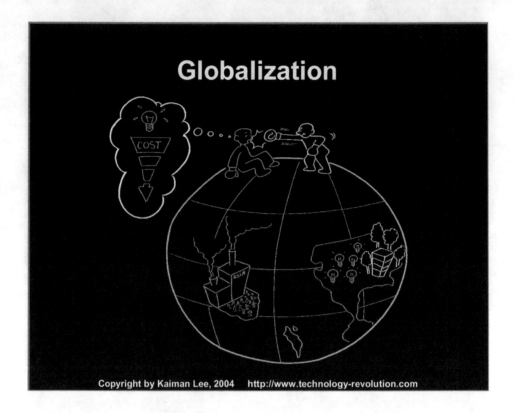

The Internet with its ubiquitous telecommunications and media access is globalizing businesses and leveling the playing field between big and small companies and countries. With universal connectivity, countries, companies and individuals that were not able to participate in the industrial revolution have the opportunity to play a role in the Internet revolution.

Globalization allows businesses to generate new markets, and get new supply sources. They can not only get low-skilled/low-cost labor, but state of the art contract assembly plant, and pools of technically specialized workers all from other countries.

Globalized economy will foster innovation. Competition will force companies to come up with ever more creative ways to increase productivity and keep costs down.

Although globalization opens up opportunities and increases diversity for the poor around the world, it can lead to economic inequality. The leading countries benefit from low-cost products and low inflation, while people in the less developed countries may feel they can not control their own economic destiny.

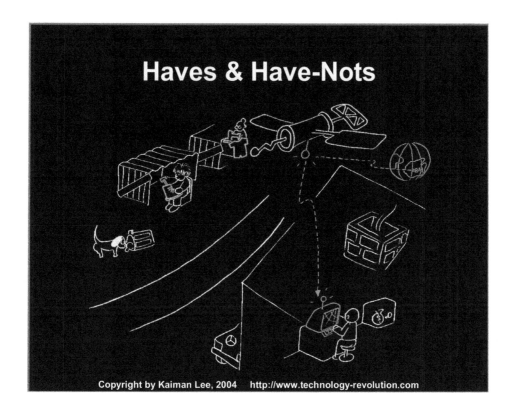

Haves & Have-Nots

Copyright by Kaiman Lee, 2004   http://www.technology-revolution.com

Technology can be both democratizing & segregating.

About 25% of the world population of 5.9 billion live in countries where there is less than one phone line for every 100 people. Or, two-third of the world's people have never made a telephone call.

We have already created classes of people who have access to the Internet and those who do not. Education is starting to favor those who have access, and those who do not are being left behind. As e-commerce continues to grow, whole classes of people will be unable to take part. As electronic access to the government grows widespread, whole classes may become disenfranchised.

Access to technology will not by itself level the playing field: if you wire them, they will not necessarily prosper. Computers might become as common as TVs, but they require initiative and creativity to use them fully. Knowing how to play computer games is not the same as knowing how to use them productively.

In the Santa Cruz district of Bombay, very, very rich computer programmers with cozy houses are right next to very, very impoverished neighbors with tin roofs. When the extremes are close together like that, can domestic tranquility be maintained?

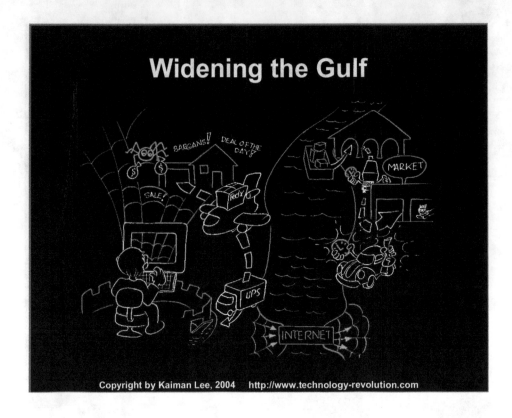

There may now be "two worlds," the haves and the have-nots. The division between is getting wider.

The haves benefit from online auctions, real-time pricing, and "deals-of-the-minute."

The wardrobe warriors work up an appetite, and order a pizza, Chinese food, or a "cybermeal" without picking up the phone. They do not waste time driving to local stores or banks. They recognize that "time" is the most precious commodity they have, and they save time in everything they do.

The Milton S. Eisenhower Foundation issued a report called "The Millennium Breach" in early 1998. It says: "the rich are getting richer, the poor are getting poorer, and minorities are suffering disproportionately." "The top one percent of Americans have more wealth than the bottom 90 percent."

Where do we go from here?!

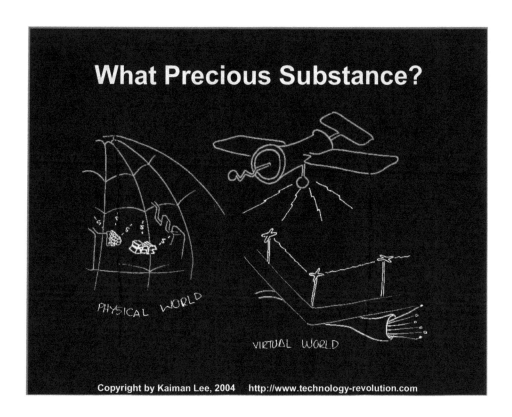

What Precious Substance?

PHYSICAL WORLD

VIRTUAL WORLD

In the <u>physical world</u>, <u>gold</u> is the precious substance. What is the precious substance in the virtual world? The information highway is only a trek across virgin territory. The <u>minerals of the new world of cyberspace are still in formation</u>.

It is not so much a question of "<u>where is the precious gold</u>?" but "<u>what is the next precious substance</u>?" It could be <u>access speed, targeted content, or artificial intelligence</u>. Ultimately, it has to do with <u>time</u>, biologic and virtual.

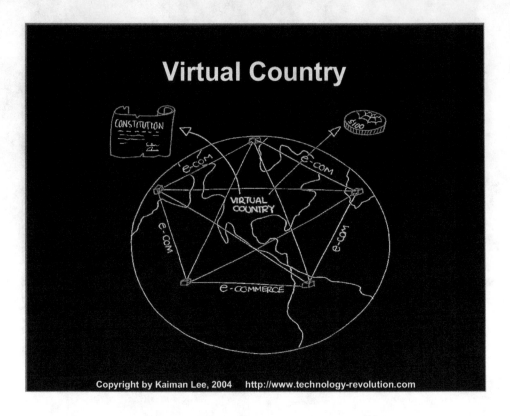

The Internet could create virtual "countries" or electronically-developed "nations" that exist without physical boundaries.

They will challenge the existing authority and control, and even the sovereignty of nations.

We have instantaneous commercial transactions happening from one country to the next. We have visual, verbal, and written communications happening across country lines. We have unimpeded flow of money to and from banks around the world. Traditional concepts of national sovereignty have been blurred.

Companies are creating "currencies" that are such as loyalty points or frequent-flyer miles, thousands of currencies which can be freely traded, but almost none of which is issued by governments.

With or without the realization of virtual countries, the significance of traditional countries has diminished, and will continue. The world is being governed more and more by virtual marketplaces.

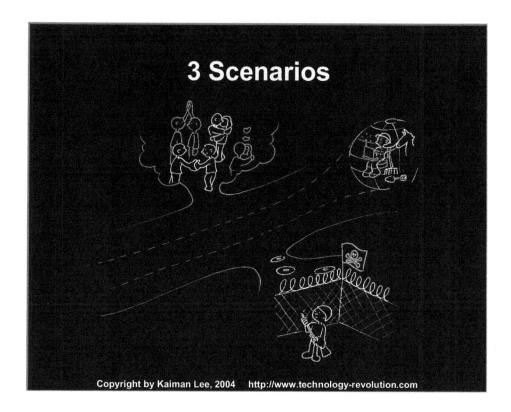

What can happen to the information superhighway? Three possibilities:

1. <u>Utopian scenario</u>: The Internet will be instrumental in <u>solving all the problems of the world and bringing peace on earth</u>.

2. <u>Monolithic backlash scenario</u>: The government will slam down on the Internet with "<u>border controls</u>." Even though their efforts are expected to be futile, that is unlikely to stop some governments from trying to tame the beast.

3. <u>Middle of the road scenario</u>: <u>Life will go on</u>, and people will slowly but surely <u>use the Internet for their own benefit</u> in their own way. There are reasons for optimism -- the information age has four key qualities that will result in its ultimate triumph: decentralizing, globalizing, harmonizing, and empowering. Internet is a general model that <u>figures out what it will be used for as people use it</u>. It is like starting out with the idea of a machine, and having that machine adapt itself to different tasks as needed.

Do you want to bet on the <u>middle of the road</u>?

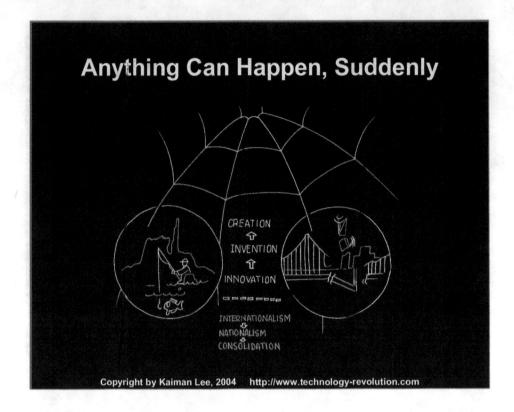

It is easy to understand that the <u>Internet</u> with its <u>serendipity</u> nature can let us <u>quickly innovate, invent and create</u>. But it might be comparatively difficult to visualize its down side.

Internet's <u>global business</u> is highly <u>competitive</u>. Those who <u>gain</u> from internationalism are the <u>strongest and most-competitive</u> people. Those who <u>lose</u> are the <u>weakest and least competitive</u>.

<u>Internationalism</u> causes a <u>clash between elite and ordinary people</u>. It causes widespread job cutting and sky-high CEO salaries while moving plants abroad. Too much internationalism could lead to a pull back <u>toward nationalism</u>.

Nationalism could lead to a <u>consolidation of reliable information</u> into fewer and bigger organizations. <u>Competition dwindles</u>.

<u>Local and state law-enforcement authorities</u> cannot effectively deal with <u>hackers</u>, scam artists and such. <u>Online transactions across borders are difficult to trace</u>. As a result, the <u>federal government</u> has assumed an ever-larger role in <u>tracking and prosecuting criminals</u>.

<u>State and local sales tax collection</u> on online transaction is messy and inefficient. <u>Federal</u> assumption of online sales tax would let Congress <u>redistribute</u> this revenue to <u>special interests</u>.

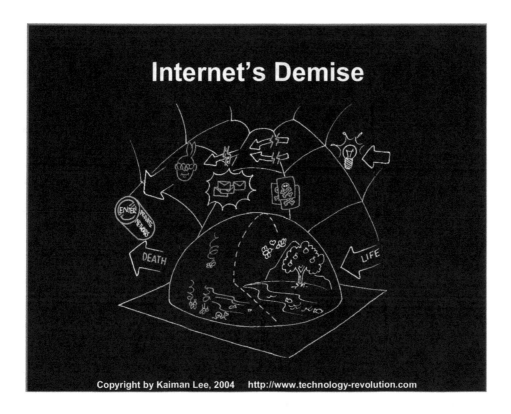

A study was made on a <u>male</u> and a <u>female</u> <u>fly</u> that were placed in a small glass enclosure. They were given an <u>unlimited supply of food and water</u>. As the population grew, the habitat became so <u>contaminated with waste and pollution</u> that all the flies <u>died</u>.

In just a few years, the <u>Internet</u> has already become <u>profoundly polluted</u>. If the industry and government do not figure out a way to clean it up, it could become a glorified game-playing, spam-advertising, sex-pandering, fraud-inducing platform.

Now that most ISPs provide the ability for everyone to have his or her <u>own Web page</u>, <u>millions</u> of pages per day are <u>generated</u>. The flood of <u>poorly updated and managed</u> pages is creating a navigation nightmare, with dead links and moved Web sites.

Internet's contamination could eventually lead to its demise. In the next 10 years, the Internet could assume a role not unlike <u>network television</u>. Serious companies and businesses will splinter off to <u>private networks</u>, <u>similar to cable TV</u>, where each customer will be <u>charged</u> extra for access.

The Internet as we know it could go the way of the <u>typewriter</u>, becoming a once-valuable tool that is no longer efficient or productive. It could become a <u>catchall conduit</u> that appeals to the <u>lowest common denominator</u>.

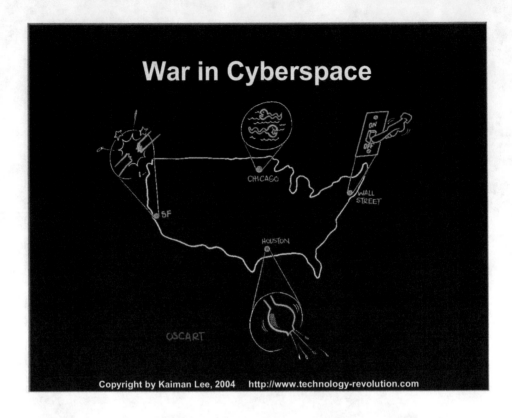

War in Cyberspace

CHICAGO

SF

WALL STREET

HOUSTON

OSCART

In the war of the future, power comes from the ability to deliver or withhold something that someone else wants. The ability to use the cyberspace while denying or exploiting the opponent's use of it will be the key to surviving a 21st century war. This is the U.S. concept of information superiority.

Techniques of 'information warfare' may be employed by terrorist organizations with no less effect than the traditional bomb. They could include hijacking air traffic control systems to crash planes, using ultra-high-frequency radio waves to scramble hard drives and fry computer chips, and cutting power supplies.

There are super-secret agencies with names such as "Office for Cyber Warfare" and the FBI's "Threat Assessment Center."

Could cyberterrorism really happen? "Absolutely," says Deputy Assistant FBI Director Michael Vatis, who heads a new cyberdefense agency, the National Infrastructure Protection Center (NIPC). "We have concrete information about several foreign countries that are developing programs to target the U.S. and our critical infrastructure in particular."

In a cyberwar, the offensive force picks the battlefield, and the other side may not even realize when it is under attack. The intruders are "sophisticated, patient and persistent."

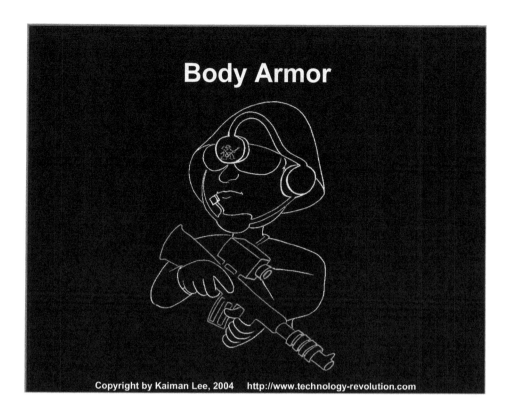

Body Armor

The U.S. Army is developing a <u>body armor called Land Warrior</u> for future foot soldier combat.

It gives soldiers a digital <u>battlefield map on a helmet video display</u>. They can read orders of commanding officers on the monitor. They can also hear the commands. A hand unit controls the helmet-mounted display and computer.

Specifically, the monocular video display gives the soldier navigation data, command and control instructions and target coordinates. The information can also be viewed through a <u>night vision, flip-down eyepiece</u> mounted on the helmet visor.

A <u>video camera</u> on the weapons subsystem is <u>connected to the eye piece</u>, so soldiers can fire a weapon overhead, around corners or behind them while reducing their exposure to enemy fire.

The computer and radio system, carried in a soldier's backpack, sends the soldier's coordinates to a <u>Global Positioning System</u> satellite. The signal is returned to a receiver in the backpack so the soldier <u>knows where fellow squad members are</u>.

IT STRATEGIES

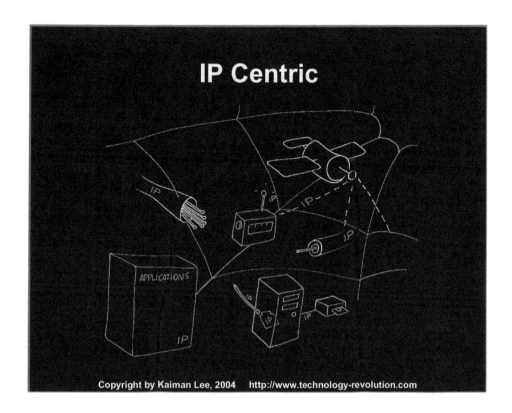

With the ubiquity of the Internet, we should move to connections entirely based on Internet protocol (or IP in short) to all applications.

When everything is running on IP alone, the systems architecture or topology can be upgraded without requiring application modifications. If all SCSI peripherals were migrated to IP, we could use 10-MBPS Ethernet today, Gigabit Ethernet tomorrow and Terabit Ethernet next year. The peripherals and IP devices will just work.

With all networking abstracted to IP, everything on the Internet could serve as a peripheral, a coprocessor or even a CPU cluster. You can talk to anything from anywhere. Voice, video, and data can be combined over virtually any transport system.

IP networks will allow everything to be interoperable. Imagine what would happen if Intel puts IP intelligence on its chips. All legacy protocols including IBM's SNA, Novell IPX, Digital's DECNet, and AppleTalk, could become a thing of the past.

You will also see IP over satellite, cable and vertical blanking interval (VBI) of analog TV signals. In summary, the most important 2 syllables in digital technology is IP.

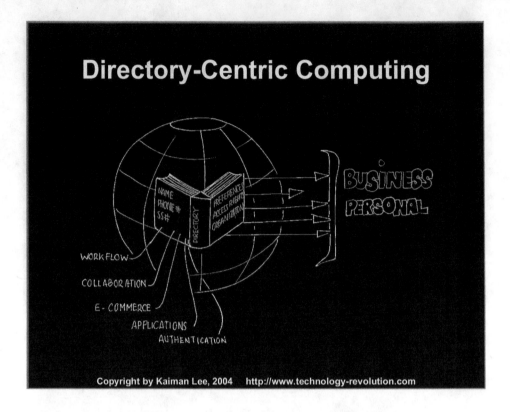

Directory-Centric Computing

Directory-centric computing extends the traditional directory that stores employee names, phone numbers and other personal information, etc.

A universal corporate directory captures data about all the people who need to access information in the organization, including contractors, subcontractors, consultants, partners and employees.

You can categorize users by the organization they are with, the projects they are on and the levels of access they have.

By having a centralized directory, single source, you put the data in once. When people leave, you can remove them from the central directory and know they have been removed from all applications. You can assign security rights to each field within the directory server, e.g., certain fields are updateable by users, while others are updateable only by company officials, and what fields can be viewed by whom.

Universal pricing codes, bar codes, and class of data are things that could also be stored in a directory.

One day, the Internet could contain a series of directories listing almost everyone on the planet.

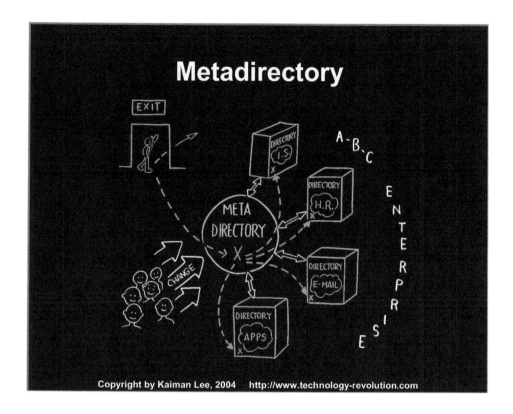

Metadirectory

A typical Fortune 1000 company might have more than <u>100 directories</u>, each containing crucial, unconnected administrative information scattered about the enterprise: <u>E-mail addresses, telephone extensions, physical locations and computer assets</u>.

Information changes constantly. <u>Employees move</u> to new buildings, get <u>married</u> and change their last names, have their security clearances upgraded, or <u>laid off</u> and need to be removed from multiple company directories.

A <u>metadirectory is a directory of directories</u> that you can get a single view of say Kaiman Lee wherever he may live throughout the organization. <u>Meta</u> is the Greek word for <u>with or among</u>. a metadirectory can interconnect standards-based and legacy directories and synchronize them.

You can use a metadirectory as a <u>central data repository</u>. Compile personnel attributes from disparate directories and you can now centrally manage it all. Changes made there automatically disseminate to other connected directories and applications.

The target directory standard is the <u>X.500 directory</u>. <u>Users can update their own profile</u> and contact information which will then propagate to every directory in the company.

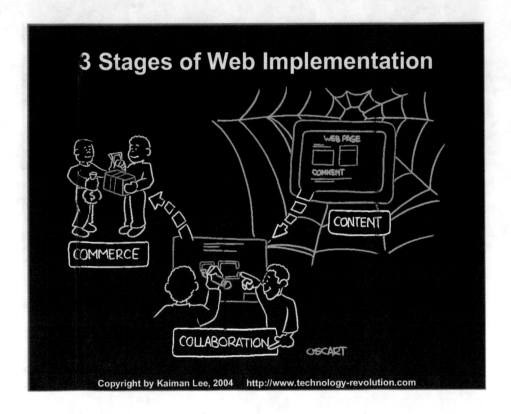

There are three progressively more difficult stages for Web business implementation.

a. <u>Content</u>: The simplest is to publish all the printable materials as static Web pages. The basic purpose is information access. Examples of this type of Web contents are: <u>departmental description, phone list, address book, manuals, policies and procedures</u>.

b. <u>Collaboration</u>: There are two categories.
- <u>Anytime or asynchronous</u> collaboration is collaboration at different times on the same document. I do something now, and you do something later, then I come back to do more even later.

- <u>Real-time or synchronous collaboration</u> is when people work on the same page and make decisions at the same time. Doing things at the same time eliminates the time float.

c. <u>Commerce</u>: For effective e-commerce, it has to be <u>real-time, synchronous, or concurrent</u>. This is where <u>transactions</u> take place. It requires <u>interactivity</u> much more than just real-time collaboration. It requires concepts such as data warehousing, full integration of automated business processes (finance, purchasing, accounting, sales, marketing, etc.). It makes interactive sales and marketing possible.

Daily Web Page

Web sites are not built, they evolve. The ultimate Web site for a company is a corporate portal. But you have to begin somewhere.

Begin with a daily Web page, and you will see how fast it can evolve to a full-fledged Web site.

A daily Web page may consist of:
- top 10 goals of your company
- the boss' message to the troops
- lunch menu
- visitors of the day
- issues of the day for every department
These items may be hot-linked to other Intranet sites and pages.

The daily Web page should not repeat anything from before. Therefore, it is assumed that all employees will read every daily Web page whether they are in the office or not.

Paperless

I WILL PRINT FOR FOOD

HELP THE PRINTLESS

Copyright by Kaiman Lee, 2004   http://www.technology-revolution.com

One 1998 report estimates that the amount of information in offices is doubling every one to three years. So, despite the digital and electronic conversion of documents, the amount of paper continues to grow by 10% to 15% per year.

But, with all kinds of data soon to incorporate <u>voice and/or video</u>, we can see the beginning of the end of paper. How can we <u>print out 3-D, simulation, virtual reality</u>, etc..?

More and more of our information will be <u>dynamic, transient and transaction oriented</u>. How can we print them?

Pretty soon, <u>incentives</u> will be given to people filing <u>federal and state reports electronically</u>. The private industry has gone ahead of it already, e.g., ticketless plane ticket.

In the business world, <u>business intelligence</u> is derived from <u>linking information</u> from one database to another. Paper-mode operation will be a detriment to business progress.

It seems likely that once people have become accustomed to paperless, they will <u>not go back to the paper-based world</u>. Would you go back to using a horse and buggy when you are used to your car? It is <u>not</u> a matter of <u>if</u>, but <u>when</u>. For those who want to get ahead, the sooner the better.

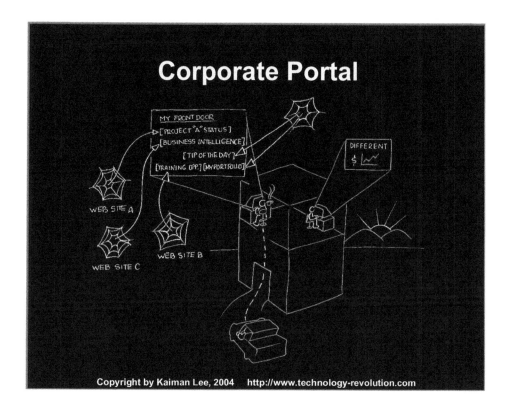

Corporate Portal

A corporate portal can <u>combine information from multiple sources</u> such as Intranet, data warehouses, enterprise resource planning (ERP) system (SAP, PeopleSoft/J.D. Edwards, Oracle and Siebel), and the Web, based on your <u>role, profile and preferences</u>.

Indexing and linking to Internet- and Intranet-based content, a corporate portal provides users with a <u>single point of access</u> to their important information.

With a corporate portal, a sophisticated profiling system could alert you to the arrival of new information that matches your profile and suggest related documents or subject matters. It could also use your profile to automatically <u>connect you to people with similar interests</u>.

The <u>ideal</u> corporate portal may include functions for <u>document management, knowledge management</u>, Web-based data <u>analysis, and enterprise reporting</u>.

351

Intranet Key Strategies

The key strategies to reap the benefits of Intranets are: <u>big fat servers, big fat pipeline and webifying and/or Web-enabling almost everything</u> so that everything can be seen using an Internet browser.

When all data are webified, you can see them with just a browser and you can copy it. Get a <u>few data elements from this Web site, a few from another site or Web page</u> and so on, and combine them in various ways to get the information you need.

Larger servers will allow you to have a more centralized configuration where the computer becomes a peripheral to the Intranet.

Start with <u>over capacity</u> ("fat") so that you do not need to worry about transmission and server capacity for about 18 months.

An Intranet can be thought of as merely the vehicle that you choose for information delivery and collaboration. It is a tool, just like the phone or the PC, but it is hard to think that way about it out-of-the-box. It is like asking the people who <u>invented the automobile to envision suburbs</u>.

Your use of an Intranet is <u>limited only by your imagination</u>.

Bird's-Eye View

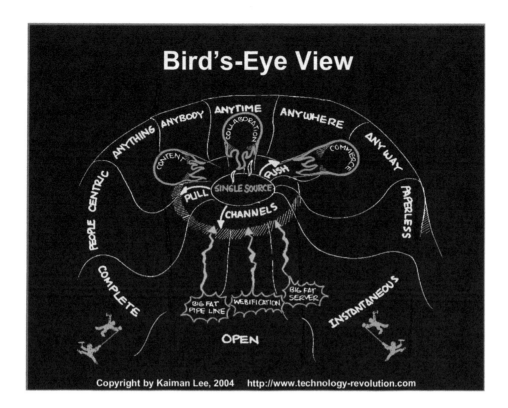

To be successful in implementing information technology for your company, try to remember this bird's-eye view of a volcano that summarizes many strategic concepts.

Information must be <u>complete, open and instantaneous</u>.

Information deals with <u>anything, anybody, anytime, anywhere and any way</u>.

The computing environment must be <u>people centric</u>.

The medium of information exchange must be <u>paperless</u>.

The information system infrastructure must consist of <u>big pipeline, big servers, and data webification</u>. How information is transported must make use of <u>both push and pull</u> technologies.

The implementation stages are: <u>content</u> (publish, get comments and republish), <u>collaboration</u> (anytime and real time) and <u>commerce</u> (transaction).

The core concept is "<u>Single Source</u>" where people check into a document and do something, then check out. It is like going into a library, doing some reading and copying, then leaving it.

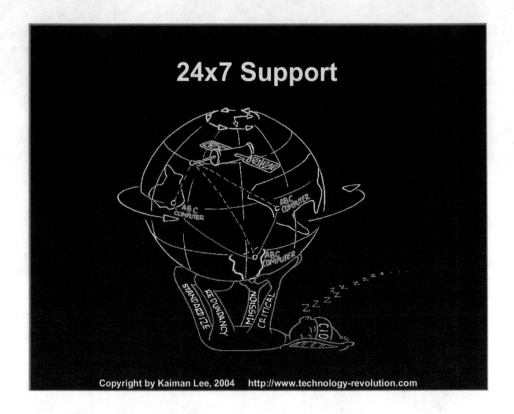

24x7 Support

Your network is mission critical. When your competitors' networks are down and yours is up, you win. If you are running a global business, 24-hours-7-days support becomes mandatory. When your network is down, it is like locking the front door.

To keep your business going continuously, you need reliability, availability and serviceability (RAS) --100 percent uptime for mission-critical applications and fast recovery from disaster.

You should standardize on computers, routers and switches, etc. and keep extra inventory of them.

You should build redundancy into servers. Have two or more servers running in parallel with the same operating system and applications, acting as a backup to each other.

It might seem overindulgent and costly for doubling up on key devices and keeping extra inventory, but the price will never add up to what it would cost, say an online bank, in terms of business lost in the event of a systems failure.

You should provide round-the-clock remote management software and after-hours online backups. With all that, the CIO can sleep tight at night.

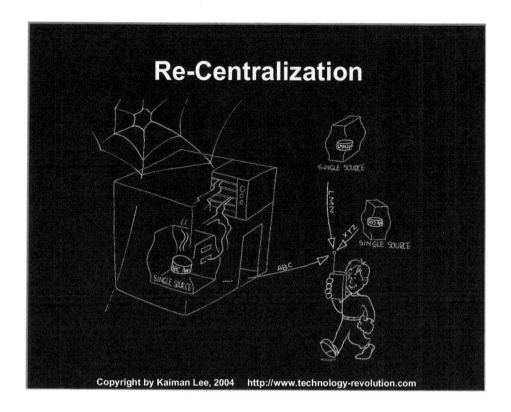

Re-Centralization

How do you know <u>which are the current sales figures</u>: the ones on your laptop or the ones on your desktop machine? Now that handhelds have entered the mix, the <u>synchronization problem</u> has gotten worse.

It is time to <u>return to a centralized database</u>, in which one server keeps all of a company's data. All PCs, laptops, and handhelds are <u>thin clients</u>. A thin client is a computer that depends on a network for storage; it is also known as a <u>network computer</u>.

Oracle had eliminated 2,000 server computers scattered around the world and consolidated them on 158 machines at its Redwood Shores headquarters. All the company's data are stored on one central database accessible via the Web.

You <u>do not need to centralize everything physically</u>. You can centralize <u>logically</u>, i.e., keeping physical servers someplace where they can get the best care. Inevitable <u>high bandwidth</u> and transparency of most corporate wide area networks make <u>location a non-issue</u>.

<u>Centralized</u> computing architectures are <u>much easier to manage than distributed computing environments</u>.

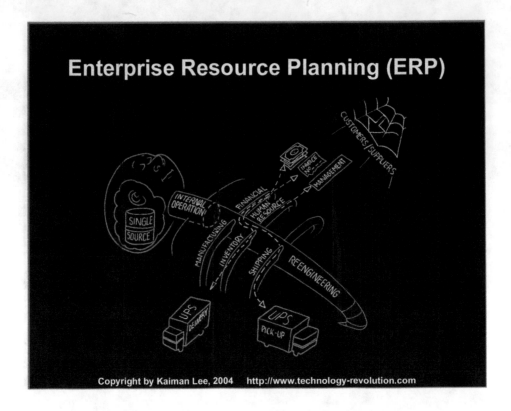

Enterprise Resource Planning (ERP)

Enterprise resource planning (ERP) began with the integration of manufacturing and financial applications. Now it is an integrated backbone of your key business and management processes. ERP tracks company finances, human resources data and manufacturing information including production, procurement, inventory & materials management, sales & distribution.

For example, the financial module can cut a check as soon as the loading dock clerk confirms that the goods have been received in inventory. Similarly the accounts receivable module can generate an invoice as soon as the shipping clerk says the finished goods are on the truck to the customer.

Because all the functions share the underlying databases, information must be entered only once. For example, when a new employee is hired, the computerized records of his or her pay rate, benefits, retirement account, office location and phone number, and so on are available to all who need the information.

The most progressive companies are placing less emphasis on improving internal operational efficiencies and more on how to reach customers and suppliers more quickly and inexpensively. The Internet excels at the latter; ERP, the former.

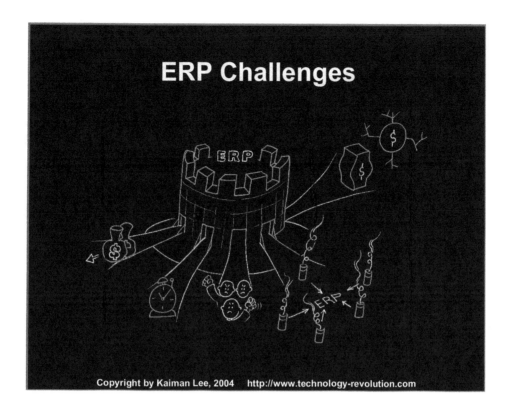

ERP Challenges

Copyright by Kaiman Lee, 2004   http://www.technology-revolution.com

ERP implementation cost could be many many times the software cost because it involves changing business processes. Employee resistance to changing job contents, changing work group assignments, changing reporting procedures and so on can be a major challenge.

ERP concepts go against the mantra of decentralization, which spurs innovation among business units. They are now required to switch from a functional to a process orientation because ERP modules often cut across traditional departmental lines. That is tough for companies with independent business units that are unaccustomed to sharing information or coordinating with other divisions. Mergers and acquisitions make it even more vexing.

As packaged or commercial off-the-shelf software (COTS), ERP systems can be inflexible. You have a choice of modifying your processes to match the software or modifying the software to fit your processes. If you modify the software you will lose at least some of the benefits of COTS. For example, you may find it more difficult to connect your ERP system with other enterprise systems, and you will not be able to update your system readily when improved versions of the software become available.

Traditional ERP is too inward-looking, which must be morphed to be Web based.

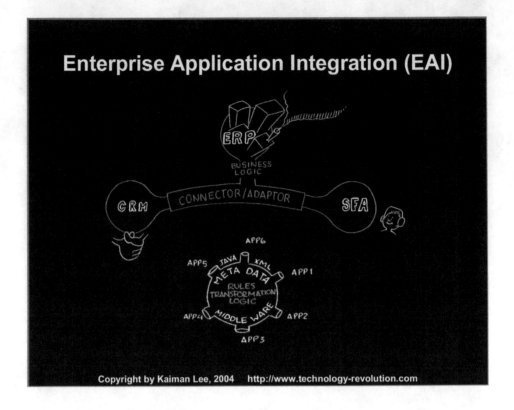

No need for hard-coded interfaces for software applications anymore. Place a special integration layer between applications for the easy management of data connections and formats.

EAI solutions offer pre-built or "productized" connectors or adapters to applications such as off-the-shelf enterprise resource planning (ERP) and customer relationship management (CRM) offerings. They create a bridge for applications to share business logic and coordinate information flow.

For data sources from unique applications, you can build middleware in a central (hub-and-spoke) fashion using meta data tools without modifying the current application code. The central area (hub) provides a standard documentation point for critical interfaces. Messages can be placed on the central queue and be picked up by other applications when needed. This central area carries rules and transformation logic, allowing you to modify either one independent of the applications.

EAI allows companies to use the best-of-breed approach, and not to be locked into one suite (single source) of applications.

The building block technologies for middleware are: Java and XML. Java provides portable programs to everywhere. XML provides common data elements.

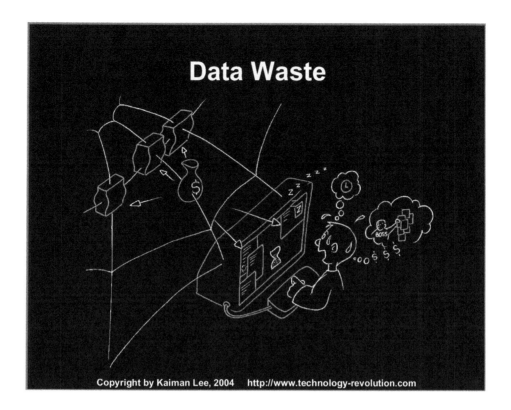

Data Waste

Data waste can be <u>defined as the amount of online data you purchase minus the data actually used by your company</u>. Does your home page feature <u>a news stream</u> along the upper end of the desktop screen? If these tickers serve <u>no decision-producing intelligence</u>, they are data wastes.

Data waste can come from <u>data overload</u> when a <u>worker can not find critical information</u> in the sea of irrelevant data flooding your company's networks. When you start wading through useless information or hunting for lost data, it is decreasing your productivity.

When you buy data from an outside source, a lot of it is irrelevant. Your company may be buying too much, or badly chosen data. Volatile business markets can cause you to react and <u>buy even more data</u> rather than use the data in your existing data pool. This is a particular problem in fast-moving industries such as telecommunications, pharmaceutical and financial services.

You might be <u>obsessed with new data sources</u> in hopes of learning something new that will help you <u>stay ahead of your rivals, more effectively support customers or merely survive</u>. You might want the <u>latest and greatest information</u>, whether you need it or not. But, eliminate some and buy smartly!

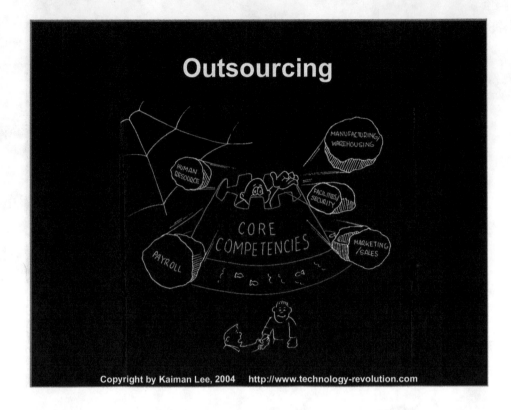

Outsourcing

You should consider outsourcing everything that is not a core competency, i.e., context. The mantra used to be OPM -- other people's money. It is now OPR -- other people's resources.

You could move to distributed and network-centric computing, and speed Internet development. You could outsource the purely technical positions in your IT department, such as programmers and database administrators.

You will be required to nurture your own staffs to become more strategy-, architecture-, and business-process-oriented.

Proper outsourcing could save money, increase flexibility, and improve quality, efficiency and technological competence.

It could also allow you to focus on your core competencies and cope with globalization, and increased competition.

Drivers for outsourcing range from increased privatization and deregulation, the ability to incorporate emerging technologies, structural change, budget cuts, increased merger and acquisition activity, poorer than expected performance of systems and organizations, Euro currency, and a shortage of "human capital" in the IT arena.

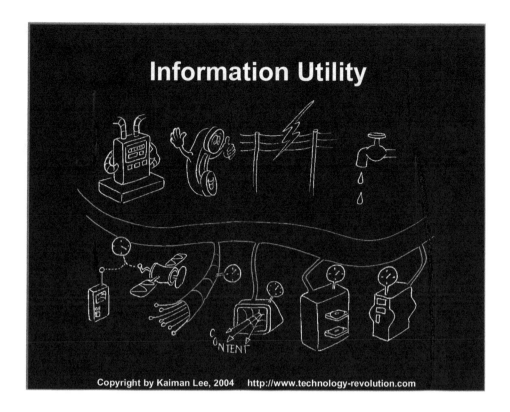

Information Utility

Computing in households or by individuals will become more like using a utility such as electricity or telephone. You pay for what you use, and it will be easy to use.

Information appliances such as personal digital assistants (PDA), cellular phones, and smart cards, will hook into the "information utility" infrastructure. The access to Internet and the Web is the first step toward making use of the information utility.

Information utility as a computing environment is independent of devices, locations and users. It is ubiquitous and worldwide.

Further, hundreds of different types of special-purpose devices could act together as a virtual computer with everything else on the information utility network.

All kinds of intuitive information appliances will be built to plug in to this new utility. That is the pervasive computing environment we are marching onto.

Melenovsky Effect

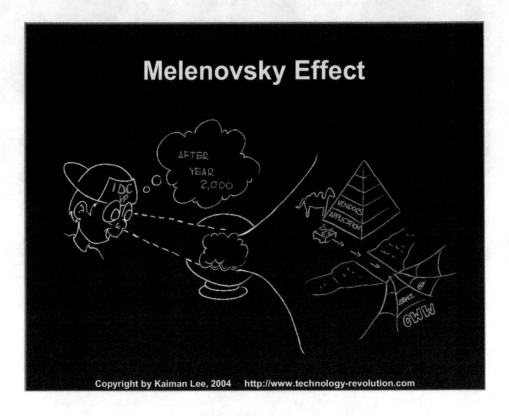

Mike Melenovsky, a vice president at International Data Corp. (IDC) predicted a <u>shortage of trained computer service professionals</u>. Coupled with the ever more <u>complex applications and network environments</u>, it would create an <u>exodus of staff from user organizations to service and outsourcing firms</u>, which would offer them better career paths and money.

It takes only a <u>few good programmers</u> to write a piece of <u>middleware</u>, or an <u>application</u>. But it <u>takes an army to support it</u>.

The training and assimilation problem caused by such a mass migration could prompt major user companies to <u>pressure vendors to slow the rate of technological obsolescence</u>.

The falling product growth rate will <u>lower the market valuation</u> of these product vendors. With stock options no longer the lure they once were for the brightest of the bright, a reverse <u>brain drain from product companies</u> such as Intel and Microsoft <u>to service firms</u> could begin.

We will use computing resources the way we use utilities. <u>Time-sharing</u> would be reincarnated on the infrastructure of the Web, thus the <u>application service providers (ASP)</u>.

362

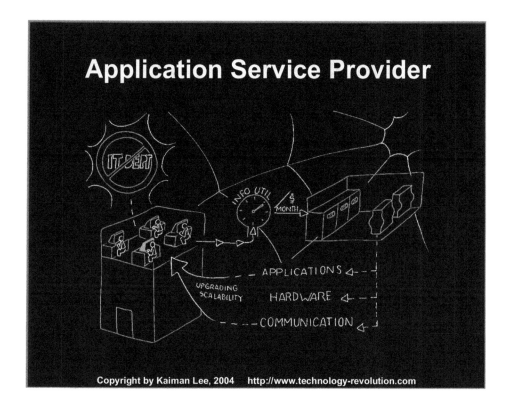

Application Service Providers (ASPs) set up off-site "pay-per-use," "taxi meter," or "applications on tap" based computing services. ASPs spare you the burden of buying and installing hardware and software. You pay a fee for the "information utility."

With ASPs, you can eliminate the high capital costs of constantly upgrading hardware and software. ASPs allows you to refocus on your core competencies.

ASP services are almost ideal for call centers, distance learning and teleworking. They must go over secure high-speed digital networks, i.e., virtual private network (VPN).

Small to midsize firms may convert to ASP service wholesale. Larger companies may consider this option for new sales channels, marketing, or e-commerce application.

The appeal of the ASP model can be to get a highly functional Web site up and running quickly, with the potential to scale it up rapidly, and not have to worry about hiring a staff of expert.

ASP returns us to the bygone days of service bureaus and time-sharing but as an updated, and more productive reincarnation.

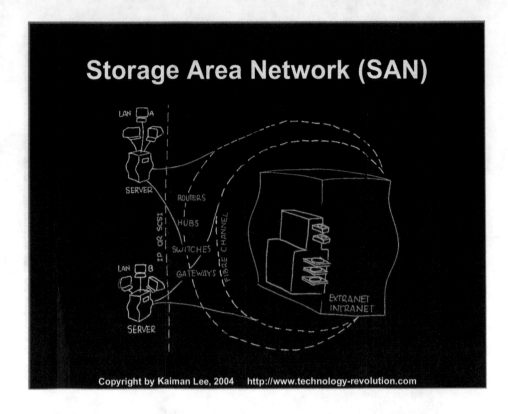

Storage Area Network (SAN)

A storage area network (SAN) is a network separate from the LAN with unlimited storage capacity.

SANs can comprise of any number of storage systems -- RAID (redundant array of independent disks), tape backup, CD-ROM libraries or simply a bunch of magnetic disks. SCSI has a 16-device bus limit while fibre channel can support up to 128 devices. They are linked via optical-speed (e.g., 100 MBPS up to 10 kilometers) fibre (not spelled "fiber") channel to servers.

SAN servers can access data directly from any device in the dedicated storage network; no need to go through the LAN.

Two servers can have access to the same storage devices over two separate loops. If one server fails, you still have access to data from the other server.

Data backup can be done concurrent of operation with no down time required, because of optical-speed transmission in SANs.

On top of storage devices and servers, a SAN consists of three basic components. First is a fast network pipe (e.g., SCSI or Fibre Channel). Second is interconnects to channel traffic (e.g., switches, gateways, routers, or hubs). And the third is a protocol (e.g., IP or SCSI).

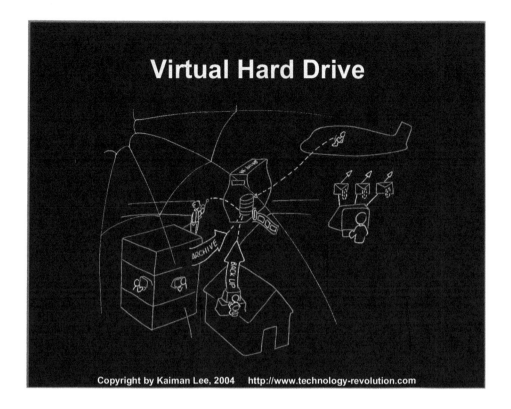

Virtual Hard Drive

A virtual hard drive or "data garage" is basically some storage space on a remote server where you can park your data and access them over the Internet from anywhere.

You can use the virtual hard drive to back up or archive your business-critical and home-critical files or just store data.

If you do not have your own Web site, you still can post documents, e.g., resumes, online for others to access. Rather than sending a big attachment with an E-mail, you can include a hyperlink in the E-mail body to a file stored in a virtual hard drive.

A free virtual hard drive service could offer say 25 megabytes of free storage and users may purchase more. The service provider could generate revenue from advertisement and other value-added services.

The software can provide automatic, on-line backup from servers, workstations and stand-alone personal computers including laptops. It could transmit only those parts of your files that have changed. It could run automatically each day, on selected days, or on demand.

Virtual hard drive blurs the distinction between the PC and the Internet -- towards a real distributed computing model.

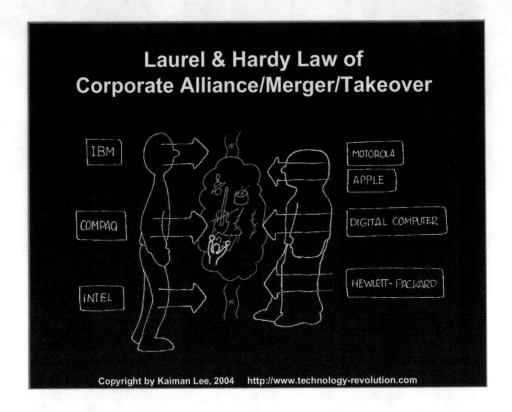

Laurel & Hardy Law of Corporate Alliance/Merger/Takeover

IBM
COMPAQ
INTEL

MOTOROLA
APPLE
DIGITAL COMPUTER
HEWLETT-PACKARD

Kevin Maney, in his technology editorial on June 4, 98 USA Today defined the Laurel and Hardy Law of Technology Alliances. It says that "whenever two or more giant companies get together to create complex new technology, the result is another fine mess." His insight was brought on by the Intel and Hewlett-Packard Merced's delay.

Creating an effective alliance is an art as much as a science. Each is like a symphony that has a single composer.

PowerPC partnership was launched in 1991. The partners Motorola, IBM and Apple Computer pooled their people and moved all 340 of them into a three-story office building called Somerset in Austin, TX -- far from any of the partner's headquarters. They took away dress codes and all wore badges with a Texas logo. But despite the badges, everybody at Somerset knew whom everybody worked for. The different companies pulled in different directions.

Apple and IBM alliances in the early 1990s, Taligent (to develop an advanced object-oriented operating system) and Kaleida (to develop multimedia products) were shut down by 1995.

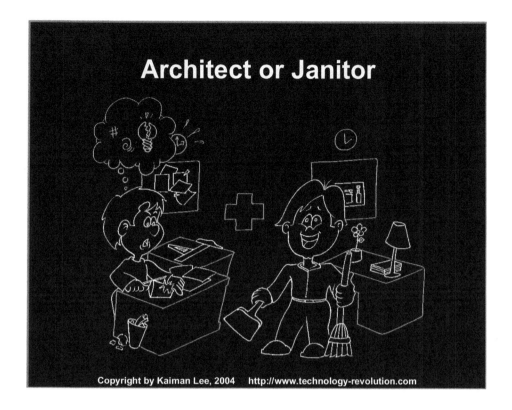

Architect or Janitor

Copyright by Kaiman Lee, 2004   http://www.technology-revolution.com

Two leadership qualities are crucial to <u>CIO's survival and success</u>. The first is the ability to create a set of <u>value expectations</u> (architect) shared across all departments. The second is the ability to <u>deliver</u> (janitor) those expectations.

Do you like to ask "<u>what if</u>?" Do you like to constantly <u>question assumptions</u> about your business? Do you feel urged to <u>try new technologies</u> and apply them to your company's need? Are you <u>not bothered by messiness</u> that may lead to something great? Does embarking on new projects and <u>making a concept a reality</u> give you a thrill? If you like these things, then you have the qualities of an <u>architect</u>.

On the other hand, do you strive to <u>efficiently</u> maintain computer systems for your company? Do you react to customer needs in a <u>timely</u> manner? Do you like to <u>fix things</u> that are broken? Does it <u>bug you</u> when something does <u>not work</u> the way you think it <u>should</u>? Are you <u>happiest</u> when nothing is going wrong and things are <u>smooth</u>? "Yes, yes," then you are like a <u>janitor</u>.

IT departments, like great buildings, <u>need both</u> architects and janitors. So, make sure that your IT department operates like clockwork, the users are happy and the <u>backups</u> are being done on schedule. But also make sure you are <u>building for tomorrow</u>.

367

Ideal CIO

Traditionally, CIOs tend to focus on tactical planning and implementation of specific information technologies. They were seen as super computer specialists.

Their role is now moving toward global strategic business planning at the highest levels of their corporations. This is because corporations are trying to maximize their competitiveness and growth through technology.

The CIO has taken on one of the most challenging and dynamic leadership role in the business world. They are at the center of many of the most volatile and costly changes in a corporation.

An ideal CIO should have some of the following mentalities. I am in charge of reinvention. Technology means revolution. I do not think outside the box; I do not even see the box. My role is to lead. I can work with young and weird talents. I will attack the corporate cultural issues head-on. "Ready, Fire, Aim" is okay. We do not want to be the best of the best; we want to be the only one doing what we do.

The ideal CIO should have technical/engineering qualifications, plus a background in finance, marketing and strategic planning.

CIO titles could be: CIO and executive vice president, CIO and senior vice president, CIO and vice president, chief information officer, chief technology officer, or Vice president of IT.

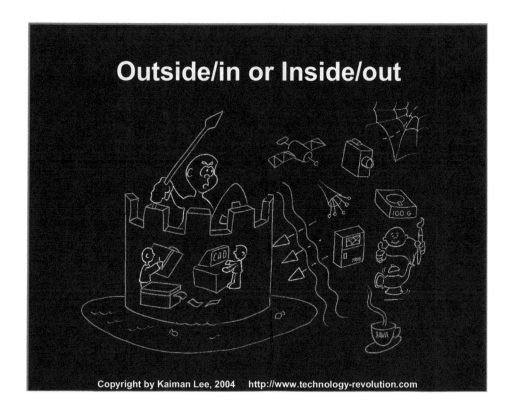

Outside/in or Inside/out

The successful, thriving giant companies of the world are always the ones that change before the industry, or before their competitors force them to change. That is challenging.

It is not difficult to explain the need for change to people when there is a problem, but getting people to change when things are going well is almost impossible.

" ... when the pace of change outside an organization becomes greater than the pace of change inside the organization, the end is near."
--- John R. Walter, President of AT&T, just before its break up.

Is change happening to you from the outside/in or from the inside/out? The difference between the two approaches is whether you are reactive (crisis management) or proactive (opportunity management) to change. Consequences of the reactive approach can be deadly.

However, change or not, to quote the legendary management consultant Dr. W. Edward Deming: "It is not necessary to change. Survival is not mandatory."

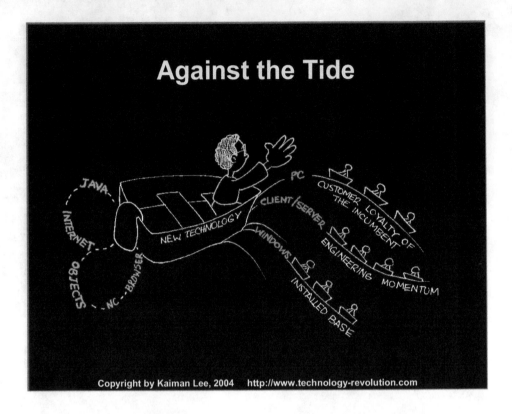

Why is it <u>so difficult to implement new technologies</u>, such as network computing and Java?

From the computer manufacturer's point of view, those with a <u>vested interest in PC technology fear a loss of market share</u>. Historically, however, the market share loss to the next generation computing has been trivial in comparison with the stimulation of new application opportunities. Bringing lower cost computer technology to the user has always generated increased product demand.

User organizations with a <u>big installed-base</u> say that they can use the current technology to satisfy the network computing needs of users. And, the <u>momentum of using current technology</u> prevents them from changing direction. But the PC-centric client/server can not be easily extended into the network-centric systems environment.

Connectivity changes everything. <u>Personal computing must become personal communication</u>.

Whether used for work group collaboration or Intranet access, a PC becomes a <u>communication tool</u> that is only useful if it is consistently available.

Windshield or Bug

"It is <u>not the strongest</u> of the species that survive, nor the most intelligent, but the <u>most responsive to change</u>."
--- Charles Darwin

It has been <u>true</u> for millions of years in the wild world of <u>animals</u>.

It is just as <u>true</u> in the world of <u>business</u> where technology changes everything so rapidly and so often.

What would you rather be, a <u>windshield or a bug</u>?

Yuck!

Better to be the <u>driver</u> who can respond to change like his/her second nature in driving, and think "<u>outside the box</u>."

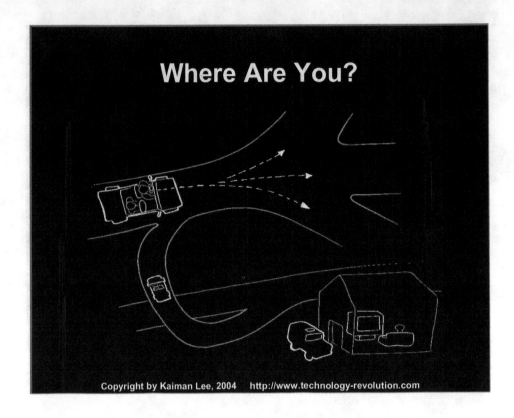

Where Are You?

Using "information superhighway" as the metaphor, are you a <u>driver</u>, <u>passenger</u>, <u>getting on the on-ramp</u>, or <u>not even on the road</u>?

You can <u>ride</u> the Internet wave confidently, be <u>carried along</u> by it, or find it <u>crashing over you</u>.

The Internet, a.k.a. the Net or Web, is <u>the most important technological development of the past 20 years</u>. A 1997 survey had it tied with the personal computer and cable television, with the VCR as the third most important.

In an environment of rapid technological changes, <u>many will resist the Net, most will tolerate it, and a visionary few will embrace it</u>.

EPILOG

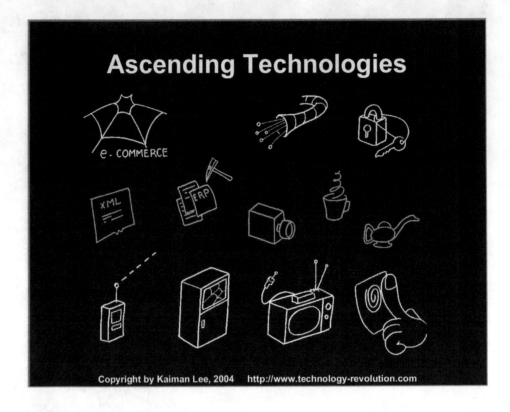

The following are <u>top technologies</u> to watch for:

- business-to-business e-commerce (B2B)
- customer relationship management (CRM)
- dense wavelength division multiplexing (DWDM)
- security (e.g., biometrics) and privacy protection
- eXtensible Markup Language (XML)
- open source (e.g., Linux)
- IP everywhere and everything (e.g., VoIP)
- wireless networking (e.g., packetized IP over air)
- computer-telephony integration (convergence)
- information appliances (embedded devices)
- set-top box devices (e.g., cable modem)
- objects (e.g., Java, Jini, etc.)
- database applications (e.g., data mining, ERP, etc.)
- distributed Internet-based computing (+ ubiquitous computing)
- enterprise and universal directories
- policy-based management

With <u>infinite storage</u> available on the horizon, maybe the one technology that will affect everybody in a most profound way is the <u>WebCam technology</u>. WebCams could be on every wall and everything.

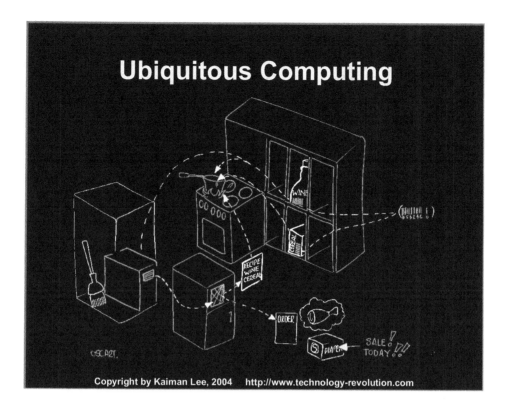

Ubiquitous Computing

"Ubiquitous computing," will bring together many <u>embedded and networked computers</u> that will react to us and serve our needs reflexively. It can transform the <u>energy of a footstep</u> into electrical power. A standard <u>ink pen</u> can write on paper but also records your messages for downloading to a computer later.

A visionary scenario of ubiquitous computing is a hyperconnected household. It would use an <u>Intranet Web server</u> that could be located <u>in a broom closet</u>. It should work as simply and seamlessly as your oil burner or electricity. We will get to the point where Internet service will flow through your house all the time. Internet will become so popular that it will be ubiquitous and unexciting.

A <u>flatpanel screen</u> that is attached to a refrigerator or cabinet could keep an <u>updated inventory of your pantry</u> by reading <u>bar codes</u> when you bring the food home. The cooking database in your home server or a <u>Java recipe</u> downloaded from the Web could recommend how to cook a good meal using the items you have stocked in the pantry.

Your Intranet server cold remind you that you are <u>out of Spam and paper towels</u> and send an E-mail order to a delivery service. It could also automatically take advantage of <u>this week's sale</u> on the brand of paper towels that you prefer.

Gauge for Internet Success

Using a computer should be just <u>as easy and reliable as the telephone</u>. It is not going to be with a PC, but with the Internet.

People should be able to safely get exactly the information they want or need any time, from any place in the world. The key is to deliver a 'web-tone' anytime you <u>turn on your computer</u>, be it a PC, a laptop, palmtop, or any Internet-embedded device. Web tone must have the same dial-tone-level reliability.

There is no complexity in using a <u>telephone</u>. As long as you <u>get a dial tone you can connect</u>. Web tone not only allows you to get connected with others, but also get any data anywhere anytime.

Eventually, you will use the <u>Internet for everything just like the telephone network</u>. When Internet becomes ubiquitous, the place we call the Net will cease to exist.

The time sequence for this to happen is first the dial tone, then data tone (e.g., data and voice merged on telephone line), IP (Internet protocol) tone (e.g., voice over IP), and Web tone.

Web-tone success depends on <u>bandwidth abundance</u>. With <u>ISPs doubling their network capacity every few months</u>, and the practical use of Dense Wavelength Division Multiplexing (DWDM) technology, it could be only a few years away.

Internet Serendipity

It could be a lot of the fun when you <u>stumble on some strange, Web page</u> developed by someone working in a basement, or a college computer laboratory.

In 1999, you could get Internet serendipity by using sites such as eTour (no longer in business) and Uroulette (also no longer in business).

When you sign up with <u>eTour</u>, you <u>select your interests, e.g., cooking</u>, mountain climbing, etc. from a large list. If you like, you can make it your <u>browser's home page</u>. Then, every time you fire up your browser, you will find yourself <u>looking at something new</u>.

<u>Uroulette</u>'s ("<u>Random for your pleasure</u>") name came from a play on URL, the acronym for Uniform Resource Locator, computerese for Web site address.

You do not select your interest with Uroulette. All you do is <u>click</u> on an on-screen <u>roulette wheel</u> randomly. Your first click on the Uroulette wheel could <u>take you to any site in the world</u>, e.g., Smithsonian, Lexus, etc. The result could be <u>totally surprising</u>, and you achieve <u>serendipity</u>.

The <u>innovation age</u> will be accelerated by Internet serendipity.

Major National Concerns

Copyright by Kaiman Lee, 2004   http://www.technology-revolution.com

Currently, the top areas where the U.S. government is concentrating on are: <u>encryption (whole egg into scrambled egg and back to whole egg again), consumer privacy, antitrust (e.g., Microsoft, Oracle's bid for PeopleSoft), and Internet taxation</u>.

<u>The government is concerned about the threats to democracy</u> that arise from the concentration of power in <u>fewer hands</u> with high-power software, high-speed transmission, and precious media.

The government's major concerns touch upon the <u>physical impacts</u>, but leave the <u>intangibles and psychological issues</u> to the people themselves.

Major Personal Concerns

Information technology (IT) as society's nervous system is a strategic component in every life-support function. It has become United States' largest-economic sector.

Organizations and individuals have difficulty coping because IT causes rapid changes with unintended consequences, some of which are psychological and they alter human attitudes and behavior.

Message traffic has soared in volume and speed. Systems are increasingly vulnerable to sabotage and dysfunction. Integrity in contents and sources are highly uncertain.

The loss of eye contact and body gesture imparts loneliness. Resulting stress and anxiety foster the urgent instead of the important.

Worry Like Crazy

Our brain of human knowledge and wisdom is expanding exponentially in volume and speed, fueled by technologies that enable anything, anybody, anywhere, and anytime communications.

On the other hand, we humans, with about 64 kilobits-per-second data-processing speed, are being swamped by information. We are being rendered obsolete by machine-to-machine communications networks.

As the economy shifts from human labor to nonstop machine-driven operations, humanity's economic, social, cultural, and political environments will be changed profoundly.

Technology changes everything. Everything is new from every direction.

"What, Me Worry!"
--- Alfred E. Newman, Mad Magazine, 1955

You should worry like crazy about the Internet and the age of innovation that it will bring, unless you are as lucky in everything as Alfred E. Newman was.

Be As Vigilant As Hell

"The expansion and use of the <u>Internet</u> will be as commonplace as <u>electricity</u> is today."
--- Bill Gates, Chairman & CEO Microsoft Corp.

Among the exhibits gathered by the Justice Department in its case against <u>Microsoft</u> was a number of <u>internal memos</u> and presentations dating 1995-1996.

One states unequivocally: "This is not about browser. Our competitors are trying to make an <u>alternative platform to Windows</u>. They are smart, aggressive and have a big lead. This is not Novell or IBM we are competing with."

Other documents make the same point with even greater urgency: "Netscape/Java is using the <u>browser to create a virtual operating system</u>. <u>Windows will become devalued, eventually replaceable</u>." "This is <u>make-or-break</u> time: the next six months are critical."

The greatest improvement in productivity, and the greatest change in work habits, e.g., "single source" operation, will be brought about because of the Internet, and its nature of universal connectivity. <u>Internet is revolutionary</u>. We <u>should be as vigilant as hell</u>.

The Future

Today's <u>college students</u> constitute the "<u>Net Generation</u>." They read fewer print newspapers, watch less TV and listen to less radio than their non-college counterparts.

They are <u>unconsciously integrating cyberspace</u> into their daily lives. They <u>internalize technologies</u> just as previous generations internalized the automobile and television, integrating them into every aspect of their adult lives.

They will insist that <u>choice is a human right</u>. They will insist that there is such a thing as a <u>free</u> lunch, e.g., free E-mail. With the use of E-mail and instant messages, they will believe that building trust does not require knowing others in a <u>face-to-face</u> way. Internet will serve them as a primary source of entertainment. They are <u>Net-centric</u>.

They will be the ones who will <u>define the "human protocols"</u> on top of electronic protocols for the <u>communication era</u>. They will lead the world to the <u>innovation age</u>.

We are still in the <u>startup phase of the Web</u>. When we look back a few years from now, today's Internet will seem as primitive as a black-and-white television.

The <u>kids will build the future</u>.

This is the <u>Dancing Baby (DB)</u>: the slightly demonic, diapered dudelet who had been appearing all over the Web in 1997.

The original dancing baby was created as a computer-animation by a San Francisco software company (©1996-1998 Burning Pixel Productions) using 3DStudio Max and Character Studio (from Discreet/Kinetix), as a product demo. DB quickly migrated onto home pages and into E-mail, acquiring a symphony of eclectic soundtracks along the way, from Earth, Wind and Fire to Ziggy Marley to Genesis.

In early 1998, DB had expanded its incarnations into <u>Car Crash Baby, Psycho Baby, Rasta Baby and Drunken Baby</u>, ready for prime time.

Try to send the video clip as an <u>E-mail attachment</u> in your <u>holiday-greeting card</u> mailing and see what happens to the Net! <u>If nobody talks about the possible breakdown or slowness of the Net</u>, we have truly <u>arrived at the Net age</u>.

Thank You

Copyright by Kaiman Lee, 2004   http://www.technology-revolution.com

After reading this book, you should realize that we are in the information age of rapid innovations. You must not consider information as your competitive edge because information has become abundant. How you convert information into innovations and be a pioneer of the innovation era should be your focus.

Because of universal connectivity powered mainly by transmission technology, Internet technology, and embedded technology, you can access any data, any body, from anywhere, and at anytime.

You will demand single source to avoid the complications and errors caused by data duplication and synchronization.

Single source and universal connectivity together will enable you to do real-time collaboration, a ten-times effect on productivity, performance, and value, a phenomenon that Intel's chairman Andy Grove referred to as "strategic inflection point," when a convex curve changes to a concave curve or vice versa.

Please direct all comments and suggestions to the author Dr. Kaiman Lee at: *kaiman_lee@yahoo.com*

www.ingramcontent.com/pod-product-compliance
Lightning Source LLC
Chambersburg PA
CBHW060922060326
40690CB00041B/2993